Wild Love

Discover the magical secrets of freedom,
joy and unconditional love

GILL EDWARDS

piatkus

PIATKUS

First published in Great Britain in 2006 by Piatkus Books Ltd
This paperback edition published in 2009 by Piatkus

A CIP catalogue record for this book
is available from the British Library

ISBN 978-0-7499-4001-0

Text design by Briony Chappell
Edited by Liz Dean

Set in Times by Action Publishing Technology Ltd, Gloucester
Printed in Great Britain by
Clays Ltd, St Ives plc

Papers used by Piatkus are natural, renewable and recyclable
products sourced from well-managed forests and certified
in accordance with the rules of the Forest Stewardship Council.

Piatkus
An imprint of
Little, Brown Book Group
100 Victoria Embankment
London EC4Y 0DY

An Hachette UK Company
www.hachette.co.uk

www.piatkus.co.uk

CONTENTS

Gill Edwards is a chartered clinical psychologist, a leading spiritual writer and teacher, and the author of the best-selling titles *Living Magically, Stepping Into the Magic* and *Pure Bliss*. She trained in metaphysics, shamanism and energy psychology, and runs Living Magically workshops. She lives in the heart of the Lake District.

ACKNOWLEDGEMENTS

My deep love and thanks to Esther and Jerry Hicks, and Abraham, whose clarity about emotional guidance led me towards understanding the links between love, reality creation, energy psychology and co-dependency. Mere words could never convey my heartfelt gratitude to you. An infinite thank you to those in the unseen realms who kept nudging me in the right direction, whispering in my ear, wrapping me in their wings and helping me trust in the unfolding journey. My thanks also to Gary Craig, Donna Eden, David Feinstein, Tapas Fleming and other pioneers of energy psychology and energy medicine; and to Bert Hellinger for his invaluable insights into guilt, loyalty and the family soul. Thanks to David Whyte, Mary Oliver, the remarkable Rumi and other poets who are lovers of life, and help us to live with 'a foot in both worlds'. My gratitude to everyone at Piatkus, especially Gill Bailey and Helen Stanton, for being so helpful, positive, supportive and patient. And my love and thanks to Bev, the golden ray of light who runs my office so brilliantly, allowing me the time and space I need to write and teach.

A big bear-hug and thank you to Neale Donald Walsch, for so graciously offering to write the sparkling Foreword to this book, and for his enthusiasm and support for my work. (Also to Anthos, who gifted Neale a copy of *Living Magically*. Bless you for being such an angel.)

More personally, oodles of love and thanks to my parents (as always) for their endless love and support, for proof-reading the manuscript of *Wild Love* with infinite care and thoughtfulness, and for the gift of growing up with the boundless love they share. My love and gratitude to my close and loving friends, who supported me with such caring, patience and compassion through my long, painful and enlightening journey into a new life – especially Trina, Andrea, Ian, Sally T, Sue R and Jana; also to John, for loving me enough to set me free, and for still being my friend. Thanks to Margaret Lyth and Dave Evans for their caring support and help. Thanks to Jay Ramsay for being there, for understanding the rocky path. And a huge cuddle to my gorgeous son Kieran, for putting up with a mother who was often 'lost' in her own painful process and writing; you have your mum back at last – and with more love to give than ever.

Finally, my eternal love and gratitude to P – for blasting my heart open, for changing my life, for helping me understand so much, and for waking me up to my forgotten dreams and the magic of unconditional love. We have often walked this path together, and I wish you so much happiness and joy. This book emerged from our journey together, and – though you might never read it – *Wild Love* is dedicated to you.

My grateful acknowledgements to Penguin Books for permission to quote from *The Essential Rumi*; to HarperCollins for permission to quote from *The Soul of Rumi*; and to David Whyte and Many Rivers Press for permission to quote from *The House of Belonging*. Thanks to Esther and Jerry Hicks for permission to quote from Abraham, and to publish my own version of the Emotional Scale; and to Donna Eden and David Feinstein for permission to quote from *Energy Medicine*, and to include Donna's exercise Heaven Rushing In. Thanks to Brian Patten and HarperCollins for permission to quote from *Love Poems*; to Random House and the Wallace Literary Agency for permission to quote from *The Moon is Always Female* by Marge Piercy; to Beacon Books for permission to quote from *The Kabir Book* (transl. Bly); to Bloomsbury Publishing for permission to quote from *Poems* by Anne Michaels; to HarperCollins for permission to quote from *Selected Poems of Rainer Maria Rilke* (transl. Bly); and to AP Watt on behalf of Michael B Yeats for permission to quote from *Selected Poems* by Yeats. At the time of going to press, no reply had been received from Beacon Books for permission to quote from Mary Oliver's *New and Selected Poems*, and *The Kabir Book* (transl. Bly), or from Robert Bly for permission to quote his translation of Goethe from *News of the Universe*; these will be remedied in future editions. (All poetry in the text which is unattributed is my own.)

Gill Edwards
April 2006

FOREWORD

What it is, is that we have to remember how to love.

That's what it is.

What it's not is what we *think* that it is, which is about protecting ourselves and regulating ourselves and stopping ourselves. If we could just walk up to every person we meet and say, 'I'm wild about you!' If we could just embrace every circumstance and condition in our lives and say, 'I'm just wild about this!' if we could just look into every mirror and say, 'I'm wild about *you, too*!' we could change our lives – and, not coincidentally, our world – overnight.

The world is the way it is because we don't love wildly. We don't love life wildly, we don't love each other wildly, and we don't love ourselves wildly. If we just did that ... if we just *did it* ...

Ah, but what's the use? We wouldn't know how, even if we wanted to.

Okay, some people might. A tiny handful. But most people wouldn't.

Isn't that crazy? We don't know how to love. Not wildly. And anything less than wild love is not love at all, but a limp and lukewarm imitation that can't come close to the fire and passion, the explosive ecstasy, of the Real Thing. That's because love *is* wild, by definition. It is that which is untamed, unlimited, unrestricted. It is the Ultimate All, the Complete Totality, the Absolute Everything.

We do not know how to love wildly because no one has ever taught us.

Wait. It's worse than that. We've been taught just the *opposite*. We've been taught how to love sanely, how to love safely, how to love appropriately, primly, properly, limitedly. We've never been taught how to love *full out*.

Here's a wild idea: let's all of us learn!

We can, you know. It's not too late. *It's never too late to learn to love.* Really love. Totally. With no expectation, demand, requirement, or boundary. With no neurosis, unhealthy attachment, or stomach-twisting pain. With no holds (or embraces) barred, with no punches (or smooches) pulled, with nothing but naked desire and naked truth.

Of course, we will not be learning anything, we'll merely be remembering. You see, when we made the journey from spirituality to physicality most of us left a ton of awareness at the portal. It's not necessary to go back to the other side in order to regain that. It can be regained during your time of physicality. In fact, that's the whole purpose of physicalisation. Life is God made physical. So I've been told, in a couple of conversations that I've had ...

I've also been told that when the student is ready, the teacher will appear. So I'm not even a little surprised that a book titled *Wild Love* should pop into the space. We called it forth, you and I, and we used the part of Us that names Itself Gill Edwards (to whom we owe effusive thanks) to tell ourselves about ourselves in this way.

We're always doing that. That's what's so wonderful about life. We're always calling forth exactly what we need precisely when we need it in order to move to the next level in our experience. In this sense it can be said that we never need anything at all. Even before we ask, we will be answered.

You asked for this book, or you wouldn't be holding it in your hands. Trust that. Then dive into this very special writing with wild abandon. Love this book wildly. It will remind you of many things: how the world is and how it works; the energy system that is life itself, and how to – quite literally – tap into that system; and the only true and real definition of love and life and of that which some of us call God.

Get out your highlighter – you're going to need it. If you're one of those who turns down pages on which there's something you really want to remember, you're going to make a mess of this book. They should have just published the thing with every page pre-crimped. It would have been neater. On the other hand, if you want neatness you shouldn't pick up a book about love. There's nothing neat about it. Not about real love. Not about wild love. Wild love messes the sheets. Wild love messes your hair. Wild love messes with your mind.

And what a lovely mess it is.

So let's mess around. This book is a delicious wisdom. Let's invite humanity to gobble it up.

Neale Donald Walsch

CHAPTER ONE

Invitation To The Dance

> …Then comes the moment
> of feeling the wings you've grown,
> lifting.
>
> **Rumi**

I sit on my favourite blue bench in the garden, watching the doves fly and swoop around the dovecote. Dragonflies hover over the reeds in the tiny pond. A robin hops along a nearby branch, cocking its head. Sunshine dapples through the oak tree onto craggy rocks below, and a warm breeze caresses my skin. My heart sings in this beautiful garden, and I am filled with gratitude for the unfolding path of my life.

How did I come to be here? Three years ago, my life seemed so settled – with an apparently stable marriage, a young child and a large family home where we had planned to stay for at least 20 years. My future felt secure and predictable – or so I had imagined. I now reflect in wonder on my chaotic and tumultuous journey, a journey that catapulted me out of my marriage, out of my home and through every extreme of joyous and anguished emotion. A journey that was to return me unexpectedly to the Lakeland hamlet I had long thought of as 'home', and to this gnarled and ancient homestead where I gave birth to my son, nine years ago.

Through this rich period of transformation, my heart has been opened. I have learned the true meaning of unconditional love – for myself, for others and for life. I understand, more deeply than ever, how our inner and outer realities are intertwined, and how we consciously shape our lives in quite magical ways. I have learned so much about the origins of suffering, what causes conflict and what makes relationships joyful and fulfilling (or otherwise). I have gained a fresh roadmap for life, and a delicious sense of freedom and expansiveness. It has been far from easy, yet this crucible has been a precious gift. These days I see the world so differently. I *feel* so different – as if I've given birth to a new Self.

❤

This book is revolutionary. It will take you on a long and deep journey. It is a journey that might well change your life.

Wild Love invites you into a new and magical reality, a reality in which we are apprentice gods and goddesses. It offers an energy-based approach to our emotional and physical well-being. It gives a liberating perspective on God, religion and the purpose of life – which can free us from guilt, duty and self-sacrifice for ever, and allow us to be who we really are. It makes some startling and heretical suggestions about what it really means to be spiritual, how to be happy and how to make our relationships work. It takes you through my own personal journey of inner-outer transformation, and the unconventional insights that emerged. It shows how and why relationships usually go wrong. And it suggests a radical new model for love – a model that could transform our stifling, conventional approach to marriage, make all our relationships more joyful and rewarding and potentially consign our need for personal or global 'enemies' to history. When we love ourselves, others and life more wildly, we begin to create heaven on earth.

Let me walk you through the journey of *Wild Love*, so that you have some idea of where this book might lead you. I suggest that you do not attempt to read it in one sitting. That would be like stuffing down a banquet. It needs to be absorbed bit by bit – then probably to be re-read several times, or dipped into at random – taking your time, often pausing for breath or sitting down to admire the view, as if you were climbing a mountain. S-l-o-w-l-y. At times, the path might feel like drifting through a meadow of wild flowers on a summer's day. At other times, the way might seem steep, rocky and challenging, like forging an uphill path through a dense green forest. But if *Wild Love* does not change your way of being in the world for ever, you have probably not read it thoroughly – or you have read it without putting it into practice, and are trying to avoid its profound implications. You have been warned!

Wild Love will turn your common sense upside down and inside out – and you will need time to think. You will also need time to *feel* – to tune in to your emotions, to listen to your gut feelings, the language of your soul. The message of this book challenges many of our core assumptions about life, love and relationships. Yet it might feel as if you're awakening from a deep sleep – and hearing what your heart has long been whispering, though you hardly dared to believe it.

Our journey begins, in the next chapter, by exploring the dramatic new world view that is emerging from science. We are living in the midst of a rare paradigm shift – a massive change in our way of understanding reality. Instead of seeing the world as made up of solid objects that are separate from each other, we are shifting towards an energy-based perspective in which everything is interconnected. The surface reality of everyday life is not all that exists. Hidden beneath the visible world is an interconnected web of energy-consciousness – the level of deep reality, or Source. And it is this deep reality that is the source of our freedom, joy and empowerment. You do not have to accept this new vision of reality; you just need to entertain it as a possibility. Just for now. If you are reading this, you are already on the cutting edge of a thrilling new approach to life.

In chapter 3, I look at how the immature ego lives in surface reality – and will convince us that there is nothing else – even though the magic of deep reality lies just beyond our noses. It is the ego that separates us from the limitless energy of Source, imprisoning us in a fearful, insecure and fragmented Self. As I see it, our personal challenges form part of a bigger picture of global awakening. Collectively we are being called to undertake what mythologist Joseph Campbell called the 'hero's journey' – to leave behind our old ways of being and give birth to a more expansive Self, which can help transform our world.

Chapter 4 explores the emerging field of energy psychology and energy medicine. It shows that whenever we are stuck in fear or judgment, we short-circuit our energy system. Our negative emotions are simply a signal that we are not aligned with Source energy. Everyone has energy habits, such as fear or guilt or denial, which keep us trapped in our ego. These habits form deep riverbeds – well-worn tracks in our energy system that feel easy and comfortable to run along. Yet they disconnect us from Source energy. By allowing our energy to flow – by forging new riverbeds – we build a bridge to deep reality, which lies beyond the limitations of space and time. When Source energy flows through us, we liberate our true human potential. And the key to free-flowing energy is unconditional love: wild love.

In chapter 5, I ask whether God needs therapy – or whether it is our crazy concepts of God that need a complete overhaul. I look at how religion has promoted fear and judgment as an agent of social control – and how splitting the world into good and bad, right and wrong, safe and dangerous, merely strengthens the ego. It tames and limits us. Rather than throwing God out, perhaps it is time for us to mature into a more grown-up philosophy: an understanding of our creative Source that honours our essential goodness, and frees us to become the 'apprentice gods' – the conscious creators of our lives – which we already are.

Chapter 6 offers a new approach to spirituality. Instead of trying to be good, which splits our energy and makes us neurotic, it suggests that we should aim to be happy. As an energy-based approach can demonstrate, this brings us into harmony with our deep Self – and this leads us towards wild love. Our emotions constantly guide us towards deep reality. As we pay attention to our emotional guidance, we re-align ourselves with Source energy, and with love.

In chapter 7, I explore how we come to lose touch with our authenticity, our deepest truth, by getting lost in relationships – by trying to please others, to fulfil others' needs and expectations, or trying to be 'good' by external standards. Through sharing my own personal crisis, I outline some ways of reclaiming the authentic Self, and setting out on the hero's journey towards a new way of being.

Chapter 8 outlines the process of reality creation – how we create our lives from the inside out – and why unconditional self-love is crucial to making our dreams come true. It shows how we can live with a foot in both worlds, aware of both surface and deep reality, and learn to be conscious co-creators with Source. By following our bliss – by choosing to be happy, rather than trying to be good – we can create our own heaven on earth.

In chapter 9, I explore how, as we transmute lead into gold, our personal wounds can become our gifts to the world. I look at the true purpose of suffering, and how it can be a catalyst for a more joyful, loving and harmonious future. By sharing my own journey through wild and tame love, I show how difficult experiences can clarify our desires, and expand our consciousness – and why duality creates most of the world's problems. I suggest that we need to move beyond fear and judgment – beyond duality – towards wild love.

The final three chapters explore our current practice of tame love and its origins, and a visionary future of wild love.

Chapter 10 looks at how the ego always makes 'love' conditional – and thereby wrecks our relationships. Love can heal and transform us, but only if it is wild love. Tame love is insipid or restrictive, needy or controlling. It merely strengthens our ego defences, and makes relationships shallow, painful or imprisoning. Tame love makes us fall into patterns of what I call 'blaming, shaming and taming'– which split our energy and squash our human potential. It tries to control others from the outside in. I look at how co-dependency is promoted through pressures to be good and loyal and dutiful, and why our models of love and marriage need to radically change.

Chapter 11 explores our family patterns, and shows how dysfunctional 'riverbeds of relating' – based on fear, shame and misguided loyalty – flow down the generations. The good news is that the current chaos in our personal relationships is due to these old riverbeds drying up and fracturing. Our awareness is expanding. Our dreams are calling us towards a new future. We are pioneering paths of real love – wild love – which take us beyond the ego.

Finally, chapter 12 explores what wild love means in practice. I offer a radical model of what love really means, and suggest ten ways to transform our relationships – with Self, with others and with life – by loving more and more wildly. Once we know that we create our own reality, and that relationships always mirror the signals we emit, we can no longer hold anyone else responsible for what we feel, or what we experience. Everything is a dance of co-creation. Then we can love wildly. We become conscious co-creators – and a miraculous new world opens up to us. Instead of becoming fatter and fatter caterpillars, we are transformed into butterflies. We become wild and free.

Wild Love opens the door to an adventurous reality. A world of joy, freedom, creativity and boundless love. Heaven upon earth. It shows that you are holding the key to that ballroom door – and instead of peeking through the keyhole, it invites you to come and join the dance. I hope you will accept this gold-leafed invitation to an expansive and magical new universe, in which *you* can create the life and love of your wildest dreams – a life that truly belongs to you.

CHAPTER TWO

Our Looking-Glass World

What I thought was unreal now, for me, seems in some ways to be more real than what I think to be real, which seems now more to be unreal.

Fred Alan Wolf, physicist[1]

A journey of a thousand miles begins with a single step ... so let us begin by exploring the stunning new vision of reality that is emerging from science. This is a rocky and challenging part of the path, but getting to the top will be well worth the climb! If you have not come across this model before, you will need to suspend your judgment for a while, since it shakes up all our common-sense assumptions and leaves them reeling. The new paradigm suggests that the 'solid world' we live in is not as it appears to be – that we live in a looking-glass universe in which the outer world mirrors the inner. And it is only when we fully realise that life is created from the *inside out* that we stop trying to control it from the *outside in*.

♥

Twenty-five years ago, while studying for a postgraduate degree in clinical psychology, I stumbled across a strange book about the nature of reality. It was a book that would change my life. It scrambled my brain cells and turned my understanding of the world upside down; yet the ideas in it seemed curiously familiar, as if I was recalling a long-forgotten dream. At that time, I was struggling to integrate years of scientific training with my longstanding interest in mysticism and the paranormal. I had so many questions. How does mind relate to matter? What is the nature of God? Is science compatible with mysticism? What is the meaning and purpose of life? *And where does love fit into all of this?*

Having grown up in a haunted house, I had an acute awareness that unseen realities mingle with our ordinary lives. There was no mistaking the 'electric' atmosphere in our home on days when the ghost was around. I also had strange lucid dreams and frequent out-of-body experiences, which I learned how to induce. I knew there was more to life than met the eye. Yet I also had a practical, no-nonsense, down-to-earth streak that liked things to make sense, to fit together, to be integrated. Sometimes I felt split in two, as if I lived in two separate worlds which lay uncomfortably back to back – like partners in a marital bed who refused to speak to each other – while I flip-flopped uneasily between the two.

I read books about the new physics – about the wonders of time running backwards as well as forwards, apparently disconnected particles 'communicating' beyond time and space, and how the mere observation of an event has a crucial impact upon what happens. I knew that some scientists believed we had not yet grasped what quantum physics revealed about the nature of the universe – that it implied that we are not merely objective *observers* of an independent physical reality, but instead conscious *participants* in what happens 'out there' in the world. I pondered whether consciousness was somehow built into the very fabric of the universe.

Then I read *Seth Speaks*,* which suggests that we are multi-dimensional beings who are currently focused in physical form, and that it is consciousness that shapes, forms and even creates physical reality. As a psychologist, I was riveted by the possibility that the mind is the prime creative force in the universe – that our thoughts and beliefs and desires literally create our lives. Was that really possible? It sounded so magical. Yet somehow it felt so right. I caught glimpses of how science and mysticism might come to merge, with staggering implications for our everyday lives.[3]

Centuries ago, people accepted without question that the earth was flat, and that the sun moved around the earth. (And from their limited perspective, this was 'true'.) Then we became aware of a wider perspective – and slowly accepted evidence that the earth is round, and that the planets of our solar system revolve around the sun. We shifted from a flat, two-dimensional earth to a round, three-dimensional model. In the same way, might we be expanding our awareness again, and moving towards a more multi-dimensional view of reality – a quantum leap in our world view?

SURFACE AND DEEP REALITY

Let us take a peek at the new world view that is emerging from pioneers in scientific thinking. According to the new physics, there are two levels of reality. At the superficial level of reality, objects *appear* to be separate. A chair can be moved away from a table. A football can be kicked into a goal. A stone can fall into a river. And a stone is 'obviously' dead, inert, lifeless. A stone has no consciousness. (What a ridiculous idea!) This is the material world that we have been culturally brainwashed into believing is the only reality. It is a mechanical universe of mindless atoms and molecules, in which life emerged as an unlikely result of random events.

It is a lonely planet of separate people, disconnected objects, statistical accidents, chance encounters and innocent victims. It is a depressing, empty world devoid of any meaning or purpose. This is the limited world of the ego, the divided, fragmented self that sees itself as separate from the world, and separate from other people. It is a model of the universe that many still believe in as dogmatically as any religion – accepting it without question as 'how things are' – as if, because it can construct jet planes and computers, and predict the orbit of Mercury around the sun, science has also had the final say about the nature and meaning of life.

Yet at the cutting edge of science, a more expansive world view is emerging – another level of reality. We are living in the midst of a rare and exciting paradigm shift, a huge change in how we see the world – a merging of science and spirituality, of rationality and intuition. Science is transforming its mindset from a dead, meaningless, materialist universe to a vibrant, conscious and ever-evolving universe.[4] And this mirrors a shift in our own consciousness, a shift so dramatic that it might be compared with a caterpillar turning into a butterfly. We are expanding beyond our old world view, and maturing into a world view that is broader, deeper, more loving and more empowering. We are becoming aware of hidden dimensions of reality, of a magical connectedness between mind and matter – and of our own amazing power as creative beings.

In 1981 – while I was reading my first Seth book – *Wholeness and The Implicate Order* was published, a groundbreaking book about the nature of the universe by physicist David Bohm, a brilliant former student of Einstein's. Bohm stated that there must be higher dimensions of reality, otherwise the properties of subatomic systems made no sense. He viewed the physical world that we can see, hear, touch and smell as just one level of reality, which unfolds from a deeper, hidden level of reality.[5] I call these two levels 'surface reality' and 'deep reality' respectively.

At the level of deep reality, the universe is a massive interconnected web of energy. As countless mystics throughout the ages have suggested, everything is one. This is the level of the deep Self, the higher Self or soul. At this unseen level, everything affects everything else. It is a level of unbroken wholeness. The visible and invisible realms – surface and deep reality – are seamlessly interwoven, and the two levels constantly interact, flowing in and out of each other. In fact everything, including a human being, seems to be a packet of pulsating energy that dances in and out of deep reality, the energy field that interconnects all that is.[6]

What is more, this web of energy is inseparable from consciousness. (Are you still following this? It is a crucial point to take in – because until you understand how our inner world is linked to the outer world, you cannot love wildly. This won't make sense yet, but it will soon. Just you wait.) David Bohm and others suggest that consciousness, rather than matter, is probably the basic building block of the universe. In other words, matter emerged from consciousness – from a unified field of conscious energy that is the Source of all being. Within a materialist model of the universe, God is absent, distant or simply irrelevant and unnecessary; but in the emerging world view, we are inseparable from God/Source, and realise that God/Source is evolving itself *through us*. Just as mystics have said since ancient times!

According to this viewpoint, consciousness shapes and moulds and even creates what we experience. The world 'out there' is connected to what happens 'in here' – in the privacy of our own mind – in ways that boggle the imagination. Our view of reality needs to be turned inside out. As mystics have always said, there is no real separation between inner and outer.

> Like the world of the magician, the world of the
> physicist is full of unseen connections traversing
> apparently empty space.
>
> Rupert Sheldrake[7]

THE CONSCIOUS UNIVERSE

Physicist Amit Goswami suggests[8] that the curious paradoxes
of quantum mechanics *only* make sense if we assume that
consciousness creates physical reality. (Take a deep breath.) It
is *consciousness* that collapses the wave function of any
quantum event – and this in turn determines what happens
in the outside world. Quantum physics is all about possibilities; and which 'possible event' actually manifests in the
world depends upon our consciousness.

Despite what the mundane world view tells us, this
means there is no real, solid world 'out there' that is separate
from our inner world. Nothing exists independently of our
consciousness; it only *appears* to be separate. Mind and
matter are interwoven like different-coloured threads in a
multi-dimensional tapestry. We perceive the world according
to our own awareness, and – more magically – 'pull' events
from the outside world that correspond to our own state of
mind: our desires, beliefs and expectations.

William Tiller of Stanford University, California, one of
the world's leading scientists on the structure of matter,
suggests that we are moving towards a model of the universe
in which consciousness creates energy which creates matter.[9]
According to this model, energy is the bridge between mind
and matter. *Energy is the link between our inner world and outer
reality.* This is central to understanding wild love, since it is
the *flow of energy* – as you will see – that determines whether
we create heaven or hell, or something in between.

Einstein discovered that energy could be converted into
matter, and vice versa – but we are now grasping that

consciousness comes into this too, and that consciousness, energy and matter are *all* interconvertible.

Consciousness ⟷ Energy ⟷ Matter

Tiller has constructed a ten-dimensional model of the universe that provides a scientific framework for understanding how our thoughts, intentions, beliefs and expectations affect physical reality. He suggests that the world is rather like a huge, interactive television set which both receives and transmits information, according to what is held in our consciousness. According to this view, 'what appears to us on the <u>outer</u> is just a materialised reflection of that which is on the <u>inner</u>'.[10]

As scientist Joseph Dispenza points out in the film *What The Bleep Do We Know?*, 'We've been conditioned to believe that the external world is more real than the internal world. This new model of science says just the opposite. It says what's happening within us will create what's happening outside of us.'

> *A new door has opened, and we once again seem like babes 'crawling on the floor of the universe'.*
>
> **William Tiller**[11]

Within this new paradigm, physics is blending into metaphysics. We are beginning to fathom the amazingly interactive nature of reality. The new model tells us that *everything* – whether it is a ten-ton truck, a pleasant thought, a rush of anger, a handshake or a ghost – is just organised energy, vibrating at different frequencies which determine what form that energy takes. It also says that consciousness determines the outcome of quantum events, which in turn determine reality. Similarly, countless mystics and channelled sources suggest we are like radios that emit and receive patterned energy.[12] As we emit certain vibrational patterns of energy-consciousness – for example, as repeated thoughts – these attract corresponding realities towards us. We attune ourselves to certain radio stations, and tune out others.

According to the universal Law of Attraction, like attracts like. You get what you focus upon. If you focus upon problems, you attract more of the same. If you focus upon what you love and appreciate, you attract more of the same. If you focus upon lack and scarcity, you get more of it. Vibration always precedes form. Energy turns into matter – as events or situations. In other words, we are creative beings who literally birth our reality, moment by moment, through the vibrations that we emit.

As I see it, many of these vibrations are habitual energy patterns, or 'energy habits' – whether of thoughts, feelings, behaviours or ways of relating – which have been passed down the generations, or practised for many years, and have formed deep riverbeds; hence our tendency to repeat old patterns. It is always easier not to change, to remain stuck and stick to our old habits, even if we realise that they are limiting or imprisoning us, or wrecking our relationships. However, we *can* shift our energy habits through conscious intention, or by unblocking and balancing our energy flow, so that we emit different frequencies, tune in to different realities, and thus transform our lives. And this psychoenergetic view of reality – which might sound rather like Alice in Wonderland – is consistent with the new paradigm in physics.

> For any speculation which does not at first look crazy, there is no hope.
>
> **Freeman Dyson**[13]

Unlike the disconnected view of surface reality, this new paradigm offers a rich and eloquent reality in which the appearance of a rainbow or a butterfly can be meaningful and significant, since it is linked with the vast, universal, conscious energy that we might call Source, God, Spirit or the Universe. Such events are not necessarily random, but might be *meaningful* coincidences – or what Jung called 'synchronicities'. They might emerge from the connectedness of deep reality. Those who live in surface reality would dismiss such a notion as hogwash or 'wishful thinking' – but they inhabit a shallow, limited and fragmented reality that corresponds to the physics of the 19th century, a physics without a heart or soul. At the level of deep reality – the hidden and meaning-ful reality that underlies our everyday experience – everything is interconnected, and the basis of the universe is conscious energy.

In this new model, energy and consciousness are two sides of the same coin, so everything from the trees and the wind to a computer or an armchair *must* have its own consciousness, albeit different from yours and mine – just as mystics have always suggested. According to Seth, there is consciousness even within a nail, and there is no such thing as dead matter.[14] In fact, the whole cosmos might be seen as a unified and conscious organism.

Some years ago, an elderly woman was walking on the clifftops in New England when she fell down the cliffs on to an isolated beach. She was too badly bruised and hurt to move, but just as she was abandoning hope of surviving, she saw a seagull hovering above her. She and her sister had regularly fed a wild gull at their home, a mile away – and had named the gull Nancy. Acting on a hunch, she cried out, 'For God's sake, Nancy, get help!' Minutes later, her sister was disturbed by a gull flapping and tapping at their kitchen window. She was unable to shoo it away, and eventually went outside, somehow sensing that the gull was trying to tell her something. She followed it towards the beach, with the gull alighting at regular intervals as if checking that she was following. The gull finally landed on the cliff edge where her sister had fallen – and an ambulance was called.[15]

This heartwarming true story reminds us that love and

connectedness are a natural part of the web of life. We are never alone, never separate. Everything is conscious, and all consciousness is interconnected. We have emerged from a loving Source from which we are forever inseparable – even though we have become blinkered to this bigger picture of reality, and have somehow convinced ourselves that we live in an empty, clockwork universe, or that God is distant and abandoning. Perhaps we needed to take that prolonged journey into the wasteland, but love is where we have come from, what we truly are and where we are going. Within the new model of the universe, we are apprentice gods and goddesses within a conscious, ever-evolving universe who are learning to love, learning to be conscious creators, learning how to create our own heaven on earth.

> *Learned scientists have said*
> *energy tends to disperse.*
> *Cigarettes burn into ash.*
> *Strong metals rust. Bombs are transmuted*
> *into rubble. Planes explode*
> *in fireballs. White bones*
> *leach slowly into dust.*
>
> *But on a brighter note, they add,*
> *kinetic bonding tends to hold*
> *our molecules together,*
> *keeps us from shimmering*
> *out toward loss.*
>
> *Perhaps love is its other name,*
> *abiding chemistry*
> *that binds the fragments close.*

Susan Castillo[16]

THE EVOLUTION OF CONSCIOUSNESS

The quantum world is full of *potential* – the potential for countless possible futures, for unpredictability and for freedom of choice. The possibility of change hangs glimmering in the air like a fairy godmother's wand, in each and every moment. The more conscious we become, the more genuine freedom we seem to have. The more we expand our awareness – developing our own uniqueness and authenticity, while also connecting deeply with others and the world – the more we inhabit the loving, creative, joyful and miraculous world of our deep Self. We are constantly choosing which world to inhabit, which future to create.

As in the Harry Potter books, there seem to be two worlds, a magical world and a mundane world. Yet there is an extraordinary twist. The truth is that we are *all* witches and wizards; we are simply not aware of it. We all create our reality in magical ways, through the power of our focus, desire, intention and consciousness. Life does not simply happen to us. It is actively created (or passively allowed) by our consciousness – including events that might seem quite beyond our control, such as other people's behaviour, accidents, illnesses, good or bad luck, and so-called coincidences.

Deep reality corresponds to the magical world of Hogwarts school of wizardry, while surface reality is the superficial world of the Muggles – the 'ordinary humans' who are untrained in magic. (And perhaps part of the astonishing popularity of Harry Potter lies in the deep intuitive knowing that these two worlds *are* mirrored in reality, and are not just a work of fiction.) If cutting–edge scientists and visionaries are right, what our culture sees as normal is but a stunted fragment of our human potential. And perhaps our current crises are pushing us towards the natural evolution of humanity, and forcing us to expand our awareness? Perhaps it is time for the seen and unseen worlds to come together – and for us to embrace our power and potential as human beings, and walk with a foot in both worlds?

In *Conscious Evolution*, Barbara Marx Hubbard suggests that those of us who are shifting into expanded consciousness are like the 'imaginal disks' in a caterpillar, which carry the blueprint for the butterfly yet to come. Initially, the caterpillar's immune system sees these disks as foreign and tries to destroy them, but as the disks multiply and mature into 'imaginal cells', they eventually break down the caterpillar and destroy it. Then the wondrous butterfly can emerge.

> *The breakdown of the caterpillar's old system is essential for the breakthrough of the new butterfly.*
> **Barbara Marx Hubbard**[17]

This means we need to get used to change, and let go of our former stability, or we are in for a very bumpy ride! Many of us feel as if we have been flung against the walls in recent years, being pushed into unexpected changes and growth, or even into releasing our old lives – as if some greater force is urging us on. No longer is it possible to sweep issues under the carpet with the vague intention of tackling them someday. We can no longer cling to our old ways of being, our self-defeating habits and addictions. We can no longer pretend that life is fine when it is not. Our alarm bells are ringing too loudly. Our forgotten dreams and desires are clamouring for attention. We are being urged as individuals to wake up – to remember who we are, to fulfil our potential – and to change our lives from the inside out.

At a cultural level, most of our social systems seem to be in crisis, on the verge of collapse or transformation. The old ways are no longer working. New perspectives are creeping in at the side doors. Those conservatives who strive to maintain the status quo (and who tend to hold positions of power) are beginning to flounder. Our imaginal cells are maturing, and becoming more and more numerous, and the pressure for change is growing. Like it or not, our consciousness is moving towards a quantum jump.

A NEW VISION OF REALITY

A psychoenergetic model of the universe is still highly controversial, and most traditional scientists would hold up their hands in horror, or laugh uproariously (at least in public) at the idea that consciousness creates reality. The current orthodoxy sees such ideas as heretical and dangerous – and many scientists dogmatically insist, with the true fundamentalism of their 'religion', that consciousness somehow emerged from matter. For them, what happens at the level of quantum reality bears no relation to what happens in our everyday lives. Those same scientists would scoff at the existence of ghosts, or telepathy, or mind-over-matter, or out-of-body experiences – despite the overwhelming evidence for such phenomena. (See Dean Radin's powerful book, *The Conscious Universe*, for the wealth of scientific evidence for psychic phenomena.)

Dean Radin[18] notes that earth-shattering ideas tend to move into cultural awareness slowly. At first, the ideas are dismissed as impossible or ridiculous, since they violate the known laws of science. Those brave souls who promote the heresy might be rejected, ridiculed, fired from their academic or statutory posts – or, in past times, tortured or burned at the stake. Science, like religion, has powerful vested interests that support the status quo, and resists any 'threat' that might overturn the orthodoxy. (I once shared a house with a theoretical physicist who would not have dared to reveal his mystical leanings within his university department.) During the next stage, the new ideas begin to be accepted as real – but they are seen as irrelevant or insignificant. Then the vast implications of the expanded world view begin to seep into mainstream consciousness, and a new era dawns. At the final stage, the sceptics claim that it was their idea in the first place, or they simply grow old, retire and die — and everyone sees the new model as common sense, as 'how things are'.

Such a cultural shift takes many decades. The first signs of the current paradigm shift can be traced back to the 1920s (with quantum physics and the 'first wave' of feminism). In the 1960s and 1970s, the implications of a holistic world view began to trickle into mainstream thought via feminism, green awareness, alternative medicine, the peace movement, new spirituality and so on. Early in the 21st century, we are still grappling with what this means for our everyday lives, and whether the most radical interpretations of quantum physics are correct — but a paradigm shift looks increasingly imminent.

At a personal level, I am still 'recovering' from the materialist world view, despite teaching and writing about the new paradigm for the past 15 years, and studying it for 30 years. I can still slip back into conventional ways of thinking. We are currently straddling two paradigms, and it can feel lonely at times to inhabit assumptions about our daily lives that are strikingly different from those of friends, family and colleagues. It is tempting to share *their* reality in an attempt to fit in and belong, or to feel less crazy! However, as more and more of us 'come out' and challenge the existing world view, the easier it is for others to join us.[19]

According to Thomas Kuhn, a paradigm shift always seems to be triggered by crisis.[20] Crisis seems to precede transformation. Serious problems arise for which the old paradigm has no real answers — such as ecological crises, chronic health problems, wars, increase in violent crime, child abuse and the breakdown of family and community. Then the emergent new paradigm offers a different way of seeing that expands our awareness of what is going on, and points towards new and creative solutions. More and more people begin to explore those new options, and eventually the world shifts on its axis.

However risky and threatening it might feel, a crisis is always an opportunity for change, pushing us into growth and evolution at both personal and cultural levels. And evolution always means higher consciousness and greater freedom.[21] As we feel more and more aware, and more and more free, we know that we are moving in the right direction. We are becoming butterflies.

> *One doesn't discover new lands without consenting to lose sight of the shore.*
>
> *André Gide*[22]

Let us suppose that the mystics and cutting-edge scientists might be right, and that consciousness *is* what creates our experience. If so, in order to change anything 'out there', we have to change our inner world – since at the level of deep reality, it is energy-consciousness that shapes, moulds and attracts whatever happens in our lives. This might sound like a scary option. After all, it means there is no-one to blame any more! We can no longer see ourselves as victims. We can no longer blame our childhood, our family, our boss, our partner, our neighbours, our body, the government or our circumstances for how we feel or for what happens to us. We can no longer try to control others in an attempt to feel good. As apprentice gods, we have to take responsibility for *whatever* we experience – whether or not we like it. (And this has radical implications for the law, politics, science, healthcare, social services and so on.) On the other hand, this new model offers us unlimited power to create what we really want in our lives.

So let us entertain the possibility, just for now, that we *are* emerging from spiritual kindergarten, and becoming apprentice gods and goddesses. Let us grapple with the mind-boggling idea that the outer world mirrors our inner world. Instead of seeing ourselves as merely human, let us open to the possibility that we are multi-dimensional beings currently having a human experience. Instead of seeing the world as made of solid stuff that is really Real, let us think in more fluid terms of energy and consciousness and love. Let us dare to become initiated into a new vision of reality.

As we shall see, this new paradigm has the potential to transform our lives and our relationships. As we connect with Source, we shift away from the 'tame love' of surface reality, which is a pale imitation of love. Our consciousness grows. We see the bigger picture. This frees us to express the 'wild love' of the deep Self – a liberating and unconditional love that gives birth to relationships based upon joy, freedom and growth, and allows us to fulfil our wildest dreams. Then we can co-create heaven on earth. But first, we must become aware of how we limit and imprison ourselves. We must accept an invitation from our deep Self to expand our awareness, and learn to love more wildly.

CHAPTER THREE

The Call To Adventure

*If you don't break your ropes while you're alive,
do you think ghosts will do it after?*

Kabir[1]

In the inspiring film *Field of Dreams*, a struggling Iowa farmer hears a voice one day in his cornfield: 'Build it, and he will come.' For weeks, he wrestles with what the voice means, whether he might be losing his sanity, and what exactly he is being called to do. He slowly realises that he is afraid of turning into his father, who rarely showed any spontaneity and seemed to abandon his hopes and desires; so he cuts down acres of crops in order to fulfil his dream of building a baseball field. Despite the threat of losing his farm and the warning voice of 'reason', he learns to trust his intuition. He then allows the voice to lead him on an epic journey through hope, forgotten dreams and the meaning of life. On returning home, he acts upon a newfound belief in himself and his vision. The ghosts of his past are healed – and a magical new future unfolds.

When we live in surface reality, we tend to lose sight of our dreams and passion and vision. We might tell ourselves we are being grown-up and realistic. We might pretend that life is fine, that we are happy enough. We might sternly remind ourselves that others are far worse off. Yet deep down, something gnaws away at us. Something is missing. Something important – perhaps something crucial.

'No-one wants to remain a prisoner in an unlived life,' says poet and philosopher John O'Donohue, 'yet most of us are lost or caught in forms of life that exile us from the life we dream of. Most people long to step onto the path of creative change that would awaken their lives to beauty and passion, deepen their contentment and allow their lives to make a difference.' [2]

Many of us secretly yearn for our own field of dreams – for a clear, unmistakable voice to shake us out of a humdrum or imprisoning reality and lead us into a joyous and enchanted life. And the new paradigm assures us that those magical realms *are* there, waiting for us, that the unseen dimensions are not just the stuff of fairytales. But first we have to break free from the prison of our old way of being. We need to stop believing in consensus reality, even if everyone around us is convinced that it is how the world is, and begin to expand our perspective. We must see beyond the ego. We have to step into the looking-glass world.

♥

Surface and deep reality correspond to two aspects of our consciousness: the ego (or personality) and the deep Self. The ego sees itself as separate from the world, separate from other people, and separate from Source/God/love, while the deep Self is interconnected and multi-dimensional in its awareness.

Our ego gets lost in surface reality, in the details and busyness and to-do lists of everyday life. It believes that the physical world is solid stuff, and sees itself as a victim of other people's behaviour, situations, illnesses or 'accidents'

that are beyond our control. It feels cut off from unconditional love, and believes it has to earn or deserve love – so it
tries hard to be good and dutiful and perfect, sacrificing itself
for others, or it judges others as bad or wrong or imperfect
so that it can feel better. It is forever seeking love and
approval, and forever sure that it is not quite good enough
to deserve it.

At a consciousness level, the 'skin encapsulated ego' – as
Buddhist philosopher Alan Watts called it – is the part that
sees us as lonely and isolated beings, adrift in the universe.
Rather like an iceberg, the ego is what we see on the
surface, and might easily be mistaken for the whole – but it
is only a tiny proportion of the Self. Although we need an
ego in order to function in physical reality, the ego can be
defined as those aspects of the personality that disconnect us
from Source.

At an energy level, everyone has a garden hose that is
connected to an infinite supply of 'the water of life', or
Source energy. Source is the universal web of energy-
consciousness-love, and when we are tapping into that
energy supply our natural state is unconditional love, joy,
exuberance, freedom, growth, passion, vitality and creative
expression.

However, we tend to tread on our garden hose or put
kinks in it, or fail to open the tap fully, so that our water
trickles out pathetically instead of forming a beautiful and
abundant fountain. As a result, we might feel tired, frustrated,
angry, blaming, critical, depressed, anxious, overwhelmed,
hurt, sad, guilt-ridden, fearful, insecure or not fully alive –
which are just signals that love, the water of life, is not
flowing freely through us.

Those kinks in our hose mostly take the form of negative thoughts or beliefs, based upon childhood experiences
or the influence of others. Our ego has long-practised
energy habits that feel comfortable and familiar, and which
it is keen to hold on to – even if they make life miserable

for us and everyone around us. It strangles the life out of us, making us anxious, guilt-ridden or negative, and disconnects us from our boundless inner Source of joy, freedom and unconditional love. It is too fearful and insecure to be capable of wild love.

THE PRISON OF THE EGO

Based upon its illusion of separateness, the ego has three core beliefs:

✧ I am not safe.

✧ I am not loved (or loved only if I am good).

✧ I am not in control.

These three negative beliefs, which simply arise from being disconnected from Source, give rise to three corresponding needs: the need for security, the need for approval, and the need for control. What the ego really needs is to connect with deep reality, but instead it searches 'out there' for the approval, control and security that it craves. It is a search that is guaranteed to backfire.

Since the ego feels separate from love/Source, it tries to jump through hoops in an attempt to find love, keep love, be worthy of love or gain others' approval. However, *seeking* love and approval means we are affirming its absence. We are affirming our unworthiness and unlovableness – and this insecurity will be mirrored back in our relationships, which will offer only conditional (tame) love. Similarly, if we search for security while feeling unsafe, the world will mirror back those fearful beliefs. Or if we try to control others, believing that *they* need to change or adapt their behaviour in order to make *us* feel happy or loved or secure, they will resist, feel resentful or long to break free.

If the ego understood the Law of Attraction – that like attracts like – it would not anxiously search for a partner while feeling needy, lonely and unloved. After all, when our vibrational frequency is emitting 'needy, lonely and unloved' signals, we will either attract no-one, or a partner with whom we will feel needy, lonely and unloved! (Then our ego will blame the outside world – 'He's afraid of commitment.' 'All women are fickle.' 'All the decent women/men are married.' 'He is wedded to his work.' 'Men can't express their feelings' – instead of looking within.)

If the ego understood the Law of Attraction, it would not install extra locks and burglar alarms in an attempt to feel safe and secure. It would know that, at an energy level, such measures are more likely to *attract* a burglar, since we get what we focus upon (whether real or imaginary). If our thoughts and actions are emitting vibrational frequencies that say, 'The world isn't a safe place. There is a lot of crime about. My house would be attractive to break into,' then we pull that quantum possibility towards us. We prove ourselves right.

I remember hearing of someone putting up smoke alarms in every room of their house. Just a week later, a fire started in their kitchen and they had to call out the fire brigade. 'What a good job you put smoke alarms in,' they were told. But at an energy level, the prolonged focus on the fearful *possibility* of a fire was exactly what had pulled it into their reality.

Our ego constantly tries to protect itself – locking doors and windows, buying insurance, keeping children off the streets, fretting over violent crime, obsessively planning for retirement funds, watching share values, hoarding and clinging in the belief that there is never enough, that it might be taken away, that danger lurks around every corner. It is always looking over its shoulder, always worried that someone or something might smash into it. It has no faith, no trust, no ability to surrender and go with the flow. It does not know that feeling safe comes not from locks or weapons or insurance or wealth, but from a connection with deep reality.

> We do not see things as they are, we see things as we are.
>
> **The Talmud**

Our ego feels lonely and frightened. It sees life as a struggle against a cruel, unpredictable and threatening world. It feels under constant threat of hurt, damage, rejection or annihilation, and strives to keep itself safe by shielding and protecting itself – and forever pointing the finger at others. The ego tries to create peace by going to war, and controlling, banishing or killing the 'enemy'. It tries to exclude what is bad, so that it can feel good. Although it is striving to feel safe and loved, it only succeeds in dividing and disconnecting. It maintains the illusion of separateness.

Within the new paradigm, *we live in a blameless universe*. Whatever happens in our lives is always a dance of co-creation that we have attracted into our reality. Blaming or judging someone else is like giving them a script, then criticising them for accurately reading the part we have written for them! The deep Self understands this bigger picture, but our ego gets lost in victimhood, loving to wag its finger and feel self-righteous. (Or even graciously 'forgiving' others, then feeling self-righteous for doing that!)

This victim/battle mentality also operates at a global level. The war against terrorism. The war against poverty. The war against crime. The war against cancer – and so on. Every war that opposes a current problem is simply perpetuating it, by the Law of Attraction. It keeps on activating an energetic vibration that says: 'Here is an enemy. I don't want the world to be this way – but this is how it is. I don't like it – but it is the truth.' And the world has to keep on reflecting that 'truth' back until we change our vibration. And the more frequently we activate that vibration – by watching the news, reading newspapers, talking about it, thinking about it or actively fighting it – the more we pull that particular experience into our own personal reality. It becomes a self-fulfilling prophecy.

The ego struggles *against* what it does not want – not realising that whenever we focus on problems or lack or threats, we reinforce the status quo. What we resist persists. We always get what we focus upon, whether we are focusing upon what we do not want, or what we do want. Our natural tendency is to try to resolve a problem by focusing on it – analysing it to death, trying to get to the bottom of it, working out what might have caused it, complaining about it, worrying about it, talking it over with friends – but this means that we hold on to the same old vibration. We affirm, over and over again: 'I have this problem or issue.' And so the world continues to mirror that belief back at us.

Since its feeling of separateness is deeply painful and threatening, the ego develops well-practised strategies to try to feel safe, loved and connected. These are usually familiar (*family*-ar) patterns we learned by observing our parents or relatives, or worked out in response to our own childhood experiences. Some of the most common patterns and defences are:

✧ Trying to be 'good' or perfect

✧ Conforming to what others expect; seeking approval

✧ Trying to be special, a shining star, an over-achiever

✧ Saying what we believe others want to hear, instead of speaking our truth

✧ Feeling self-righteous; needing to be 'in the right'

✧ Being loyal and dutiful, regardless of our own feelings or wishes

- ✧ Putting others' needs first; feeling responsible for others' happiness

- ✧ Trying to fix or rescue others (to feel 'better than' or avoid looking at self)

- ✧ Concealing whatever thoughts, needs or emotions feel unacceptable to others

- ✧ Hiding behind roles and masks

- ✧ 'Playing small' (hiding our potential) in an effort to be accepted

- ✧ Withdrawal and distancing; learning to be self-contained

- ✧ Wanting a relationship to be exclusive; being clingy, jealous or possessive

- ✧ Clinging to a relationship, money, status or possessions as a source of security

- ✧ Agreeing or 'merging' with others to avoid conflict, or the risk of abandonment

- ✧ Pretending everything is fine – even when frightened, hurt, angry or confused

- ✧ Blaming, criticising or judging others

- ✧ Projecting our own rage, negativity or destructiveness on to others

- ✧ Being a martyr (secretly angry about others' demands and expectations)

- ✧ Being a control freak – for example, being obsessively clean and tidy, counting calories

- ✧ Controlling or manipulating others

- ✧ Being arrogant and egotistical (as a defence against feeling not good enough)

✧ Avoiding change, staying stuck in negative situations

✧ Being forever busy or workaholic

✧ Compulsive shopping, TV-watching, web-surfing and other addictions

✧ Quelling anxiety with food, drink, drugs or obsessive exercise

All of these defensive strategies are the ego's attempts to cope with its feeling of separateness, and its resulting needs for approval, control and security. All of them are counter-productive, since they reinforce our feeling of disconnection from ourselves and others. They are based upon conditional (tame) love. And all of them become unnecessary when we reconnect more fully with Source energy.

The ego is not wrong or shameful. It just sees the world from a limited perspective. It lives in a narrow prison from which it needs to be liberated. If we see the ego as a road-block to happiness and enlightenment, we can fall into the trap of trying to battle with it – and as soon as we reject *any* aspect of our wholeness, we create inner conflict (neurosis). The ego is not bad or evil, any more than a toddler is bad for not being able to climb a mountain, or recite Shakespeare. It is better to compare the ego to a young child who hasn't yet grasped the bigger picture of reality, since he or she is still figuring out such essentials as how to handle a knife and fork, and how to cross a road safely.

Our ego is essential to being a healthy and whole human being. Without an ego, we would be psychotic and unable to function in physical reality. The ego gives us feedback about what is happening 'out there'. It also allows us to be aware of ourselves as individuals, with our own emotions and desires, visions, uniqueness and boundaries. On the other hand, if we *identify* with the ego – seeing it as who we are – then we remain imprisoned in a limited, mundane and fearful reality. Instead we need to take our ego gently by the hand and help it to mature, to evolve, to expand beyond its old limitations and ways of seeing, and to connect with the deep Self – to connect with wild love. Then we can live with a foot in both worlds and become apprentice gods. Life becomes a magical adventure of joyful co-creation.

> *The breeze at dawn has secrets to tell you.*
>> *Don't go back to sleep.*
> *You must ask for what you really want.*
>> *Don't go back to sleep.*
> *People are going back and forth across the doorsill*
>> *where the two worlds touch.*
> *The door is round and open.*
>> *Don't go back to sleep.*

Rumi ³

THE WORLD OF THE DEEP SELF

Our deep Self knows that there is no real distinction between inner and outer reality – that it is all One. It has three core beliefs (or knowingness), which come from its connectedness to deep reality:

✧ I am utterly safe.

✧ I am loved unconditionally.

✧ I create my own reality.

The deep Self is completely free. It has no need to seek approval, control or security, since it already has these. It knows that we are always safe. (Even if we die, we are utterly safe, since death is an illusion; it is merely a transition from one state of consciousness to another.) The deep Self knows that it is inseparable from love, that it is loved unconditionally by Source. It does not need to search for love or

approval because its very core is love; it radiates unconditional love – and so attracts love, too. And it does not need
to control others or the outside world, because it understands that we consciously create our own reality, and that
what the ego sees is an illusion, a holographic projection of
consciousness, rather like marionettes on a stage.

According to the new paradigm, our thoughts are the
biggest contributor to our vibrational frequency. Thoughts
attract our reality, pulling certain events and circumstances
towards us rather than others. Any thought that makes
you feel joyful, expansive, glowing, peaceful, optimistic,
trusting, heart-centred, relaxed, free, loving or empowered is aligned (at an energy level) with the deep Self.
For example: 'Everyone is always doing the best they can.'
'I can create anything my heart desires.' 'There is plenty
of time.' Any thought that makes you feel anxious, sad,
angry, depressed, closed down, blaming, critical, guilty,
negative, confused, mistrustful, hopeless, frustrated,
regretful, overwhelmed, diminished, tense, limited or
disempowered comes from the ego.[4] For example: 'Life
is a struggle.' 'It's all his/her fault.' 'If only I had made a
different choice ... ' And as you *feel* any thought, you
align with its vibrational frequency, and so begin to attract
corresponding events and situations, whether positive or
negative.

Happily this does not mean that you have to feel
concerned about every single thought you have, since physical reality includes the 'cushion' of time – which softens the
impact of being a conscious creator, since it means that your
thoughts do not manifest immediately. You need to repeat
the same thought many times *and* align yourself with its
energy (that is, feel it or believe it), before a corresponding
event turns up in physical reality. However, the more *strongly*
you believe in a thought, or focus on something you desire
(or fear), the more rapidly it will show up – in some form –
in the outside world.

> *Freedom comes from knowing that nothing and no-one 'out there' is responsible for what you experience or how you feel. What you attract into your reality – and how you choose to interpret it – is all an inside job.*

THE HERO'S JOURNEY

In *The Hero With A Thousand Faces*, Joseph Campbell shows how all the great stories and myths of the world have one central theme: the hero's journey. This archetypal drama forms the backbone of most powerful stories and is an immensely helpful framework for understanding the path of growth, awakening or transformation. It is a journey that you might take, on a dramatic scale, once or twice in a lifetime, especially at major turning points. But on a smaller scale, you face this journey every day – as you make choices about whether to speak your truth in a situation or be defensive, whether to repeat a familiar pattern or make a different decision, whether to criticise or appreciate someone, whether to play safe or take a risk, whether to blame someone else or take responsibility for what happens to you, or whether to 'do your duty' or follow your heart.

The hero's journey outlines the process of growth – that is, the expansion of the ego towards the deep Self – in its raw, essential form, freed from the barrage of everyday details that often make us lose sight of who we are and where we are going. It involves six stages:

✧ The Call

✧ Refusal of the Call

✧ Crossing the First Threshold

✧ The Road of Trials (or Initiation)

✦ The Elixir of Awakening
✦ The Return Home (with the Elixir)

According to Campbell, the hero's journey begins with immersion in the ordinary world of surface reality, in which you live the predictable 'me-too' life that others expect of you. You take on beliefs, values, demands and expectations that are not your own. You walk on the daily treadmill of the unawakened life. You work in order to pay the bills. You drift along in superficial relationships, chatting and gossiping, doing the housework, avoiding true intimacy. You go shopping in hope of 'buying' happiness or fulfilment – or just to fill the vacant time. You might pop pills, smoke, drink or use other addictions (such as work, compulsive exercise or TV) to squash your emotions, to soothe your anxiety, to quell your hidden longings. And you keep yourself busy, far too busy, in order to silence the 'still small voice within'.

Then comes a wake-up call – a Call to adventure, an invitation to change and growth. It might be a challenge, a crisis, a mystery, an opportunity. Or perhaps an unnameable discontent nudges its way into your life, a gnawing frustration, a wordless yearning, a sense of wasted time. The Call might come from a conversation with a friend, an inspiring book, or a sudden desire for change. Or it might take the form of an illness, an accident, falling in love or an unexpected bereavement.

The Call is a finger that beckons us across the threshold into deep reality. Sometimes a Call tiptoes into the silence of our night, as vivid dreams, visions or angelic messengers that tear the thin veil between physical reality and other realms. Or it might blast into the midday sun of our lives as fierce shaking thunder that threatens to shatter our old self into sharp fragments – perhaps a malignant lump, a sudden bereavement, a road accident, an unexpected redundancy, a devastating flood or a heart-stopping betrayal. Sometimes a Call is simply an odd or inexplicable event that makes us wonder about the nature of reality, or ponder whether someone up there is trying to tell us something.

A woman at one of my workshops told me that she awoke one morning to find a long purple ribbon lying on her bed. Just that. She had no idea how the ribbon came to be there, and quickly ruled out all plausible explanations. For months, she carried the ribbon with her, like a holy relic, sometimes fingering it as if it might reveal some secret to her. The mystery led her to read about Jung and symbolism, which led to an evening class – and before long, she had embarked upon a spiritual quest that led to a new career and a new life. After a few years, the ribbon disappeared one day as mysteriously as it had arrived. Presumably its work had been done.

At its simplest, a Call is a reminder that life is not what it seems, that appearances can be deceptive, that there is an ocean of meaning and connectedness beneath the choppy surface waters of our everyday lives. It plunges us into deeper waters. It is an alarm sounding. 'Wake up! Wake up!'

When a major wake-up call comes along, your everyday world shifts on its axis. It offers a stark challenge: will you choose to carry on as before, repeating your old patterns and clinging to your familiar life, or will you say 'Yes' to the invitation, and step into the unknown? If you do say 'Yes,' you will never be the same again. It is as if the river of your life changes course, you begin to flow into a new riverbed – and a richer, deeper journey begins.

> It is a basic principle of spiritual life that we learn
> the deepest things in unknown territory.
>
> **Jack Kornfield[5]**

Initially, the Call to adventure is usually refused. Most of us prefer to pull the bedclothes over our head rather than venture out into the dark woods, at least until we know there is no other choice, or life becomes too uncomfortable, dull or downright painful. However, if we do reach the doorway and peer out into the woods, we often face Threshold Guardians who urge us to turn back – well-meaning people who mirror our own fears, who try to dissuade us, offering grave warnings of what might happen if we abandon our old way of being, of the price we might pay, of the risk we will take or what others might think of us. But the Call is usually repeated, and eventually it becomes impossible to remain in the old world. Staying the same is no longer an option, and all that once seemed so solid and reliable begins to vanish like the morning mist.

At this point, says Joseph Campbell, we are usually sent guides and helpers who urge us to follow the Call. It is often with a nudge from the magical realms (deep reality) – such as a wise friend or stranger, a helpful coincidence, or an irreversible change in circumstances – that we finally accept the Call. The possibility of a new world begins to feel more enticing than what we are leaving behind, or there is no longer any choice since our old world is collapsing. We pass through a metaphorical wall into a new reality: we cross the First Threshold, and our hero's journey begins.

> *And so long as you haven't experienced*
> *this: to die and so to grow,*
> *you are only a troubled guest*
> *on the dark earth.*
>
> **Goethe** [6]

As we travel along the Road of Initiation, we meet with many trials. The outer journey that we take is, of course, a metaphor of *inner* growth and transformation – and as we answer the Call, we commit ourselves to profound inner change. Our inner demons are likely to materialise in the outer world – our old habits of thought, our fears, our resistance, our projections, our family patterns, our unresolved emotions, our unfinished business from the past – and we must confront these if our journey is to be a success. We have to face the death of our old self. Like a snake, we have to slough off our outer skin: our old self-image, our old ways of thinking and relating, how we used to present ourselves to the world, our old limitations. We might even fear that we will die physically, or feel that we *are* dying. But it is ultimately a journey of healing, of reclaiming our wholeness, of reconnecting with deep reality.

In time, if you are willing to let go, you can be resurrected as a new Self, who returns to the ordinary world with the Elixir of Awakening: fresh wisdom, awareness or gifts from your own experience that have the power to change the world. Your journey of personal awakening then becomes a tool for social transformation. Lead is transmuted into gold, as your ego merges with your deep Self.

Your choices are now different. Your way of seeing is different. You are no longer dependent upon others, or seek anyone's approval. You are not 'tamed' by fear or guilt or duty, or limited by what others tell you to expect from life; nor do you blame anyone else for what you experience, or how you feel. You are free from the past. You are a walker between worlds – an awakened one – living from your own centre of self-awareness, inner strength, deep stillness, truth and unconditional love. You are aware of your creative potential as a god in the making. And you begin to lead a wilder, more authentic life – a life that is truly your own.

On the hero's journey, you learn to stop doing whatever you usually do – trying to stay safe, clinging to external sources of security, seeking love and approval, leaning on your addictions, blaming or controlling others – so that you release the expanded awareness and love of your deep Self. The ego fondly believes that it is protecting us, but the reality is that it separates us from love, from freedom, from aliveness, from joy, from growth. It is the ego that keeps us imprisoned within our false self, blocking us from what we truly long for.

Along the Road of Trials, we have to face the painful consequences of our ego's limiting beliefs in separateness over and over again, removing its defensive layers and connecting with hidden strengths and deeper truths, until we finally 'know' that we are safe, we are loved and that we create our own reality. Then we are free. Then we are joyful. Then we radiate unconditional love, wild love. We live with a foot in both worlds, in both surface and deep reality. This is what our personal transformation, our conscious evolution, is all about.

OUR GLOBAL AWAKENING

On a recent trip to the States, I saw newspaper headlines which announced that Rosa Parks had just died, at the age of 92. She was known as the 'mother of the civil rights movement' in the USA. Fifty years earlier, Rosa Parks had been asked to give up her seat to a white man on a city bus in Alabama. She refused to do so – which broke the laws of racial segregation. She was arrested, and lost her job – yet this simple act of civil disobedience changed the course of American history. In an interview I heard, Rosa Parks was asked why she had taken this courageous stance; she replied that she was no longer willing to conform, and be treated with such disrespect. As I see it, she had answered a Call from deep reality, which urged her to love and respect *herself* – to treat *herself* as an equal human being – instead of giving in, and doing what was expected of her. She paved the way for countless other black Americans to find their own self-respect, and insist upon racial equality.

In 1984, when Bob Geldof watched the harrowing TV footage of starvation in Ethiopia, reaching for his cheque-book felt like an inadequate response. He wanted to *do* something, to make a difference. He decided to do what he could as a musician, songwriter and pop star. The resulting single 'Do They Know It's Christmas?' sold more than 3.5 million copies in the UK alone. The charity Band Aid was set up, and fund-raising concerts were organised on both sides of the Atlantic, watched by nearly half the world's population. Twenty years on, the Band Aid Trust had raised more than £77 million pounds for famine relief in Africa. Perhaps even more importantly, Bob Geldof threw pebbles of compassion into our waters, setting ripples off across the world. He is an unlikely saint – the image of him, unkempt and exhausted, angrily thumping the table and ordering us to 'F . . . ing send us your money!' remains with me still – but thanks to him, the world became immeasurably kinder, more loving, more compassionate and more grateful.

Few of us will have as much impact as the Mahatma Gandhis or Nelson Mandelas or Rosa Parks of the world, or even lesser saints such as Bob Geldof. But we can, and do, make a difference. Every time someone reaches out with love, it makes the world more loving. Every time someone makes peace with a friend or colleague or neighbour, it makes the world more peaceful. Every time someone follows their heart instead of merely doing what is expected, it makes the world more heart-centred and courageous. We can all make ripples, each in our own way. The ripples go out – and the world subtly changes, like a kaleidoscope shifting into a new pattern.

Every day we have countless opportunities to expand our consciousness, to choose love rather than fear, joy rather than duty, freedom rather than imprisonment, reaching out rather than holding back. We can wake up or carry on slumbering. The hero's journey is an opportunity to find a new sense of freedom and joy, to become more of who we truly are. It is the Call towards spiritual adulthood. It is the Call to become fully alive. Our deep Self calls on us to let go of our old security blankets and learn to have faith and courage, to be passionate, to open our hearts, to be honest and vulnerable, to be bold and visionary, to live more expansively and to love more wildly. Then we may step into a bigger Self which has been waiting in the wings.

> *Humans have long sensed that something transcendent calls us on, often framing their intuition in myth, poetry or philosophic speculation.*
>
> **James Redfield, Michael Murphy and Sylvia Timbers**[7]

The hero's journey is nothing new. It has been recognised as the central human drama for thousands of years. But what *is* new is the current frequency and intensity of these Calls in the lives of ordinary people. Until recently, people could fall asleep for years, even decades, in a lonely marriage, a boring job, an unchanging routine – and deep reality might give them an occasional dig in the ribs, but nothing more.

As we move deeper into the 21st century, everything is accelerating. On a global scale, we are awakening. Our consciousness is evolving, and unresolved issues can no longer be put on hold. Unfulfilling or stuck relationships are being flung into crisis. Jobs end in redundancy or getting fired. Serious illness makes us face issues that we might have chosen to ignore. No sooner do we resolve one personal challenge than another comes up.

Then there are our global issues. Our beliefs in separateness are the source of most of our global problems. War, terrorism, violence, greed, the disappearing rainforests, water pollution, our vanishing topsoil, third-world debt, child slavery, religious fundamentalism, over-population, the destructive power of multi-national companies – you name it, and it can almost all be traced to the ego's belief in separateness and its resulting fear and defences.

In the past 3,000 or 4,000 years, we have focused on developing our yang energy, our masculine energy, our desire to move apart. It is now time to reconnect: to express more of our yin energy, our tendency to move together, our connectedness, our feminine energy not as an alternative to our yang energy, but in addition to it. It is time to re-balance ourselves, to become aware of both our individuality *and* our oneness. We have reached the furthest point of disconnection – from ourselves, from each other, from our earthly home, and from our creative Source. It is time for us to wake up and reclaim our wings.

So what is it we are waking up to?

Connectedness. Connectedness to each other, connectedness to nature, connectedness to the invisible realms, connectedness to our own self – and to unconditional love.

Remembering. Remembering our dreams and visions, remembering why we came here, remembering who we are, remembering we are all one.

Awareness. Awareness of the wonder of life, so that we no longer sleepwalk through the ordinary miracle of our everyday lives. Awareness of freedom and joy, beauty and gratitude. Awareness of mystery and magic. Awareness of our vast human potential, of which we catch only occasional glimpses. Awareness of the truth about who we are, how we feel, what we genuinely want – and what we have come to give.

The world might seem to be in chaos, but chaos is a necessary precursor to change. If we are clearing our clutter, we have to empty all the drawers and shelves, dust the cobwebby corners, poke around in the cupboards and face the dark cellar. And it might get messy for a while. But in order to move on, we have to look honestly at what we are experiencing, and decide whether that is what we want to create in our world – or whether we need to make fresh choices.

Personal and global challenges might be seen as wake-up calls from our collective consciousness that are *forcing* us to change – radically, exponentially, by leaps and bounds. We have to learn to see things differently, to look through new eyes. The whole of humanity needs to take the hero's journey: to die and be reborn.

However personal our wake-up calls might seem, they belong to the bigger picture of global awakening; and by confronting our own personal issues, we are also healing our global issues. Perhaps the *only* way to change our world is by changing ourselves. By holding a vision of heaven on earth in our own lives, we begin to create a more heavenly world. By holding peace in our own hearts, we can begin to create a more peaceful world. By holding love in our hearts, we begin to create a more loving and harmonious world; whereas blaming or judging others only maintains our splitting and projections, and keeps a war going within us. As Sir George Trevelyan noted, it is far better to light a candle than to curse the darkness.

Mystics have often said that there is no real division between inner and outer. Mahatma Gandhi urged us to *become* the change we want to see in the world, and this is surely what he meant. There is no Other – your outer world is inseparable from your inner world – so battling *against* what you see as wrong in the world is like stabbing yourself in the chest. Instead you need to become, to express, to visualise, whatever you *do* want. Reality is not as solid and real as our ego-self fondly imagines. Whatever you are focusing on 'out there' is simply mirroring what is happening 'in here' – and it is *inner* change that will revolutionise the world.

Once you really understand that the world is a mirror that dances to the tune of your own energy-consciousness, you know that everything you need to change is within. Battling *against* anything merely perpetuates it. This is tame love – which says 'No' to what it sees as bad or wrong, and fights self-righteously to overcome or exclude it. When you love wildly, your approach is different. You still take action in the world, you still reach out with love and compassion, but your action is inspired from deep within – from joy, from desire, from vision – and avoids the endless efforting, repetition, busywork and projections of the ego. The deep Self always knows the right action to take, at the right time, in the right place, so that miracles will happen.

This is the greater journey of humanity that was sparked off by our separation from deep reality, from the divine feminine, from unconditional love:

✧ It begins with the birth of individuation, as we face the trials, defences and illusions of our immature ego-self.

✧ Slowly we develop our inner strengths and uniqueness, and discover our own authenticity, our mature ego.

✧ We overcome the illusion of separateness, as we reconnect with deep reality, with love.

✧ Finally we return home with our Elixir of Awakening – with a new awareness of our individuality *and* our oneness, our separateness *and* our connectedness. This is the sacred marriage within – and our eternal growth and expansion continues.

What our culture currently sees as normal and healthy – the isolated ego-self – is but a stunted fragment of our human potential. For centuries, Western society has collectively denied or denigrated so much that is linked with the divine feminine – our emotions, intuition, dreams, imagination, vision, mysticism, passion, sensuality, divine sexuality, reverence for nature, peace, cooperation, balance, empathy, compassion, interconnectedness, our sense of the sacred. We have exiled ourselves from unconditional love, from wild love. But now, at last, we are reclaiming the Holy Grail. The new paradigm that is emerging from science and spirituality marks our re-awakening, our rebirth – personally and globally. Everything that has been kept under wraps for centuries is now bursting forth, like a garden emerging from a long hard winter into the warm flush of spring. We are becoming wild and free.

So how can you liberate yourself from the prison of the ego? What is the key to stepping into that beautiful garden full of vibrant flowers? How can you reconnect with Source energy, and become who you really are? A surprising clue to this quest came from my own professional background of clinical psychology. Not from the traditional psychotherapy that I originally trained in – therapy that sees mind and body as separate, therapy that ignores the deep Self, therapy from the old paradigm – but from an emerging new field known as energy psychology.

 PRACTICAL SUGGESTIONS

1. Do you have any sense that you are not living the life you were meant to live – that a deeper, more expansive, more meaningful life is waiting for you? Do you feel imprisoned by old beliefs, childhood patterns, fears and doubts, or by social norms and expectations? Do you feel as if your real Self has yet to be born, as if you are somehow being 'tamed'? Sit with these questions. Give yourself time to reflect. Perhaps get up an hour earlier than usual for a while, and spend quiet time alone with yourself. Allow any divine discontent to bubble up to the surface, trusting that it comes with a priceless gift, the gift of a life that truly belongs to you. You do not need to take any action. Or not yet. Just allow yourself to face your own truth or uncertainty, without fear. Keep a feeling of openness and curiosity.

2. When have you faced your own Calls to Adventure? Turning points which offered a choice of possible futures? Times when you could have broken through your old patterns of limitation, and created a new reality? Have you accepted these Calls? Either way, what was the outcome? You might want to write your notes in a journal. Have you

noticed that it is when we refuse a Call – usually because we are trying to stay safe, or trying to please others, or to feel worthy, or avoid guilt or rejection – that we feel most regret? Are you facing a Call right now, whether minor or major? If so, will you say Yes this time? Will you say Yes to the Call of your deep Self, and allow a richer and wilder life to unfold?

CHAPTER FOUR

A Bridge Across Eternity

> Dis-ease is an expression of how we have tried to
> separate ourselves from our deeper being, our
> essence.
>
> **Barbara Ann Brennan**[1]

Like so many breakthroughs, energy psychology was discovered almost 'by accident'. It all started with Mary. Mary had suffered from a severe water phobia since infancy – so badly that she had to close the curtains when it was raining, was terrified by the mere sight of the ocean and was forced to bathe (under severe stress) in very shallow water. She had tried almost every form of therapy, and clinical psychologist Roger Callahan had been working with her for more than a year, with little sign of progress. However, he had been studying the meridians (the energy pathways used in acupuncture), and one day he had a flash of intuition. Mary mentioned that she felt her anxiety about water in the pit of her stomach. In Chinese medicine, the stomach meridian is linked with obsessive worry and anxiety. Since his usual approaches were not working for her, Roger asked Mary to think about her water phobia while tapping just below her eye, on the acupoint at the start of the stomach meridian.

After two minutes of tapping, Mary announced that her phobia was gone! She leapt to her feet and ran laughing to the swimming pool outside, splashing her face with water happily. The next day, she waded up to her waist in the ocean without a trace of anxiety. Many years passed, and Mary's phobia never returned. Roger Callahan went on to develop Thought Field Therapy (TFT) – and energy psychology was born.[2]

♥

Energy psychology builds a bridge to a new world view in which we see ourselves as conscious energy systems – rather than as bundles of bones, genes and biochemistry with a mind somehow stuck on top. It vividly demonstrates that thoughts, feelings and even emotional or physical symptoms are, like everything else in the Universe, just energy – and can therefore be healed or changed *at an energy level*. In other words, our thoughts and emotions can be changed by working directly with our energy system. With success rates of 80–97 per cent, energy psychology holds the potential to revolutionise psychology and medicine – as well as our everyday lives. And it holds a crucial key to understanding how we separate ourselves from Source energy, and trap ourselves within the limited ego.

The methods of energy psychology still seem wacky to our old-paradigm way of seeing, and its impact can be so miraculous that it causes controversy among those who believe that emotional and physical problems cannot be resolved so easily. Its results are often ignored or dismissed as impossible, rationalised as suggestion or simply denied, even by those who have experienced dramatic cures.

I have to admit that I was a sceptic until I saw the evidence with my own eyes, a few years ago. When you watch someone with chronic asthma being apparently cured in 40 seconds by gently tapping on their face and body, it does challenge any conventional views about health – and I immediately pursued training. I had seen profound shifts in myself and others using energy methods such as flower essences and homoeopathy, but energy psychology can be so immediate and dramatic that it leaves no room for doubt. Phobias that have resisted any other treatment can disappear in five or ten minutes; 20-year depressions might be gone in a flash; migraines can be forever stopped in their tracks; panic attacks dissolve like sugar lumps in hot coffee. For those of us who trained for many years in psychotherapy, it is disheartening to realise that we have wasted so much time, using such a plodding and unreliable method as merely *talking* to people, when a simple-to-learn method has such remarkable and rapid results.

Of course, few cases can be resolved as simply and dramatically as Mary's. Nevertheless, practitioners of energy psychology have found remarkable success in treating almost every emotional or physical symptom and disease, including anxiety, addictions, depression, eating disorders, jealousy, guilt, insomnia, allergies, attention deficit disorder, chronic pain, asthma, headaches, arthritis, dyslexia, high blood pressure, chronic fatigue, premenstrual tension, psoriasis, carpal tunnel syndrome, lupus, irritable bowel syndrome, heart arrhythmia, numbness, joint pains and the side-effects of drugs. And much more besides.

EFT has been shown to reduce the dangerous clumping of blood cells (in a disease known as Rouleaux) in a matter of minutes. It has apparently cured deathly dengue fever, in a case which doctors had given up as terminal. It has had striking success in treating post-traumatic stress disorder of all kinds, from childhood abuse to road accidents. Vietnam veterans who have suffered for decades, despite extensive psychotherapy, have been freed from their incapacitating symptoms within a few hours. And it has also been used for improving performance skills – such as golf scores, athletic ability or public speaking – or rapidly instilling positive new beliefs. In short, energy psychology can create miracles![3]

So what is energy psychology? The most popular form is EFT (Emotional Freedom Technique), developed by engineer Gary Craig. Like Roger Callahan's TFT, this involves tapping on the meridians while focusing on a troubling issue or symptom – and although it takes skill to use it for complex issues, the basic self-help method of EFT can be learned in a few minutes.[4] Other methods include EMDR (Eye Movement Desensitisation and Reprocessing), TAT (Tapas Acupressure Technique) and Emo-Trance.

Energy psychology works mostly with the meridians, the energy pathways used in acupuncture for the past 5,000 years, and finally confirmed by modern science 20 years ago.[5] The meridians seem to be an interface between the physical body and the etheric body, which is the innermost layer of the human energy field, or aura.[6] According to Chinese medicine, most symptoms result from our flow of vital energy (qi or chi) being blocked or imbalanced, and acupuncture helps our energy to flow well and stay in balance. Energy psychology does the same, and can be seen as a form of psychological acupuncture without needles. It is based on the idea that any form of emotional distress or physical symptom is simply a warning sign that our energy system is out of balance or short-circuited – that we have kinks in our garden hose, that we are disconnecting from Source energy. Hence the so-called Discovery Statement of EFT:

> The cause of all negative emotions is a disruption in the body's energy system.
>
> *Gary Craig*

When I first came across this statement, it was a revolutionary thought to a clinical psychologist like myself. It twisted my belief system in knots, as it forced me to radically rethink my way of understanding emotional and psychological issues. After all, it suggests that issues such as anxiety, depression, phobias, shame, rage, addictions, unhealthy relationship patterns, low self-esteem or self-sabotage can all be healed *at an energy level*. The 'cause' is not a childhood event or recent trauma, nor complex psychodynamic issues that might take months or even years to unravel. The cause is not the past experience itself, but a thought or memory that triggers a short-circuit in the *energy system*. Energy might be blocked, reversed, weak, scrambled or imbalanced – it is simply not flowing properly – and that disrupted energy is *experienced* as negative emotion or physical symptoms.

Once the energy system is corrected, the problem tends to dramatically diminish or disappear – permanently. There are often side-benefits, too. Other symptoms might vanish; you might feel more joyful, energised, think more positively or see things differently. (I remember one of my EFT clients gasping as she felt an unexpected burst of sadness, bordering on compassion, for the uncle who had sexually abused her as a child. She suddenly realised that he, too, had probably been a 'victim' of childhood abuse. Her heart opened to him, at least a little; and she began to catch glimpses of all that she had learned from this childhood trauma. After 20 years of boiling rage and resentment, this shift came as a real surprise to her.) As blockages are released, you often gain novel insights and make new connections. If your energy system is flowing smoothly, it liberates vibrant health and your higher potential. You are free to become who you were always meant to be.

The first step in using EFT involves pairing the emotional or physical symptom with an expression of self-love and self-acceptance. For example, 'Even though I have this migraine, I deeply love and accept myself.' 'Even though I felt embarrassed when I forgot my lines, I deeply love and accept myself' or 'Even though I'm terrified of heights, I deeply love and accept myself.'

Whenever you criticise or shame yourself for showing any weakness or imperfection, you create inner conflict which blocks your energy flow. Your self-love becomes conditional. You are saying 'No' to part of your wholeness. You are rejecting 'what is' – and since whatever you resist persists, you cannot move on. By saying 'Yes' to the problem or issue, if only for a few minutes, this first step in EFT helps you move through resistance. By saying yes to yourself, despite your pain or imperfections, you relax and open to the possibility of change. *Self-love and self-acceptance – as well as acceptance of others and the past – allow your energy to flow.*

Then you simply tap on each meridian's acupoint, while focusing on the memory, symptom or underlying issue, which instructs energy to flow through that meridian. (A basic self-help guide to EFT is given in the Appendix.) Sometimes this process clears the problem within minutes; sometimes it needs to be repeated regularly, or it brings up related memories or issues that also need to be cleared.

Of course, energy psychology is not a panacea, nor is it an instant cure for all human suffering. It does not take away normal human emotions, but it does clear emotions that have become stuck or extreme, so that we can flow into new riverbeds. It offers a way of clearing our energy system so that old wounds do not become magnets for repeated patterns of experience, or a source of emotional or physical symptoms. It is a tool for moving beyond the energy block-ages and low vibrations of the ego.

Tapas Fleming, an acupuncturist who developed Tapas Acupressure Technique (TAT)[7], suggests that what turns any event into a trauma is saying 'No' to it. If what happens feels too shocking, too hurtful or too much to bear, part of us stamps our foot like a toddler and says 'No.' Saying 'No' creates an energy blockage that paradoxically keeps us trapped in the trauma. It freezes us in time, and means that the short-circuit in our energy system is always there, ready to be reactivated by any thought, memory or situation that reminds us of that earlier trauma. (And thanks to energy psychology, we now know that talking therapies often *re-traumatise* us, by repeating a trauma verbally without giving the energy system the new instruction to 'Flow' – to relax, to say 'Yes' – while focusing on that memory.) Saying 'Yes' to an event does not mean accepting that what happened was okay. It simply means accepting *that it happened*, so that we are no longer resisting it.

Using TAT allowed me to clear my lifelong allergy to dairy products, as well as other allergies (after 20 years of trying other 'alternative' approaches). After treating a patient for an allergy to salt, Tapas Fleming had the fascinating insight that allergies are linked with trauma. This particular woman had been sexually abused as a child, and had been given a packet of crisps as a 'reward' after each episode. Her body had linked salt with danger, and so identified salt as an enemy. Another woman was eating red grapes when she heard that her mother had been killed in a car accident. From that day on, she became allergic to grapes. Similarly, I suspect that my allergies to dust and mould began after being locked in a musty wardrobe by my brother when I was three years old. The terror of that episode was still held in my energy system, along with the allergies, until the trauma was released using energy psychology.

One of the steps involved in clearing a trauma, using TAT, is to focus on the statement 'It happened, it's over and I'm okay,' while holding certain acupoints around the eyes and at the back of the head. (You can *feel* how this reassuring statement makes your body breathe a deep sigh of relief.) The trauma then becomes a mere memory, with no emotional charge to it. We can learn from it, but we see it differently. It belongs to the past. One of my clients, after clearing a serious car crash from her energy system, found herself laughing: 'That car accident was seven years ago. Why was I still hanging on to it?' Once you say 'Yes,' your energy flows again, freeing you to live in the present.

Flowing energy means that there are no blockages, which is essential to our mental and physical health. It means we are saying 'Yes' to our lives, 'Yes' to ourselves, 'Yes' to others. This is wild love. It is our natural state of unconditional love and acceptance, and ever-flowing vitality. Lack of flow, by contrast, might reveal itself as physical clutter and disorder, as stagnant relationships or unfinished business, as emotional stuckness or negativity, or as physical illness or pain.

Any negative emotion that you recycle over and over again gives clues about which of your meridians might be disturbed – which, in turn, indicate energy habits, or well-practised patterns of thought or feeling, that are disconnecting you from Source. For example, if you are stuck in guilt and self-loathing, your liver meridian is likely to be disrupted. If you are critical and judgmental towards others, your gall bladder meridian is probably affected. If you tend to feel hopeless and despairing, your bladder meridian is unlikely to be flowing well. If you feel vulnerable and insecure, your central meridian might need strengthening. Such energy habits can be passed down the generations, and can therefore result in illness or disease that looks inherited – but what is being passed on is a set of emotional *habits*, which result in certain patterns of dis-ease. The 'black sheep' in a family – the renegades who dare to break the family rules – tend not to suffer from the family diseases![8]

The body sometimes gives us clues about habitual weakness in our meridian system. For example, one client I saw stroked the side of her thumb repeatedly while talking about her problems. Since she was stroking the start of her lung meridian (which is linked with grief), I asked about loss and abandonment in her childhood, which led quickly to the root of her relationship issues. Another woman kept tucking her hair behind her ears, which suggested to me that her triple warmer meridian was overactive – since this action is a subconscious way of soothing the triple warmer. This gave me a starting point for the energy healing we did together.

The body is constantly 'talking' to us through symptoms, dis-ease and body language, nudging us towards health and wholeness. Each meridian is linked with different emotions or psychological states, depending on whether energy is flowing smoothly through that meridian. Negative emotions can be precursors to physical disease connected with the organs that lie on that meridian; so chronic fear, for example, can eventually lead to kidney disorders, and so on. These links are rather like a dream dictionary – they are a starting point, rather than a definitive guide – but they do show how our body's energy system is interwoven with our emotional and physical states. Our body, thoughts and emotions are inseparable forms of energy, which are either flowing and connected, as they are meant to be, or staccato and disconnected, resulting in emotional or physical symptoms.

MERIDIANS AND EMOTIONS[9]

	DISCONNECTION	CONNECTION
BLADDER	Sense of futility; suspicion.	Hope, trust.
CENTRAL	Feeling vulnerable.	Feeling centred and secure.
CIRCULATION-SEX	Bewildered by choices, neglecting heart's needs.	Clarity about own desires and needs of heart.
GALL BLADDER	Rage or judgment towards others.	Tolerance, kindness.
GOVERNING	Lacking courage to move forward; no backbone.	Inner strength; standing tall.
HEART	Heartache.	Love for self and others.

KIDNEY	Fearful isolation, shame.	Moving towards others; gentleness with Self.
LARGE INTESTINE	Controlling, holding on.	Releasing.
LIVER	Rage against self, guilt.	Kindness towards self, self-acceptance.
LUNG	Grief, defensive detachment.	Breathing in (inspiration), letting go, having faith.
SMALL INTESTINE	Feeling pulled in more than one direction.	Decisiveness, discernment.
SPLEEN	Over-compassionate towards others.	Compassion for self.
STOMACH	Obsessive worry/anxiety.	Trust in bigger picture.
TRIPLE WARMER	Fight, flight or freeze; extreme stress.	Feeling safe.

For each meridian there are acupoints you can tap (or other techniques, such as holding each acupoint while taking one full breath), *while focusing on an issue linked with that negative emotion or state.* This instructs energy to flow through that meridian again – and relieves the negative emotion or physical symptom by reconnecting you with Source energy. It sounds almost too simple to be true, but it works! For example, the tapping point for the small intestine meridian is the karate chop point on the side of the hand. For the triple warmer, simply hold the temples in your palms for a minute or so. For the bladder meridian, tap the inner edge of the eyebrow. For the large intestine, tap at the flair of the nostrils. For the heart meridian, slap the inside of your wrist (where a watch strap lies). Or simply practise EFT – see Appendix – which tackles *any* emotional or physical symptom.

Of course, just tapping for a minute or two does not

permanently reconnect your energy system. We are complex beings, with a labyrinth of interconnected beliefs, thoughts and ways of coping – and old energy habits die hard. As we shall see, our energy system also has its own in-built way of resisting change. But the fact that we *can* relieve negative emotions by briefly tapping an acupoint should make us aware that our emotions are energy, and that any negative emotion is simply a signal that our energy flow is disrupted. Our ego is turning off our tap, or putting kinks in our hose. The cause is not 'out there' in the world, nor 'back there' in our past. It is right here and now – in our energy system.

What is more, our meridians seem to be a direct link to our multi-dimensional Self, our deep Self. The meridians are an interface between surface and deep reality. Through them, we can receive higher guidance, or pick up intuitive information from the universal web of energy-consciousness, and also transmit our beliefs and desires to Source as vibrational patterns, which attract the appropriate people and circumstances towards us. Energy is the bridge between mind and matter. The more coherent, balanced and flowing our energy, the more easily we connect with our intuition, and the more efficiently we can tell the Universe what we want to create. The meridians allow us to have a two-way conversation with God. No wonder, then, that many energy practitioners simply tap all their meridians, several times a day, in order to keep instructing Source energy to flow.

Energy psychology is still in its infancy – Gary Craig often reminds us that we are on 'the ground floor of the new healing high-rise' – but already there are exciting developments that point towards the future. There are countless anecdotal reports of using 'surrogate tapping' (that is, tapping on behalf of another adult, child or animal) with great success, often at a distance and when the recipient is not aware it is happening. A recent report found that EFT could correct vitamin and mineral deficiencies – with impressive success – without any change in diet.[10] Many people use 'imaginal tapping' with good results, just visualising that they are tapping the acupoints – useful if you are in a public place, or immobilised by pain. More and more practitioners use intuitive approaches, finding that we get even better and faster results when we let go of the 'right way' to use these energy tools, and instead trust our inner guidance. We can even heal ourselves by tapping along with someone else on *their* issues, after first deciding upon a trauma we wish to clear from our own energy system. Other healers are developing the use of colour, sound, crystals, magnets, flower essences and other energetic ways of re-aligning our auric field to create emotional and physical well-being. Such possibilities boggle the mind if we are stuck in a conventional, left-brained world view, but they make perfect sense if we adopt the new energy-consciousness paradigm.

The new paradigm tells us that energy, consciousness and the love that surrounds and interpenetrates everything is all there is in the universe. Energy psychology helps us build a bridge across eternity – going beyond the limitations of space-time to the deep Self – by combining energy, consciousness and love. It heals the resistance in our body's energy system, which is caused by lack of self-love. It breaks through the false shame, guilt, unworthiness, judgment and fearfulness of the ego. It reconnects us with wild love.

> When all your energies are brought into harmony, your body flourishes. And when your body flourishes, your soul has a soil in which it can blossom in the world.
>
> *Donna Eden*[11]

CONFLICT AND COHERENCE

The ego has a tendency to fragment, to split off parts of itself, to divide the world into good/right/safe/acceptable and bad/wrong/dangerous/unacceptable. As we shall see in the next chapter, the ego eats from the Tree of Good and Evil, which disconnects us from our wholeness. It disconnects us from others. It disconnects us from our aliveness and potential. The immature ego creates short-circuits in our energy system which block the flow of chi, making our energy scrambled and incoherent.

When our energy is coherent, our inner selves are all focused in the same direction – like the highly efficient and powerful light of a laser beam. Our energy waves are in sync with each other. Coherence is an expression of self-love, of self-integration. It means there is no conflict between our conscious and subconscious intentions and desires, so we experience inner peace and harmony, and can create miracles. Coherent energy is characteristic of what psychologist Abraham Maslow called 'self-actualisers' – those who are joyful, fulfilled, loving, open, free, creative and make a positive difference in the world.

Whenever we have a conscious desire that is eluding us – such as a desire to create a loving relationship, or to stop smoking, or sell our house, or get a promotion, or spend more time relaxing – we usually have a subconscious goal or belief that conflicts with that desire. One or more of our inner selves has other ideas. We are embattled against ourselves – that is, neurotic. Whenever we feel tired, scattered, confused, anxious or ambivalent, or feel *any* negative emotion or physical symptom, our energy is incoherent.

Lack of coherence is easy to demonstrate using muscle-testing. If you hold out one arm and ask someone to press down on that wrist briefly while you resist their pressure, you should find that if you are in a reasonably healthy state, your arm bounces back. The muscle stays strong, indicating that energy is flowing well. Now state a goal that is not happening, such as 'I want to stop smoking', or 'I want to sell my house' and muscle-test again. You will probably find that your arm has mysteriously gone weak. Any statement that is not true creates a short-circuit in our energy system, and this makes the arm muscle go weak. Your body reveals the truth about your hidden agenda. In energy psychology, this is known as psychological reversal, or PR.

> ... when you don't accept a part of who you are, what you did, or what you are doing, there can be a reversal in your energy system. The outcome is an unconscious act of sabotage against your consciously expressed goals.
>
> **Fred P Gallo and Harry Vincenzi**[12]

Someone who is chronically depressed, for example, is sure to be psychologically reversed. If they hold out their arm and say 'I no longer want to be depressed' their arm will go weak, while saying 'I want to be depressed' makes their arm stay strong, even though their *conscious* desire is to be happy. Why is this? Because they are disconnected from who they are. They are telling themselves lies about how worthless or inadequate they are. They are squashing their dreams and desires because they feel guilt-ridden or undeserving. They are suppressing their anger, because they want to please others. They are denying their own power. They are playing small, and denying the wonder and magnificence of who they really are. Their ego is trying to be safe and loved, in self-defeating ways that create an internal civil war – and their energy system is short-circuiting all over the place.

Whenever we are in conflict, we are in a constricted state of awareness. We are not seeing the bigger picture. Psychological reversal comes from inner conflict – lack of coherence – which blocks our energy flow. It invariably comes from seeking approval, control or security – from being stuck in our ego, with its negative and limiting beliefs. Once we transcend the conflict, we might suddenly see that freedom *is* compatible with real love, or that healthy self-assertion makes our relationships stronger and more authentic, or that we can be more helpful by being less enabling and 'supportive', or that we achieve more by working less, or that being wealthy can help us *express* our spirituality. Or, as we shall see, we might realise that we always serve the greater whole by moving towards happiness and fulfilment rather than through duty, loyalty or self-sacrifice. We shift to a higher perspective, and the apparent conflict dissolves.

Energy psychology suggests that the basis of every emotional or physical symptom of dis-ease is blocked energy – resistance – usually caused by unresolved conflicts that have been suppressed, denied or ignored. Inner conflict or ambivalence drains your energy, so it makes sense to resolve issues as soon as you can. If you sit with unfinished business for too long – perhaps staying in a job, relationship or place that you know is not working for you, yet lacking the courage or clarity to change it, or avoiding the resolution of a problem, or clinging to issues from the past – this depletes your energy. It then becomes harder and harder to change. It feels easier to remain stuck. You begin to feel defeated, resigned and disempowered.

Everyone has energy habits – or characteristic ways of approaching life and relationships, dealing with stress and conflict, and handling emotions (usually learned in child-hood). This means that your energy tends to run along well-established pathways, or get stuck in characteristic ways – so that joy, guilt, rage, depression, jealousy, martyrhood, despair or apathy can become fixed habits that feel familiar and are easy to repeat, as can your usual defences and ways of coping. Whatever situation comes along, you tend to flow down your established riverbeds, and use your old energy habits to deal with it. Even if it feels uncomfortable or painful, your ego convinces you that it is 'how life is', or that the alternative would be worse, or that it is the only way to be safe and secure, or to be loved, or to stay in control. So you tend to repeat the same patterns over and over again, and attract people and events into your life that will re-inforce those old pathways.

What can help you to change these habits? Energy, consciousness and love. You can shift ego-based habits at an energy level by re-training your energy system; or you can become aware of them, and consciously choose different thoughts and responses; or you can be blasted – or blast yourself – with unconditional love, which shifts everything to a higher level. Best of all, you can use all three. And that is what energy psychology, at its best, can do.

THE TRIPLE WARMER AND THE STRANGE FLOWS

Unfortunately, our energy system has an in-built resistance to change. Our body's immune system has two complementary aspects at an energy level, known as the 'triple warmer' and the 'strange flows'. (See Donna Eden's groundbreaking book *Energy Medicine.*) Based upon fear and love respectively, I see these as rich metaphors for our ego and our deep Self. These systems explain why we cling to our ego-based energy habits, even though the deep Self is now calling us to transform our consciousness, and move beyond our old ways of being.

The energy system known as the triple warmer is concerned with survival, so it is always on the alert. It looks out for what is dangerous, or what is going wrong (or might go wrong), and tends to react to new situations as if they were threats, based on past experiences. If you had a violent father, for example, anyone who raises their voice in later life might send you into a panic, which drains your ability to cope with the situation with any maturity. You are flung back into a more primitive way of responding. At any hint of threat, the triple warmer surges into action with a fight-or-flight response – either battling against enemies, or running away from situations that look threatening, or just freezing.

On the positive side, the triple warmer stimulates the immune system to deal with bacteria, germs and viruses, and helps you react quickly when you are in danger. If a runaway car is heading in your direction, the triple warmer allows you to move – and fast. Since survival might be at stake, the triple warmer is allowed to rip energy from any other meridian (apart from the heart meridian) whenever it fancies – rather like a government conscripting civilians into the army at a moment's notice. It triggers the release of adrenaline to deal with an emergency. However, since adrenaline excites and fires us up, going into battle can become an addictive cycle. When the triple warmer is over-stimulated, we can become stress junkies – hooked on conflict, drama, time pressures, deadlines and over-busyness, and dealing with everyday life as if it were an emergency.

An over-enthusiastic defence system becomes a threat in itself, as we see globally in the dangerous proliferation of nuclear bombs, and the staggering cost of weapons, surveil-lance and military forces. At a physical level, an overactive triple warmer is involved in auto-immune disorders such as rheumatoid arthritis, multiple sclerosis, Crohn's disease and lupus, in which the body is attacking itself. Allergies and environmental disorders also indicate that the triple warmer is going into battle unnecessarily, mistaking friend for foe, setting off false alarms when the only 'danger' around is a cheese sandwich or grass pollen.

In immune deficiency disorders, the triple warmer has taken flight and stopped fighting altogether; while in chronic fatigue syndrome (ME), the fight-or-flight response is permanently switched on. One woman I know developed ME after living in a violent, abusive relationship for many years; another after working as a journalist on a national newspaper which required her to deliver up-to-the-minute copy on the latest events, day after day; and yet another after several years as a nurse on an intensive care ward. We are not designed to live in a permanent state of emergency. Eventually we burn out.

At a psychological level, I understand the triple warmer as operating like the ego. It is fearful, judgmental, divisive, busy, hooked on struggle and conflict, and forever trying to protect itself. Its core belief is 'I am not safe.' When our triple warmer is working overtime, we have little interest in happiness, meaning, purpose or spiritual growth. Joy is not even on the radar screen. Our only concern is safety and survival, protecting ourselves, and getting through the days. We are always looking over our shoulder, and expecting the worst – or at best, doing our duty and getting on with our to-do lists.

What is more, the triple warmer is highly resistant to change, even positive change. It is designed to maintain homoeostasis. Its usual methods work, it tells us. After all, we have survived! What more do we want? The triple warmer is naturally conservative. (Buy more insurance! Get a pension! Stick to your secure job!) It prefers to flow down its old riverbeds, feeling safer with what it knows. It favours stability. It keeps on repeating the past, instead of moving on. It closes its eyes to wider horizons, and cannot see the bigger picture. Whenever we consider making a change, the triple warmer sweeps into action to maintain the status quo, to hold on to our usual patterns of behaviour. It raises our anxiety, and makes our thinking foggy. It acts as a Threshold Guardian, blocking the path which beckons us on the hero's journey. 'Better the devil you know,' it whispers in our ear.

The ego's ways of seeking approval, control and security mirror the triple warmer's strategies of fight, flight or freeze – and these are all self-defeating, since they are based upon fear rather than love. When faced with stress or conflict, you can:

✧ **Attack the enemy** (by seeing the other as in the wrong, blaming, controlling, expressing anger or rage, going into battle, or projecting your Shadow – that is, seeing denied aspects of yourself 'out there' in the world)

✧ **Take flight** (by seeking approval, giving in, conforming, agreeing that you're in the wrong, feeling guilty, or defending and justifying yourself; or by withdrawing, distancing yourself, hiding your feelings, running away, avoiding the problem, putting it on hold, or pretending everything is fine)

✧ **Freeze** (which means feeling stuck, numb, anxious, depressed, overwhelmed, panicky or paralysed)

– or some combination of these.

Most of us have energy habits based on these strategies that can wreck our personal relationships by blocking intimacy and disconnecting us from ourselves and/or others. (See chapter 10.) The triple warmer, like the ego, sees the Other as an enemy. From its place of fear and insecurity, it is always focused on perceived threat – and that threat could be a harsh word, a look of disapproval, a minor disagreement, a martyred sigh or even increased intimacy. Fear creates resistance; it stops our energy flowing. By contrast, the deep Self operates from unconditional love, which keeps our energy flowing. It reaches out and connects. Only the deep Self knows that everything is a friend, that it is always safe, that there is no Other, that we are all one.

If you have an overactive triple warmer, you will also have an underactive spleen meridian (since the two are paired). This can make you over-compassionate towards others, and neglectful of your own needs and desires. A balanced spleen meridian makes you compassionate towards yourself. *When the triple warmer is stripping the spleen of its energy, you aim to be 'good' rather than happy.* (We will see how crucial this is in later chapters.) A weak spleen meridian makes you over-responsible, dutiful and conforming; it disconnects you from who you really are. When the triple warmer is trigger-happy, it squashes you into a tiny box, then ignores your screams until you give in and resign yourself to your fate. It controls and tames you. Or it fights, controls and tames others. It leads you away from wild love, away from joy, away from freedom – and locks you in a suffocating prison.

> *Sometimes it takes*
> *a great sky*
> *to find that*
>
> *first, bright*
> *and indescribable*
> *wedge of freedom*
> *in your own heart.*
>
> **David Whyte**[14]

The spleen meridian is a crucial part of the energy system known as the 'strange flows' or 'radiant circuits', which take an entirely different approach to life from that of the triple warmer.[15] The strange flows operate from divine feminine energy, like the deep Self. The triple warmer sees a fearful world of separate particles, whereas the strange flows see a loving world of waves, an inseparable web of energy-consciousness.

If the triple warmer represents allopathic medicine – with its 'masculine' tendency to *battle against* disease, to control and suppress symptoms, and banish or overcome enemies – then the strange flows are models for holistic healthcare. Instead of being based on fear, struggle, aggressive conflict and competition, the strange flows are devoted to cooperation, health and wholeness. They see everything as a friend. They deal with causes rather than symptoms, and aim to keep the body in a state of harmony, balance and coordination, thus giving us natural resilience to disease. Unlike the meridians, the strange flows have no fixed pathways, and jump instantly to wherever they are needed in the body's energy system, like hyperlinks on the internet, interconnecting all the energy systems within the body.

Psychologically, the strange flows are linked with joy, bliss, laughter, gratitude, freedom, radiance, vitality, spontaneity, love, rapture, mystical experience, intuition and psychic abilities – and a sense of aliveness. In short, they make you feel wonderful! They help you to think positively, and be hopeful about the future. If they could speak, the strange flows might say 'Nurture yourself', 'Take care of your own needs' or 'Just enjoy life.' Whenever a new opportunity or pleasurable experience comes along, the strange flows immediately bounce around like Tigger and say 'Yes, Yes, Yes!' The strange flows adore life!

The strange flows mirror the emergent new paradigm, while the poor old triple warmer is stuck in fear and separation, conjuring up stress and enemies so that it can go into battle. Needless to say, Western society is suffering from an overactive triple warmer – and most of us need to soothe our triple warmer, calm our fearful thoughts, and strengthen our spleen and strange flows, so that we can live together in harmony, relax more and break free from our old riverbeds. If we are to resolve our global problems, we need to go beyond aiming for survival or staying safe, and express our loving depth and creative potential. The triple warmer imprisons us in fear and conformity while the strange flows set us free, opening the door to unconditional love, joy, bliss and new possibilities.

The comedy film *Meet the Fockers* personifies the potential conflict between the triple warmer and strange flows archetypes. A couple who are soon to marry reluctantly introduce their parents to each other. *Her* father is a retired CIA agent, always on the look-out for trouble and danger –

suspicious, uptight, obsessive, controlling, conformist and repressed. He is soon nicknamed 'El Stiffo' by her fiancé's family. *His* parents, by contrast, both exemplify the strange flows archetype: they are warm, caring, emotional, anarchic, passionate, sexy, alive and funny. Gradually the strange flows win out, and unite everyone through their love and acceptance.

The strange flows respond rapidly to your thoughts, feelings and imagination – so you can stimulate your strange flows through positive thinking, gratitude or forgiveness. Or you can imagine a beautiful scene, or recall a happy incident, or picture someone who is fun-loving, joyful and slightly wacky, and 'call them in' at an energy level. Even if you just *pretend* to be happy, it jumpstarts the strange flows and you brighten up. Or you can do it through stretching, wild dancing, spending time in nature, watching a sunset, having an orgasm or falling in love. (We enjoy being around people who are madly in love, since they strongly radiate the strange flows.)

Laughing uproariously also releases the strange flows. When journalist Norman Cousins, author of *Anatomy of an Illness*, developed ankylosing spondylitis, he was almost paralysed and given a few months to live. Believing in the ability of the mind-body system to heal itself, he watched comedies such as the Marx Brothers for hours every day. A few minutes of laughter, he found, gave him an hour or more of pain-free sleep. Slowly he regained the use of his limbs, and was soon able to work full-time again.[16]

Physically, laughter boosts our levels of endorphins, the body's natural painkillers, and suppresses levels of epinephrine, the stress hormone. Energetically, laughter and humour help our energy to flow, releasing those kinks in our garden hose that cause negative emotions and physical illness. Then we relax into our normal state of perfect health, vitality and emotional well-being.

> *I believe that happiness is our natural state, that bliss is hardwired. Only when our systems get blocked, shut down, and disarrayed do we experience the mood disorders that add up to unhappiness …*
>
> Candace Pert[17]

Doing anything different, original and unexpected can help to trigger the strange flows, and free you up. Go to a funfair. Take a ride in a hot air balloon. Dye your hair pink. Dance in the pouring rain. Walk through a forest at night. Ride a camel. Hug a tree. Go skinny-dipping. Make a cherry and coconut pie. Talk to a dandelion. Throw a fancy dress party. Buy a round-the-world air ticket – and use it! Too much routine, too little change, makes us less conscious and aware. We slip into an almost unnoticed depression, a trance state. If they are not frequently stimulated, the strange flows seem to fall asleep – and so do we. Conversely, the more we activate these radiant energies, the more we strengthen them, and so the more joyful we feel. Joy becomes an energy habit. So does growth and change. When the strange flows are flowing as they should, we are wilder and more spontaneous – and spontaneity seems to be an essential quality in producing the quantum leaps that take us out of old riverbeds. It gets us out of our old ruts. It wakes us up. It is creative, quirky, unpredictable, life-affirming energy, which can spark transformation.

♥

Energy psychology is dramatically revealing that *your emotions tell you whether Source energy is flowing freely through you* – whether you are connected to deep reality. In other words, feelings are the language of the soul. It also reveals that fear and judgment block this flow of energy, and are probably the primary factors in emotional and physical disease. Saying 'No' to anything blocks your energy. It creates resistance and pain. It sends you into battle. It disconnects you from Source energy, whereas wild love – saying 'Yes' – allows your energy to flow.

So isn't it intriguing that, for the past 3,000 years, the dominant religions have *promoted* fear and judgment? Would God really want us to *disconnect* from Source energy – from love – and thereby make ourselves miserable and sick? Or have we had the wool pulled over our eyes? Has traditional religion led us away from God, away from our spiritual selves, away from deep reality, and kept us trapped in our limited ego? And has its impact insidiously crept into secular society by the back door? Perhaps we need a radical re-think about what it means to be human and spiritual – and what love really means.

 PRACTICAL SUGGESTIONS

1. See the self-help guide to EFT at the back of this book. Choose a current emotion, issue, painful memory or physical symptom that you would like to shift, and follow the instructions. You can also use 'blank tapping' – just tapping each meridian point in turn while saying 'I now choose for my energy to flow freely' (or whatever statement feels good). Repeat this several times daily to keep your energy flowing, and remember EFT whenever you feel any negative emotion or physical symptom.

2. Invite the strange flows into your life, perhaps by dancing, stretching, laughing, feeling gratitude, imagining you are breathing in coloured light or doing anything that is just plain crazy fun.

You can also jumpstart the strange flows with an exercise known as Heaven Rushing In[18]: Stand up, breathing deeply, with your knees unlocked, and spread your fingers on your thighs. Be aware of energy pouring down through your fingers, down through your legs and into the ground, connecting you to the earth. Take a deep breath, open your arms and bring them into a praying position. Take another deep breath, and throw your arms wide to the heavens, looking up. Invite a blessing from the heavens – healing energies from the Universe. Scoop this energy into your arms, then bring your hands to the middle of your chest (a point known in Chinese medicine as Heaven Rushing In). The higher energies rush into your heart, carrying healing, guidance or inspiration, which will unfold in its own time.

CHAPTER FIVE

Does God Need Therapy?

> *You do not have to be good.*
> *You do not have to walk on your knees*
> *for a hundred miles through the desert, repenting.*
> *You only have to let the soft animal of your body*
> *love what it loves.*
>
> **Mary Oliver**[1]

In the film *Chocolat*, a beautiful and mysterious woman floats into a tranquil, conservative French village, and opens a tempting chocolaterie opposite the Catholic church at the start of Lent. Vianne is a shaman-like figure, a healer of hearts, wild and free, who dispenses ancient remedies and drifts wherever she is blown by the wind. She stirs up forgotten dreams and desires, and represents intuition, passion, magic, sexuality, freedom, spontaneity and sensual delight. Tensions develop immediately between Vianne and the arrogant, self-righteous mayor who is convinced that God is on his side. He sees her as an evil temptress who is surely destined for hell. She mirrors his repressed Shadow – so he abhors her, and wants to control or banish her. Yet it becomes clear that Vianne is spreading love and healing in the community, whereas his impact on others is negative and destructive. He is lost in fear, guilt, judgment and projections – hopelessly tied up in neurotic knots. As the relationships unfold, the film explores the escalating tensions between love and fear, between desire and guilt, between free thought and dogma, between wild and tame, between wholeness and fragmentation.

Traditional psychology suggests that our relationships with Self, others and the world are based largely upon what we experience in early childhood, especially with our parents or caretakers. However, if we expand our awareness, we see that our patterns of relating might also have deeper and more ancient roots – that they might lie in our relationship with Source. Whether or not we are religious, our primal relationship is with Source, God/Goddess, All That Is, the Tao, the Universe, the Divine or whichever term you prefer. (There is a joke that even atheists have a relationship with God. It's just a very *bad* relationship!) Our images of God have tumbled down countless generations, and even in a secular society these images, held in the collective unconscious, have a profound impact on our lives.

I suggest you stop reading now for a few minutes, take a notepad and pen, and jot down any words or phrases that come to mind under the heading 'God'.

Have you done this? If so, you are likely to find a hotch-potch of positive and negative concepts on your list. Typical words about God based on free association might include: creative, loving, omniscient, omnipresent, giving, powerful, vengeful, judgmental, distant, separate, in the sky, absent, abandoning, martyrdom, suffering, sacrifice, guilt, sin, forgiveness, atonement, fear, penitence, redemption, church, temple, dogma, priest, ritual, prayer.

Whatever we consciously believe about the nature of God, most of us are stuffed full of religious beliefs and concepts – often hopelessly contradictory – that we picked up in childhood. For example, God is unconditional love *and* God judges us if we behave badly. (What?) Or God loves us, but gives us brownie points for suffering, guilt and martyrdom. (What?!) Or God is pure love, *and* sent His only begotten Son to suffer and die on the cross for our sins. (What?!!) Such a God would surely be in dire need of psychotherapy for neurosis and sadomasochism. Personally, I doubt whether God is a neurotic wreck – but most of us human beings are rather muddled up!

Several years ago, my husband and I attended a church service on the remote Isle of Lewis in Scotland. In front of tightly packed rows of grim faces and strangely silent children, the preacher gave a dark sermon about the Garden of Eden and the Fall of humanity. The evil and suffering of the world were the fault of *one woman*, he boomed at us, in a rolling Scottish accent. Eve disobeyed the word of the Lord, and succumbed to the temptation of the wicked serpent. (The serpent, of course, is an ancient symbol of the Goddess, the divine feminine.) His most memorable line, delivered without a trace of irony, came towards the end: 'And Eve should a' known that the serpent was the devil – *because snakes don't talk.*' He was serious! By this time, my husband and I were rocking in silent laughter, and stuffing our scarves into our mouths. 'Repent your sins! Repent your sins!' the priest bellowed from the pulpit like a mad dog. We felt as if we had stumbled into a bygone age, and barely made it out of the kirk before collapsing in the street in hysterics!

With his hellfire-and-damnation approach, misogynist views and naïve, literal interpretation of the Bible, this type of priest is hopefully in a small minority today – yet the story does have serious consequences for our everyday lives. Subconsciously, many of us still have a demonised image of God as a strange, delinquent being in the sky who throws down thunderbolts when displeased, rejoices in our self-sacrifice and judges us to be worthless sinners, or (at best) in need of redemption – or who sits impassively at a distance while those on earth suffer and weep. (And as for His politically incorrect views about women! . . .) Yet curiously, most of us also associate the word God with love.

For those who grew up in the Judeo-Christian tradition – even if we rarely attended a church or synagogue – such muddled beliefs have been passed down our families for countless generations, and are built into Western consciousness. So what impact might such widespread and ancient concepts of our creative Source have on our relationships with ourselves, with others and with the world? And if we mistakenly see God's love as conditional and judgmental, how might it limit and distort our understanding of what love really means?

> *In music, in the sea, in a flower, in a leaf, in an act of kindness ...*
> *I see what people call God in all these things.*
>
> *Pablo Casals*[2]

❤

Long ago, the earth was seen as a paradise – the Garden of Eden, Tir na nOg, Valhalla, the Dreamtime – and this lost paradise is preserved in the myths of almost every culture. In those ancient days, people worshipped the Great Goddess. The Goddess was seen as loving and bountiful, and She walked and dwelt among us. The earth, the rivers, the mountains, the trees, the fruit and berries and all of the creatures, including humans, were honoured as part of Her divine body. Everything had a voice, and spoke to us. People believed in original blessing[3] rather than original sin, and saw all of creation as sacred and divine. The Goddess was associated with joy, gratitude, celebration and reverence for life, and people lived together peacefully and sustainably in such societies for thousands of years. Archaeologists have found no weapons of war from these ancient cultures. Yet until recently, these societies were almost completely erased from our history books.[4]

However, this earthly paradise could not last for ever. We collectively wanted to evolve, to learn and grow. We courageously decided to explore the illusion of separateness, to develop our own individuality as tiny creative sparks of All That Is. And so the era of oneness with creation slowly passed away, and a new era of separateness began. We ate of the Tree of Good and Evil: the tree of judgment, of separation, of the ego. We had *chosen* to fall from grace.

Our consciousness began to contract, to fragment, and we no longer felt so connected. The Garden began to lose its brilliant colours, to seem less alive and vibrant. The unseen realms slowly became more distant, and to fade away. We began to lose our sense of safety, our feeling of being loved, our sense of belonging. We began to feel frightened. The ego was taking over from the deep Self.

In place of the life-giving and nurturing Great Goddess, along came a fierce, judgmental sky-God who demanded blood and sacrifice. Perhaps there had been terrible storms or earthquakes, or perhaps famine or plagues, but somehow the earth became disenchanted. It was no longer seen as a paradise, but as a vale of tears, a fallen place. The Bible tells us that the temples, sacred groves and statues of the old, nature-based Goddess faith (paganism) were destroyed – and by 200 CE, almost all references to the feminine face of God had been removed from authorised versions of the Bible. Centuries later, witch-hunters would hunt down any remaining fragments of Goddess spirituality, ruthlessly torturing and murdering millions of women (and many men) in the name of God the Father.

In place of a mystical spirituality that honoured the whole of creation, and which saw God as immanent (present in all things), we created new religions based upon feeling *separate* from God – seeing God as transcendent and perfect and unearthly: religions based upon forgetfulness of our divinity; religions that split us off from our wholeness; religions based upon the limited, fearful and shame-based psychology of the ego, rather than the intuitive knowing of the deep Self. The sky-God religions are based upon the surface reality of separateness.

The patriarchal religions gave us a new and destructive belief: that we had fallen from grace *in the eyes of God*, and needed to redeem ourselves. The God of unconditional love, of divine grace, was replaced by a God of *conditional* love. Tame love. Pseudo-love that limits and controls us. Fall-redemption theology warned us that we would only be loved if we were *good*. We would only escape God's wrath if we were *good*. We would only go to heaven if we were *good*. We would only be forgiven, and return to (temporary) grace, if we did what *others* had decided was the right thing to do, and constantly examined and confessed our sins. Religion had become a political agent of social control, a way of encouraging conformity and suppressing freedom. (Shaming and guilt-tripping are a highly efficient way of controlling and disempowering people, by disconnecting them from Source.)

Over the centuries, separateness created fear, grief, rage, pain, violence and greed. Instead of living together in harmony as brothers and sisters, we compared each other, looking for differences, and judging some as 'better than' others: men better than women, Christian better than pagan, white better than black, heaven better than earth. And like the mayor in *Chocolat*, we wished to own or control or destroy what we saw as Other – those aspects of the Self which we now defined as bad, and projected into the outside world. We declared war on each other, often in the name of God. We became more and more fragmented, disconnected and fearful.

> *Why do you wash the outside of the cup? Do you not understand that the one who made the inside also made the outside?*
>
> Jesus[5]

Jesus was a true mystic who taught unconditional love and oneness; and the lost writings of the Bible (suppressed by the early Church) speak of God as earthly Mother as well as heavenly Father. However, the power-seeking, political wing of the Church took control. In contrast to the birthing, creative, life-affirming earthy Goddess, the dominant image of Christianity became an image of death: a man dying in twisted agony upon a cross. Instead of celebrating life and love and the earth, the patriarchal religions came to emphasise death, suffering, sin, guilt, atonement and the afterlife.

By the 17th century, the bearded-man-in-the-sky God had become more and more separate from us – perhaps even unnecessary – and the scene was set for the scientific revolution. Religion and science now came to an agreement: science could study the disenchanted realm of nature and the body, while religion would confine itself to morality and the soul. Science and religion, body and mind, reason and intuition, earth and heaven, were officially split asunder. Now science was declared detached, rational, objective and amoral. The natural world was seen as dead and soul-less – merely a human resource, to be used, controlled and vanquished.[6] God was fading rapidly into the distance, and we were entering a secular age in which scientists and doctors became the new priesthood. The judgmental God, the God of conditional love, gave way to a third face of God – the distant, neglectful or abandoning God. An absent and loveless God.

From there, it was a short step to banish God altogether. Towards the end of the 19th century, Nietszche could declare that 'God is dead.' People were left with no sense of meaning or purpose in life, and soon a new god appeared – the god of materialism, urging us to possess more and more, to gobble up the earth's resources in an illusive search for happiness and peace of mind. (As an ironic car bumper sticker reads, 'He who dies with most toys wins.') God had been exiled.

Exile is almost the furthest point of separation from love. Beyond exile, we forget that there ever was a Garden of Eden – and, like abandoned children, we no longer recognise our parent. Atheism and agnosticism might be seen as ways of collectively denying our pain, of 'punishing' an abandoning God by ignoring and invalidating Him, of giving in to despair. Separation or abandonment is our primal fear. It is what terrifies us most. Yet we have all been exiled from unconditional love, so completely that the very existence of deep reality has been largely forgotten and denied. Yet locked inside, there is a frightened, abandoned child within each of us – and we need to take that child by the hand, and lead it into the promised land.

We have reached the furthest point of disconnection from our true selves, from each other, from our earthly home, and from our creative Source. The good news is that it is time to begin our long journey Home – our journey of reconnection – but now with the new gift of our individuality, our uniqueness, our potential to become *conscious* co-creators.

> The separation and the return to God ...
> This is the creative pulsation of the universe.
>
> *Emmanuel*[7]

THREE FACES OF GOD

These different faces of God have vast implications for our everyday lives. Whether or not you are aware of it, your assumptions about the creative Source mould and shape you. Your core beliefs about what God/Source wants – and therefore about the nature of the universe – have a huge impact on the choices you make: whether you base your decisions on desire or guilt, on freedom or conformity, on responsibility or blame, on hope or despair, on love or fear.

They also lead to very different kinds of personal relation-ships, depending on whether you *know* that you are loved and safe (loving God), or seek love and security through your relationships (judgmental God), or abandon any hope of real love, and keep people at a distance (abandoning God).

A God of conditional love would want us to be *good* – to do what is expected, to seek approval, to work hard, to hide our emotions, to sacrifice ourselves for others in hope of a later reward. A God of unconditional love would want us to be *happy* – to enjoy life, and to express our unique, creative and loving potential. And an abandoning God is irrelevant, so we might as well aim to be rich and successful and buy lots of 'toys', or merely get through the days (while secretly yearning for what might have been).

The three faces of God

Loving God	Judgmental God	Abandoning God
Unconditional love	Conditional love	Absence of love
God wants us to be happy	God wants us to be good	God is indifferent/absent
Core values: Love, joy, freedom, creativity, self-expression	Core values: Duty, conformity, approval-seeking, self-denial, martyrdom	Core values: Self-sufficiency, survival, materialism
Core feelings: Love, joy, gratitude	Core feelings: Anxiety, shame, guilt	Core feelings: Numbness, rage, grief, despair
Belief that we are inherently good and loving	Belief that we are not good enough (but can *strive* to be good or perfect)	Belief that we are bad, empty or worthless
Desire for both oneness *and* individuation	Desire to merge	Desire to separate

Loving God	Judgmental God	Abandoning God
Fearlessness	Fear of rejection	Fear of loss
Focus on being	Focus on doing	Focus on having
Ego need: for loving and creative expression of self	Ego needs: approval, control, security	Ego needs: security, control, approval
Core belief: life is meant to be heaven on earth	Core belief: life is full of suffering and self-sacrifice	Core belief: life is lonely, empty and tough

> *God hugs you.*
> *You are encircled by the arms*
> *of the mystery of God.*
>
> *Hildegard of Bingen*[8]

The more you believe in a God/dess of unconditional love, the more you know that everyone is *inherently* good. This is a basic essential for emotional and physical health and well-being. (As we have seen from energy psychology in chapter 4, happiness and self-acceptance – saying 'Yes' to everything – allows our energy to flow.) You feel safe and loved, and you love others with an open heart. You know that you belong in the world. You serve others joyfully, knowing that you are all connected, all part of the Whole. You feel wild and free. You are fully alive in the moment, seeing every day as a wondrous gift. Your primary emotional states are love, joy and gratitude. You trust that, even when life is less than perfect, everything is unfolding just as it needs to. You have faith in your heart's desires, because you trust your feelings and intuition, and know that life is meant to be heaven on earth.

The more that you believe in a judgmental God, however, the more you desperately seek approval from others, believing you have to earn or deserve love (or happiness, or money, or good fortune, or security). This is the essence of neurosis. You focus on *doing* more and more – feeling driven, running away from yourself, striving to feel needed and worthy and busy. You see yourself as inherently bad (or not good enough), and having to struggle against your 'fallen' nature in order to be lovable. Your primary emotional states are anxiety, shame and guilt. Serving others becomes a way of feeling good about yourself. Merging with others becomes a way of feeling safe. You hide any parts of yourself that you feel are unacceptable to others, and so fail to be authentic in your relationships. You only expect (or give) conditional love, and cling to others for security. Or you might identify with your ego-based image of God, and become judgmental, critical and blaming, or holier-than-thou – putting others down in an attempt to feel 'better than' them. You feel that you do not deserve happiness, that you cannot trust your desires, that you must deny your own feelings and needs, and sacrifice yourself for others. You might subconsciously believe that there is a limit to how much pleasure, love, luck, fun or money you are allowed to have – and feel strangely relieved when a problem comes up, or uneasy when life goes smoothly.

Belief in a judgmental God makes us chronically tense and anxious, since the rules about how to earn conditional love are rarely clear – so we might strive to be good and nice and perfect (which is highly stressful), or expect others to be perfect. And we might forever expect to be judged or punished by others, or have a shame-based fear of being 'found out'. (Many successful professionals and celebrities secretly fear that, one day, someone will discover they are a fraud, that they are useless or incompetent. Such fears almost always arise from hiding behind a false self, from which we long to be set free.)

If we worship such a God, whether consciously or not, we expect life to be full of sorrow, regrets and unlived dreams. After all, we see the world as a vale of tears, and believe we do not deserve to be happy. So we work hard and deny ourselves in the hope of happiness in the future (when we find our soul mate, when this project is finished, when the children go to school, when we get divorced, when the children have grown up, when we have our new home, when we retire, when this problem has been resolved ... or at least in the afterlife). The ego is always *waiting* to live. Heaven is always *there*, not here. The rule is jam tomorrow – or yesterday. Never jam today.

If you believe in an abandoning God, you feel even more distant from joy and unconditional love, and even more in need of control. You might disconnect and try to go it alone, resigning yourself to loneliness even within your relationships. Fear of loss and abandonment might make you focus on the false security that comes from wealth or possessions, wanting to *have* more and more. Your insecurity might lead to treating a partner or children as possessions, clinging or smothering them, or being a bully. Or you might withdraw from relationships, priding yourself on your independence and self-sufficiency, rather than risk the loss and abandonment you constantly fear and expect. Deep down, you feel lonely and alienated from yourself and others. You split the world into good and bad, seeing people and events in black-and-white terms, and striving (at huge expense to yourself) to keep the 'bad' at bay. This often means swinging between numbness and emotional chaos/unpredictability, or being critical and blaming of others.

A judgmental God at least gives us hope of *earning* love – if only we are good enough – but if we see God as ignoring or deserting us then, like an abandoned child, our hope turns to grief and rage, then to despair and hopelessness. Our defences become thicker, more heavily layered, like a smoke screen. We hide behind our roles and masks. We no longer reach out for love and joy, but grimly resign ourselves to a relationship that is not working, or a mediocre life of quiet desperation. We secretly become cynical and numbed-out. We feel exiled from joy and bliss. Having given up on our dreams and visions, we put on a brave and happy face, and keep ourselves busy. (In psychological terms, this roughly corresponds to a borderline psychotic state.)

Subconsciously, most of us have muddled concepts about God, wavering between the different faces of God – and thus wavering between healthy, neurotic and borderline psychotic states of mind. For example, you might see your work as a source of self-esteem and redemption (judgmental God), as a means of escape (abandoning God), or as a joyful and creative expression of love (loving God), depending upon which of your gods is uppermost. Whenever you make a decision, you might engage in a 'battle of the gods' within you. Sometimes you might believe that you are basically good and are meant to be happy – that God offers uncon-ditional love – and make decisions accordingly. At other times, you might slip back into fear, guilt, drivenness, blame or cynicism, as the ego-based faces of God bob up to the surface.

Personal relationships likewise mirror our complex rela-tionship with our inner gods. Every relationship is a dance between love and fear; and the more our ego-based gods take over, the more we disconnect from unconditional love, and the more difficult, insecure, limiting, distant or painful our relationships become.

> *God is at home. It is we who have gone out for a walk.*
>
> *Meister Eckhart*[9]

Almost every culture in the world has a myth of the Fall and with it, ways of seeking redemption, or reconnecting with love. The Fall is our separation from deep reality, and the birth of the ego-self. It is the global wound of separation, of disconnection, of fragmentation. On the positive side, the

Fall is the process of separation-individuation, of finding our own uniqueness, of discovering our own authentic Self. On the negative side, it is the descent into fear and judgment – and all of the ego's patterns, games and defences. It is the price we have paid for separating ourselves from unconditional love, and what we must now break through in order to grow and evolve.

Fall-redemption theology is based upon the ego's false belief that *we did something wrong* by disconnecting from Source, by leaving the Garden, by choosing to develop our individuality. Since we no longer felt our connection with love, our ego (in its wisdom) decided that our father-God must be angry and disapproving, and *there must be something wrong with us.* And if only we could put it right or be good enough, God would love us again, and all would be well. It is easy to understand this if we see the ego as a young child. To a child, its parents are God-like creatures who must be in the right. So whenever a child is abused, neglected or abandoned, it tends to assume that it has done something wrong (guilt), or even thinks '*I* must be wrong' (shame): 'I must be bad, wicked, inadequate, undeserving or not good enough.' It feels ashamed and guilty. It feels frightened and insecure. It looks for ways of coping with its fear and pain – ways of making amends, of earning love, of protecting itself from further hurt, or ways of regaining a sense of power and control.

Hidden beneath the defensive layers of the ego – hidden within each of us – is a vulnerable child who *wants* to reach out its arms for love. Our inner child longs for love and connectedness, yet it feels unworthy or undeserving of that love, or afraid of being rejected or abandoned. The ego is looking for love and security, but it looks for it in all the wrong ways, and in all the wrong places. It is searching for something it already has in deep reality, and could create in physical reality – if only we could reconnect with Source.

THE TREE OF GOOD AND EVIL

Out beyond ideas of wrongdoing and rightdoing,
there is a field. I'll meet you there.
When the soul lies down in that grass,
The world is too full to talk about.

Rumi[10]

The biblical myth of the Garden of Eden tells us that it was Eve eating of the Tree of Good and Evil that led to humanity being 'cast out of paradise' – in other words, the unconditional love of the divine feminine gave way to the conditional love of the emerging ego, and we faced the pain of separation. The mystical poet Rumi reminds us that judgment divides us from ourselves and others; it prevents the soul becoming embodied; it saps us of life. 'When the soul lies down in *that* grass' – in the field beyond judgment, beyond duality, beyond good and evil – heaven and earth become one.

Judgment is conditional love. It is the ego's attempt to feel 'good' in order to be worthy and loved. Judgment makes us fearful, wary, ashamed and guilt-ridden. It can also make us harsh and critical. If we subconsciously believe that God is judgmental, we internalise that judgment and apply it to ourselves and others, constantly assessing whether we (and they) are being good or bad. We live on tenterhooks, squashing whatever emotions and desires might be 'bad,' and struggling to be 'good' in the eyes of others. We conform to external standards of morality and behaviour, doing whatever is expected of us. We suppress our freedom and spontaneity. We believe we are being good (and will therefore be loved) if we sacrifice ourselves for others; that we must not be greedy or selfish, that other people's needs must come first, or that we will get our reward in heaven if we suffer now. We might apply moralistic labels to everything from food ('healthy' or 'unhealthy') to modes of transport (ecologically sound or earth-destroying) – then congratulate ourselves for giving up sweets for Lent, or struggling around on public transport instead of buying a car.

As spiritual author Sarah Ban Breathnach notes, 'Self-sacrifice is not pretty and it is not noble'[11] – yet millions of us embody guilt, sacrifice and martyrdom as a way of life, and teach it by example to our children. Our guilt might not be attached to God nowadays – it has become secularised – but beneath guilt is a subconscious belief that we are bad, that our desires are wicked and selfish, that we need redemption. Whenever you feel 'good' for denying your own needs and impulses – whether it is a longing for gooey chocolate cake, or a desire to chill out and relax, whether it is suppressing the desire to say 'No,' or the urge to reach out to someone – you are appeasing the judgmental God within you.

Guilt always means that you are in conflict, and inner conflict drains your energy, blocks your growth and suppresses your potential. Yet for centuries, the Church has promoted guilt as a way of life. Why? Why would it have a vested interest in making people feel guilty and unworthy? Because guilt-ridden people are easy to control. In terms of our vibrational frequency, guilt is pretty much at the bottom of the ladder, close to depression and despair. Guilt splits your energy, which renders you fairly powerless. You are then vulnerable to the influence and external authority of others; you become child-like and eager to please (and more and more disconnected from your deep Self).

It is easy to demonstrate this in energy terms. If you hold out one arm, and ask someone to do a muscle-test (see chapter 4), your arm should bounce back. Energy is flowing. Now focus on anything that makes you feel guilty, and repeat the test. Your arm will have gone weak, and flop down. Guilt creates a short-circuit in our energy system, as do fear, blame, criticism, jealousy and any other negative emotions. In other words, guilt disconnects us from Source energy. (Interestingly, making the traditional sign of the cross on your body involves weakening the central meridian – since moving your hand down the centre of your body runs *against* the natural energy flow. It 'unzips' that meridian. This makes us feel vulnerable or insecure, and more open to the influence of others. The Church – whether knowingly or not – ensured that people would be wide open and vulnerable before listening to bloodcurdling sermons about guilt, sin and eternal damnation!)

Does it seem likely that God is so screwed up and neurotic, such a control freak, so pompous and self-righteous, that He *wants* us to suffer and deny ourselves, and lays down a plethora of restrictive rules and commandments to control our behaviour? Is it plausible that a loving God would set up the world as a 'trial' in which we are tempted with guilt-ridden impulses that we must resist, and burdened with dreams and desires which we cannot fulfil? Is it likely that a vast creative Source has such a fragile ego that it needs boosting by our bowing down, falling on our knees in worship, and awaiting Judgment Day in terror? It seems about as likely as stumbling across a snowman on molten lava. After all, what kind of creative Source would this be? A cruel and sadistic dictator. A lunatic God who *wanted* to create neurosis and misery. A raging God of our twisted imagination. Yet countless generations have been brain-washed into believing such a soul-destroying myth.

Only a human society that wanted to *control* people – through fear and guilt – could conjure up such a bizarre image of God, which waterfalls down the generations and (in a secular society) might be expressed through worka-holism, martyrdom or depression. Making people feel guilty and undeserving is a highly effective way of disempowering them, since it is not possible to feel guilt-ridden and empowered at the same time. And threatening negative consequences if people fail to conform – if not now, then in the afterlife – is an excellent way to manipulate their behaviour.

The immature ego, with its belief in a judgmental God, tells us that *nice* people feel guilty, and that God is somehow pleased if we criticise and judge and shame ourselves, instead of loving and accepting ourselves. The deep Self, by contrast, knows that only neurotic people feel guilty! When we are fully connected to Source energy, we radiate unconditional love and joy. We could not possibly harm anyone else, since we know that there is no Other – that everyone is an inseparable part of God/Source, and that hurting or even criticising anyone hurts us too. It is only when we are screwed up and disconnected that we hit out with sharp words, undermine others, beat ourselves up, deny our emotions or project our Shadow. It is only when we are disconnected that we suppress our own needs and desires, and try to please others out of guilt or the need for approval. And nothing disconnects us from our deep Self as effectively as guilt and judgment. *Whenever you think in terms of right and wrong, good and bad, black and white, you are trapped in the dualistic world of the ego – which puts you beyond the reach of wild love.*

The ego is quick to judge. It often tries to make itself feel better by criticising others, feeling self-righteous or superior, blaming and absolving itself of any responsibility. The ego has a great need to be 'in the right', which means that anyone who disagrees or steps on its toes must be 'in the wrong'. But as a Native American proverb wisely warns, 'Do not judge your neighbour until you walk two moons in their moccasins.'[12] The ego always views the world from its own limited standpoint. It rarely sees that everyone is always doing the best they can, from their own perspective. It rarely listens with an open heart. It rarely allows for the possibility that even if people sometimes act from a place of fear and disconnection, they are usually doing what they believe to be right or good or necessary; or they are re-enacting their own unresolved hurt and pain, or giving in to pressure from others who are disconnected. Even the terrorists, even the Nazis, even the drug-pushers and pimps. Even those in the multi-nationals who rip down the rainforests and destroy tribal communities. Even those who work in the giant pharmaceutical companies and knowingly sell dangerous drugs and silence whistle-blowers. Every one of them is a human being like ourselves. A good human being. And if we inhabited their inner world for a couple of moons, we might understand why they do what they do – and have compassion for them.

INDIVIDUALITY AND ONENESS

> ... *sometimes blocked in, sometimes reaching out,*
> *one moment your life is a stone in you, and the next,*
> *a star.*
>
> Rainer Maria Rilke[13]

The judgmental God and the abandoning God bring up and express two opposing forces within us – the desire to merge, and the desire to separate. These are both natural drives, and the tension between them pushes our consciousness towards evolution. In their healthy form, the desire to separate is our *drive to individuate* – to be authentic, to assert our individuality, to set clear boundaries, to be creative and self-expressive, to discover our own uniqueness, to learn and grow; while the desire to merge is our *yearning for oneness* – the longing to reconnect with deep reality, to love and be loved, to remember that we are all one, that the world is a magical place of unseen connections full of meaning and purpose, and (if only we can get our ego out of the way) bursting with unconditional love and joy. These desires represent the masculine and feminine energies, respectively, within each of us: the mature ego (divine masculine) and the deep Self (divine feminine).

Our immature ego, with its belief in separateness, strives to satisfy these two healthy drives in ways that fragment and disconnect us. It merges by losing touch with its own individuality and authenticity, and it separates by withdrawing and distancing itself. This reflects the judgmental God and the abandoning God within:

✧ The judgmental God leads you to *merge* with others: by sacrificing your authenticity, by seeking approval, by giving in to others' demands, by doing your duty, by pretending to agree, by prevaricating, by hiding your Shadow, by conforming – or controlling others into doing things *your* way, since you believe that love is conditional upon being 'good'. This fusion imprisons you within a false self. It means that you live a life that doesn't belong to you. It makes your relationships shallow, superficial and unreal, so that you *feel* lonely and disconnected even though you are desperately trying to *connect* – to be loved and accepted, to feel a sense of belonging. This is the immature ego's expression of our longing for oneness.

✧ The abandoning God makes you want to *distance* yourself, to withdraw, to cut off, to retreat, to escape, to hide, to disengage – both as a defence against the fear and pain of abandonment and as a way of punishing others, of expressing your rage. It imprisons you in loneliness, numbness and despair. It stops you reaching out for love. It blocks you from offering real love. It makes you retreat inside your own head, or (compulsively) into books or work or jogging or soap operas or a bottle of whisky. Or it creates distance by criticising, blaming and judging. This is the ego's version of our desire to individuate.

The battle of the gods creates the 'dance of intimacy', which makes us push forward then pull back within relationships. In fact, almost any inner conflict represents a battle between our inner gods. And such battles cannot be resolved at the level of the ego. *We have to expand our consciousness.* We have to transcend the ego-based gods, and reconnect with unconditional love. We must break free from our self-imposed prisons, and stride out into the golden rays of sunlight. We must take the hero's journey (see chapter 3) – moving through the pain of separation, discovering our own uniqueness, healing our wounds and defences, drinking the Elixir of Awakening, then returning to the world with expanded awareness.

We need both to connect deeply *and* to individuate, but the immature ego is capable of neither. It only knows how to merge or to distance. Our needs for both connectedness and uniqueness have to be expressed by integrating the mature ego with the deep Self. This means recognising that God/Source is both immanent and transcendent – that we are gods in the making, with Source energy flowing creatively through us, *and* we are loved unconditionally. Only then can we experience both individuality *and* oneness. Only then can we experience joy and bliss. Only then can we truly love and be loved.

> *Ecstasy is the dance of the individual with the All.*
> **Monica Sjöö & Barbara Mor**[14]

A GOD FOR GROWN-UPS

During the 20th century, as the bearded-man-in-the-sky-God seemed more and more ridiculous and nonsensical, a contemporary image of God began to emerge from quantum physics. At the deep level of reality, it seems there is no solid stuff, just an interconnected web of energy – and that this web is inseparable from consciousness. What is more, those who have direct experience of this level suggest, in tune with mystics since ancient times, that the web is also inseparable from love, from unconditional love. So perhaps this infinite web of energy-consciousness-love *is* what we used to call God?

At the age of 33, I experienced this web for myself. One warm September afternoon, I was sitting in my garden reading a metaphysical book on the nature of reality. Suddenly my perception of the world around me shifted. My head began to spin, I expanded beyond time-space, and everything that I could see – sky, clouds, trees, houses, grass, fence, birds – became part of me, and I was part of it. I was still uniquely myself, yet 'I' was intimately connected to All That Is. I merged into a greater whole that I had read about since my teens, but never *known* to be real. Here I was, and here was everything, and we were all the same, an unbroken field of pulsating and dancing energy. And within and above and through it all, there was love: a vast ocean of love, glittering like tiny diamonds of light in the green leaves and the red bricks and the soft autumn breeze. I was immersed in love. I *was* love. Love radiated in waves through every wisp of air, every leaf, every cell, every atom. I don't know how long this experience lasted. Time had ceased to exist; there was only the eternal Now. But as soon as I returned to the ordinary world I *knew*, beyond doubt, that we create our own reality, that I was free to do anything I wished, and that the only true reality was love. It was an experience that radically changed my life, and led to writing my first book, *Living Magically*.

Countless people have had similar mystical experiences – whether life-changing or not – either spontaneously or during meditation, trance-dance and other altered states of consciousness. Many thousands have also had near-death experiences, which consistently describe the unconditional love and oneness of the realms beyond physical reality. And the new physics likewise tells us there are many dimensions of reality, and that beneath the apparent separateness is an undivided whole.

It is time to leave behind our child-like, ego-based concepts of a judgmental, critical, disapproving God who wants us to be good and well behaved, and who sent us to earth for schooling purposes – and if we pass our lessons, *might* consider us worthy of going to heaven; an imaginary God in dire need of psychotherapy (or perhaps energy psychology!). We also need to move beyond the distant, abandoning God, or the empty, atheistic clockwork universe – concepts that have thrown us into existential angst and despair.

The time has come for an adult God/dess of *unconditional* love: a God who is consistent with psychological health and emotional maturity, a creative Source who gave us the earth as a gift, as a wondrous opportunity for adventure; a God who wants us to be happy and free, loving and creative. If God/Source is unconditional love, wouldn't it make sense if the world was designed to bring us joy and pleasure and sensual delight? We need an image of God that *connects* us with Source energy, instead of disconnecting us. Deep reality fits best with panentheism: that is, seeing God as both imma-nent and transcendent, present in all things and also beyond all things – and seeing our desires as a healthy expression of the God within us. (As St John of the Cross remarked, 'What sort of a God would it be, who only pushed from without?'[15])

In fact, we probably need to abandon the word 'God' altogether, since it has become so laden with negative or childish images that it puts kinks in our garden hose. Source, or Source energy, or the Universe, or All That Is, seem to be preferable terms, as they do not conjure up those crusty old images, beliefs and emotions; and the energy-consciousness paradigm seems an ideal way of bridging the current gap between our scientific framework of the universe and a spiritual-intuitive understanding of life.

Here are signs that you believe in a God/Source of unconditional love:

✧ Being loving and accepting of self and others

✧ Deep, loving and intimate relationships in which you feel cherished, supported and free to be and express who you are

✧ Being open, honest and vulnerable; lacking in defences

✧ Feeling relaxed and self-confident

✧ Expecting life to be good

✧ Being true to yourself

✧ Reaching out to others with open-hearted love, not with neediness

✧ Freedom and openness to change; letting life 'flow'

✧ Courage and fearlessness

✧ Trusting your intuition

✧ Being fully present in the moment

✧ Naturalness and spontaneity

✧ Being fully immersed in life – vital and alive

✧ Staying centred in your own heart

✧ Taking time for silence and solitude

✧ Being self-nurturing, as well as caring joyfully for others

✧ Honouring your emotions, and letting them flow freely

✧ Being passionate, enthusiastic and joyful

✧ Being fairly free from negative emotions such as anxiety, guilt and rage

✧ Deep sense of trust and surrender; knowing that everything is unfolding perfectly

✧ Seeing beauty and delight everywhere

✧ A fun-loving, celebratory approach to life

✧ An 'attitude of gratitude'

✧ Creative self-expression

✧ Vision and imagination

✧ Giving joyful service to the world

✧ Fulfilling your potential; living your dreams; following your bliss

✧ Being a conscious creator of your reality, an apprentice god/goddess

✧ Seeing everything as sacred and divine – including the earth itself

✧ Feeling *connected* – to Self, others, community, nature and spirit

✧ Being deeply spiritual in an 'earthy' way; embodying spirituality in everyday life (while probably not traditionally religious)

✧ Core belief that life is meant to be heaven on earth

If you believe in a God/Source who is truly loving and immanent, you do not pray for forgiveness or deliverance from evil, as in the Lord's Prayer. Such ideas can only come from a place of duality and judgment. Instead you express your love, joy and gratitude for life, and ask the God/Source energy within for an ever-increasing sense of connectedness – as in my own Prayer to the Goddess:

O Mother God,
Birther of all creation,
Bringer-forth of life from your cosmic womb:
May I know your eternal grace and beauty
And feel your divine presence within me.
May I see the Beloved in every bird and tree and rock.
May I hear your sweet Voice
In the whistle of the wind and the roar of the river.
May I cherish all beings upon earth
As my sisters and brothers –
And may I walk gently upon the face of my Mother.

Aramaic scholar Neil Douglas-Klotz has translated the Lord's Prayer from an early version written in Aramaic, the original language of Jesus. His beautiful translation begins: 'Oh you, breathing life in all, origin of the gleaming sound, you shine in us and around us, even the darkness glows when we remember.' It continues, 'May the burning wish of your heart unify heaven and earth through our harmony... Do not let superficial things lead us astray, but instead free us from that which holds us back.'[16] This is a prayer based upon immanence as well as transcendence, based upon a recognition that what we call God breathes in us and through us, that there is no separation – and that freedom comes from moving beyond duality into unconditional love. I feel sure that this is what Jesus really taught.

An immanent God is an *earthy* God. When you see God as present in all things – a flower, a candle, a teapot – you treat the earth with love and reverence. You do not see a painful severance between the perfect heaven of the afterlife that you are longing for, and the fallen world that you have to suffer in the meantime. Instead you see beauty and divinity and mystery everywhere. Heaven is here and now. The earth is our home. And you know that we are inseparable from the earth. It then becomes impossible to pollute the seas, to cut down the rainforests, to poison the soil with chemicals. You tread softly on the earth, knowing that you tread upon the face of our Mother.

If you see God as immanent – if you believe that everything is carved out of the body of God, that there is nothing that is *not* God/Source – then unconditional love and acceptance flows naturally. You believe in original blessing and divinity, rather than original sin. Instead of judging people, or seeing their imperfections as bad and wrong, you accept everyone in their wholeness, knowing that they are a spark of All That Is – not just their 'nice bits', but also their negativity, their arrogance, their impatience, their neediness, their insecurity, their despair, their self-pity . . . Nor do you judge their behaviour or decisions or values, knowing that you can never see the whole picture, that you do not know what *their* unique journey is about, that you cannot know what is right for anyone else. And you become more accepting and befriending of yourself, knowing that you are loved in your wholeness and imperfection, simply because you are part of the whole, because you are inseparable from the loving, conscious energy field of the Universe. You do not have to be perfect; you simply have to be yourself.

An immanent God is also an *evolving* God – not moving towards perfection, but moving towards expansion and creative self-expression. If God is immanent, then God is evolving and growing through us. We *are* God in evolution. If we see God as perfect and transcendent – separate from us, better than us – we set ourselves up to feel shameful and inadequate. A perfect God is an oppressive God. How could we ever aspire to be perfect? And who defines what perfect means? Aiming to be perfect inevitably means suppressing our wholeness, our humanness, our individuality, our messy emotions, our uncertainty, our authenticity. We cannot be perfect and also be green, moist and earthy. Perfect people would end up being boring clones of each other – like the empty-headed robot women in *The Stepford Wives*, forever smiling sweetly and keeping their houses immaculate. Aiming for perfection means aiming for conformity, suppressing our freedom and self-expression. A world full of perfect people would be a dull place to live: safe, predictable and boring.

When we see God as ever-evolving, it allows us room for growth, for movement, for an endless journey of being and becoming – without the implicit judgment and unworthiness of not (yet) being perfect, of trying to reach an end-point. When we are aiming towards perfection, however subconsciously, we always have a sense of not being there yet, of life not quite beginning yet, of waiting to get there. And we will lie on our deathbeds still 'waiting to get there' – because life can never be perfect. If it were perfect, it would come to a standstill. It would become a stagnant pool. It is the imperfections – the unfulfilled longings, the imbalances, the challenges, the fresh desires – that keep us alive and moving. The universe never stands still.

Life is about growth and freedom and joy, and exuberantly living the adventure, and the sheer delight of learning how to consciously create what we want. There is no perfection in this. No-one 'up there' is keeping score, or drumming their fingers with impatience, waiting for us to make the right decisions, to finish everything on our to-do list, to complete our mission, to finally 'get it right'. No-one is tut-tutting as we get lost in surface reality, expecting us to model ourselves on saints, to become beyond reproach, or to figure out how to do His will. Only a God of *conditional* love, of judgment, would have fixed ideas about what we should do, who we should become, or what the rules are.

Wild love always sets us free. We are sparks of God in conscious evolution. Life is an adventure in consciousness. We are exploring how to express our uniqueness and become conscious creators (which requires an ego) while also staying aligned with Source energy. This is not easy, but we are working on it. It is time for us to make our own choices, to create our own rules, to become spiritual adults, to become apprentice gods. It is time for us to reawaken the divine feminine, the immanent God – to reclaim our power and divinity.

 PRACTICAL SUGGESTIONS

Write four letters (perhaps over several days or weeks) to and from God. Let this writing flow from a deep place within you. Do not censor anything. Don't try to be 'nice' or rational. **Write the letters in this order**, since they represent our spiritual evolution from child to adolescent to adult:

1. Write a letter to the judgmental God of conditional love, saying what you believed (in the past) you must do in order to gain God's love and approval – and ways in which you still try to gain others' approval or sacrifice yourself, because you secretly feel unlovable, unworthy or not good enough.

2. Write an angry letter to the 'distant, abandoning God' who showed no care or compassion for humanity, saying exactly why you are so angry. (Perhaps because of your current life, or childhood, or the state of the world, or historical events.) Let rip! Hold nothing back! Express your rage!

3. Write a letter to the Source of unconditional love, about your longing to reconnect with Source – and to be bathed in love, joy, freedom, creativity and miracles all day long. Tell Source all that you long for in your life.

4. Write a letter back to yourself from Source, suggesting how to reconnect with this energy, with the God within,

more and more fully. (It might help to relax deeply or go into a meditative state before you begin this letter, and perhaps use the hand you do not normally write with.)

CHAPTER SIX

Choosing To Be Happy

When you do things from your soul, you feel a river moving in you, a joy …

Rumi[1]

In the film *The Remains of the Day*, a dutiful English butler devotes his life to serving the needs of others, while tragically ignoring the whisperings of his own heart – his secret love for the housekeeper, Miss Kenton. Personal relationships between staff are forbidden, and Stevens continues to do his faithful best for his employer, despite increasing evidence that his loyalty is misplaced. We long to see Stevens break down the walls of his narrow, self-imposed prison, and take the risk of being human, emotional and vulnerable, but he is too rigid, too repressed, too afraid to reach out and express his true self. He continues to do what is 'right and proper'. Despairing of him, Miss Kenton enters a pale and loveless marriage, and moves away. Many years on, Stevens is given a second chance to connect with her, and to be honest and authentic rather than proper – but still he hides behind his mask, and lets her go. He remains in the shadowlands, with his lonely half-life of lingering sorrow and regrets.

How many of us go through life like Stevens, following the dictates of others, seeking others' approval, being good and dutiful at the expense of our own authenticity and joy and aliveness? How many of us say 'No' to connecting more intimately – to diving beneath the surface, and making deeper and more meaningful relationships? How many have unfulfilled dreams and half-buried desires, stuffed down by the suffocating demands of convention, guilt or loyalty?

What if Alice had ignored her curiosity about the White Rabbit, and remained asleep in the garden – saying 'No' to the rabbit hole, saying 'No' to her hero's journey into Wonderland? What an adventure she would have missed. Yet so many of us do what is expected by society, remaining blinkered to more magical possibilities – even if, in some private corner of our mind, we are waiting and hoping for something more. All too often we ignore the promptings of our heart, tell ourselves to be sensible and realistic, and settle for the mundane life of surface reality.

But are we really meant to be good and dutiful and loyal, and to squash our hopes and dreams and desires, perhaps in hope of a later reward? Are we meant to keep ourselves safe, and conform to social expectations? Is this really what life is all about?

❤

Within new paradigm thinking, we are not 'children' of God, waiting to be told what to do, and striving to win His approval. Nor are we hopeless Muggles in a mundane reality. Instead we are powerful co-creators with Source energy, exploring and moulding physical reality. Life is a gift, and we are free to choose how to enjoy that gift, day by day. There is no right or wrong, no judgment from above. Nor is there any source of evil – just a Source of good, which we can be more or less aligned with. It is okay to make mistakes, to learn as we go along, to forge our own unique path. And we are not here to save the world. (Phew!) Life is a never-ending journey – and the journey itself *is* the point. We are neither rushing nor dawdling towards any final destination. *This* moment is our life – and *this* moment, and *this* moment. And an evolving, immanent God is forever longing to burst forth through us – with joy and passion and love and creativity. And all of this means giving up being 'good' in favour of being happy.

As we have seen, the patriarchal religions have urged us to overcome our 'fallen' nature, and strive to be good and perfect. The not-so-hidden assumption is that, deep down, we are not good, not worthy, not deserving, and that life is a struggle to prove ourselves, to battle against our 'bad' (selfish, greedy, rebellious, self-indulgent, nasty, destructive) impulses, and reach for what is good and pure and saintly within us. Life then becomes a battle between good and evil. And if we win the battle, we just might be 'good' enough to be loved by a God whose love is so conditional that He loves us only when we are conforming to His standards of behaviour. This splitting can only create inner neuroticism and outer conflict. *Without a healthy psychology based upon unconditional love, religion or mysticism is as likely to lead us towards enlightenment as a blind bat is to lead us into the sunlight.*

Trying to be good stems from a dualistic way of thinking. It is based upon judgment, or conditional love. Trying to be good fuels self-righteousness, which means seeing someone as 'in the right' (blameless, faultless, beyond reproach) and someone else as 'in the wrong' (guilty, shameful, bad, unworthy, imperfect). This kind of splitting – projecting our dark Shadow onto others – is at the root of all wars, terrorism, genocide, racism, sexism, family feuds, religious factions and almost all relationship difficulties in which we are convinced the other is at fault, while seeing ourselves as righteous or innocent victims. It creates a huge proportion of the misery and suffering in the world.

It is mostly the guilt-ridden or self-righteous – those

who are trying to be good, to be 'better than' others – who hurt or harm or try to control others. The politicians all believe that they are in the right as they lay down new laws and regulations. The terrorists and suicide bombers believe they are fighting evil. The righteous war-mongers think that mass murder can be justified for a good cause. The witch-hunters and Crusaders saw themselves as battling against 'wicked' paganism. Those who fight *against* pollution or pesticides, or third-world debt, or nuclear weapons, or child abuse, or any kind of perceived injustice or exploitation see themselves as in the right. But as soon as we try to be in the right, someone else (or some part of us) has to be bad or wrong. There has to be an enemy. Then we have to do battle with that enemy, or control or exclude them, and might 'justify' hurtful or abusive behaviour towards them, intimidation or even violence. We are living in fear and separateness. We are lost in judgment – and our soul cannot lie down in the grass.

We only project our Shadow, viewing others as bad and wrong, when we need to see ourselves as good and perfect since we fear, deep down, that we are bad or unworthy or inadequate, and want to redeem ourselves by comparison. Self-righteousness is pretty near the top of the ego's emotional range, so it likes to hang out there. (A bishop's wife once told me that she hoped there *was* judgment at the pearly gates, otherwise all her good works would have been in vain. Hmmm ...) Where does such fear and insecurity come from? From conditional love, which makes us split off what we see as not good in ourselves. This creates an inner civil war that is then mirrored in our relationships with others or with the world. And so the vicious circle of splitting, projection and judgment continues.

If you believe that being spiritual (or loving) means being 'good', *you're in big trouble.* After all, you have identified spirituality (or love) with the world of the ego – the world of judgment, the world of good/bad and right/wrong – so you will tie yourself in neurotic knots. Ideas about what is 'morally right' can only come from the ego, which lives in duality. It eats from the Tree of Good and Evil. And when you are being guided by the ego and its judgments, you are ignoring the deep Self and your emotional guidance. You will be imprisoned by trying to do what is 'good and right and holy', instead of choosing what Source energy is constantly guiding you towards, which is joy and freedom and unconditional love.

The ego is driven by sticks rather than carrots, and is highly vulnerable to the idea that it will be loved and safe if only it is good. But what if Source does not want us to be good? What if God/Source loves us unconditionally – which means loving *every* part of us equally, with all our messiness and apparent imperfections? What if God thinks we are dazzlingly wonderful and beautiful and amazing, just as we are? What if Source thinks there is nothing wrong with us? What if God views us as divine sparks of All That Is, having a glorious adventure on planet earth, exploring our individuality and relatedness, and learning to become conscious co-creators? What if our creative Source has no needs, no expectations, no demands – and simply wants us to enjoy the gift of life? What if trying to be good simply reinforces our ego, and *separates* us from real love, from wild love?

OUR EMOTIONAL GUIDANCE

> *Inside everyone*
> *is a great shout of joy*
> *waiting to be born.*
>
> *David Whyte*[2]

There is a healthy, life-giving alternative to being good. It is choosing to be happy. If we aim to be happy and joyful, we are not being guided by external standards, or hand-me-down rules, or social norms, or others' expectations. Our only yardstick for how we are doing is *how we feel*. Right now. Our focus is on our inner world. We are fully present to ourselves. We are Self-centred – and therefore empowered. We are not concerned with what others might think, but with how we ourselves feel in the moment. At a single stroke, this frees us from neurosis – and takes us towards wild love.

Western society teaches us to be left-brained. It encourages us *not* to feel – to suppress and deny our emotions, to be logical and analytical, to live in our heads. Our culture and education system devalues our emotions and intuition, so that by the time we are young adults, most of us have lost touch with how we feel. Boys are taught not to feel upset. Girls are taught not to get angry. Many are taught that emotions are untrustworthy, dangerous, selfish or even childish – best ignored, and not to be taken seriously. We become strange, unbalanced, half-brained creatures who have to fend off the non-rational half of our nature by cramming our days with busyness, noise and stimulation, avoiding time alone and numbing ourselves with addictions.

The problem is that your logical left brain lives in surface reality, while the more emotional-intuitive right brain is your bridge to deep reality – so if you ignore your emotions, you are also cutting off your inner guidance, your direct phone-line to Source.

Everyone is born with a guidance system that gives constant feedback about your vibrational state, and whether you are aligned with Source energy – and that guidance system is (primarily) your emotions. *More than anything else, it is your emotional state that tells you how connected you are to Source.* Your emotions convey your current vibrational frequency. When you feel joyful and free and empowered, you are in your natural state of connection to Source energy. When you feel negative or trapped, you are disconnecting from Source. It is as simple as that. As energy psychology has revealed, any negative emotion is like an alarm bell sounding. It means your energy flow is disrupted. You are putting kinks in your garden hose – unplugging from your deep Self – so that you are left to rely upon your immature ego. Which is not good news for you, or for anyone around you.

There are only two basic emotions: love and fear. Expanding or contracting. Feeling good or feeling bad. Feeling connected or feeling separate. Love comes from connecting to Source energy, and it gives rise to positive thoughts and feelings: unconditional love, joy, gratitude, appreciation, inner peace, freedom, passion, optimism, hope, trust, playfulness, enthusiasm, contentment, patience, opening up, reaching out and empowerment. Fear comes from disconnecting from Source energy, and gives rise to negative thoughts and feelings: anxiety, guilt, shame, frustration, irritation, unworthiness, depression, grief, despair, anger, jealousy, neediness, insecurity, blame, judgment, criticism, impatience, pessimism, worry, being overwhelmed, conflict, stoicism, approval-seeking, disappointment, lack of freedom, restriction, closing down, holding back and disempowerment.

> *Emotions are indicators of your alignment with Source energy.*
>
> *Abraham*[3]

When we feel bad, the outside world tends to get the blame. More often than not, we believe that someone or something 'out there' is *causing* us to feel whatever negative emotion we are feeling. And if only they would change, or the situation would change, we would feel fine! But this is the upside-down thinking of the ego, with its belief in surface reality. The ego feels separate from the world. It wants to point a finger of blame. Its happiness is always conditional on what is happening 'out there'. But the truth is that if we are feeling any negative emotion, we are disconnecting *ourselves* from Source. No-one can make us do that. We have attracted any negative events through our own vibrations, or we are selectively seeing what is wrong or undesirable, or we are allowing ourselves to be controlled by others – and we are choosing to have negative thoughts and beliefs about the situation. It is always an inside job. And there is enormous freedom and relief in knowing this. *Nothing in the outside world needs to change in order for us to feel good*. We cannot hold anyone else responsible for how we feel. We just have to take the kinks out of our own hoses.

I heard the Dalai Lama speak in Glasgow last year, and his loving presence seemed to fill the huge concert hall. Someone asked whether he could give advice on how to tackle depression. His brief chuckling answer was that he could not help with that, since he had no experience of depression! For someone who had been exiled from his homeland for 45 years, had seen his country invaded, its rich culture nearly destroyed, and countless fellow Tibetans imprisoned, silenced or treated with unspeakable cruelty, it was a remarkable statement. But if someone is connected with Source energy, it is not possible to feel depressed.

When we are fully connected, we love unconditionally – that is, our love and happiness are not dependent on any external conditions being met. They are *un-conditional*. Instead of focusing on what is wrong in Tibet and how awful it is, the Dalai Lama focuses on what he can do about it. Instead of feeling self-righteous and wagging a finger of blame, the Dalai Lama offers love and acceptance. Instead of wallowing in martyrdom, or empathising with others' suffering, the Dalai Lama maintains his own loving, laughing and joyful connection to Source. He knows that he cannot help anyone if he is disconnected – and by maintaining his hold on deep reality, he inspires countless people around the world.

Whatever our experience of life, the problem never lies out there. The problem – and its solution – always lies in here.

TRYING TO BE GOOD

But what kind of world would it be, the ego asks, if everyone aimed to be happy, and didn't stick to the rules? What kind of world would it be if people were not forced to behave well, and fulfil their duties and responsibilities? What kind of world would we create if everyone was 'selfish' enough to want to feel good? A joyful world! A loving world! A world of connectedness. A world filled with happy people who were connected to Source energy, who were fulfilling their dreams, who were able to give and receive unconditional love – and who were uniquely themselves.

But what about the 'bad' people who have to be controlled, the ego asks – the criminals, the terrorists, the invaders, the abusers, the rapists, the violent drunks? There wouldn't be any people behaving that way, if we were all connected to Source. And you cannot attract them into your reality if you are aligned with Source. They simply won't match your vibrations. In any case, there aren't any bad people, just people who are temporarily disconnected from who they really are, invariably because they have been shamed into seeing themselves (or others) as 'bad'.

Conditional love assures us that society would tumble into chaos if we aimed to be happy, that we are inherently bad (or at least *some* of us are!) so we need to be controlled by rules and laws and socially acceptable standards of morality. But genuinely happy people don't commit murder and mayhem; nor do they judge and blame and criticise others; nor do they need others to behave in any particular way to 'make them happy'. When we are fully aligned with Source, our happiness does not depend upon other people or external conditions; it comes from within. We are over-flowing with effervescent joy and appreciation, an intoxicating sense of freedom and vision and possibility, along with glorious well-being and vitality. We don't *need* love from others; we radiate love. Happy people allow others to be free, since they love unconditionally and trust in everyone's essential goodness – and what they attract towards them mirrors this.

> *As a rule, it was the pleasure-haters who became unjust.*
>
> **W H Auden**[4]

Whenever you are *trying* to be good, your emotional guidance system is sent into chaos. You are living from your head, not from your heart. You believe that you are unworthy and inadequate, and are *trying* to be worthy and lovable, or *trying* to please others (or to please a mythical God). You ignore your emotions, and even turn them upside down, believing that it is somehow good to feel bad.

For centuries, people admired saints and martyrs who tortured and mutilated their own bodies, starved and abused themselves, and denied their natural desires, revering them for their self-flagellation and neurotic suffering. This might seem crazy to us today, but it is not much different from forcing ourselves to go to the gym, denying ourselves a slice of chocolate cake, working through lunch instead of taking a proper break, feeling guilty about sexual attraction to the 'wrong' person, or about making time to relax. How often do we judge and criticise ourselves for natural desires? And how many actions are motivated by a desire to see ourselves as virtuous – such as giving more than we can afford to charity, or working late at the office, or visiting relatives whose company we do not enjoy, or gloomily munching on lettuce leaves when we long for a huge bowl of stuffed pasta in rich red sauce?

The confused and immature ego tries to convince us that what feels good is in fact bad, and what feels bad is good for us. 'No gain without pain.' 'Suffering is good for the soul.' 'You have to pay a price for success (or happiness, or love, or enlightenment).' This makes some crooked sense if you believe that we are worthless sinners in need of redemption, or that life is supposed to be tough, or that we are merely here to 'learn lessons' and get our reward later. It makes no sense at all if you believe in a God/Source of unconditional love.

The ego will urge you to do what you 'should' do, what you ought to do, to fulfil your responsibilities, to put others first, to push yourself to the limit, to 'resist temptation' and ignore your own feelings. It believes that you will be happy if you are loved – but that you will only be loved if you are good. So it urges you to be good rather than happy. To be tame and controlled, rather than wild and free. To fend off your feelings of shame, guilt and unworthiness. To be self-righteous and self-denying. And so it leads you away from the deep Self, away from unconditional love and joy, away from your true path and along a blind alley.

> *Listen, are you breathing just a little, and calling it a life?*

> *Mary Oliver[5]*

THE EMOTIONAL SCALE

If you wish to reconnect with deep reality, it is crucial to pay attention to your emotions. Instead of repressing, denying, projecting or ignoring how you feel, or pretending you are happy when you are not, you need to take your feelings seriously. E-motion is energy in motion. How you feel is a reliable indicator of how your energy is flowing – and that, in turn, determines whether you are attracting positive events into your lives, and moving towards your heart's desires, or whether you are pulling 'bad luck', challenges and difficulties towards you.

William Tiller has shown how consciousness, energy and matter are interconvertible within the new paradigm. As I understand it, these might equally be thoughts (consciousness), emotions (which mirror our vibrational frequency) and events (the 'solid stuff' that appears in the outside world). In other words:

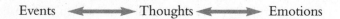

Events ⟷ Thoughts ⟷ Emotions

Our emotions arise mostly from our thoughts. If you are thinking negative thoughts – such as fearful, despairing, guilt-ridden, anxious, critical, blaming or jealous thoughts – then your deep Self sends gentle feedback in the form of negative emotion. You feel a twinge in your solar plexus, or a wave of anxiety or rage or guilt, which is a wake-up call. 'Pay attention,' the deep Self is saying, 'you are choosing thoughts that are not aligned with who you really are. You are choosing thoughts that are lowering your vibration – thoughts that will make you feel bad, and will (in time) attract events and behaviour and circumstances which you do not want.'

What usually happens is that we squash or displace negative emotion by getting busy, having a drink, raiding the biscuit tin, kicking the cat – or trying to ignore it. Or we blame our feelings on the outside world: 'He/she is *making* me feel this way! If only they would change, I would feel fine!' 'If only this had not happened in my life, I would be happy.' 'If only this was not happening in the world, I would be content.' But whatever is happening in our lives, and whatever we hear about in the world and how we choose to interpret those events, all depends upon our energy. It all depends upon what matches our vibrational frequency. The world is not a real, solid place; it dances to the tune of our energy-consciousness.

Let us suppose that you do pay attention to that twinge in the solar plexus and instead of blaming someone or something else, you take responsibility for your feelings. 'Ah, I'm feeling hopeless and disempowered in this situation. So what are my thoughts right now?' Then you can choose to have different thoughts that make you feel better – knowing that feeling better is a sign that you are raising your vibrational frequency, that you are becoming more aligned with Source energy. Then you will not only feel happier, but will also attract more positive events towards you.

Abraham – who is a channelled source, like Seth (see chapter 2) – provides an Emotional Scale which shows roughly where different emotions lie in terms of their vibrational frequency.[6] Towards the bottom of the scale are emotions such as fear, guilt, despair, grief, worthlessness, insecurity and powerlessness. Such painful emotions indicate that you are seriously disconnecting yourself from Source. At the top of the scale are positive emotions such as joy, passion, freedom, love, gratitude and empowerment – which indicate that Source energy is flowing freely in and through you. This is my own condensed version of the Emotional Scale:

THE EMOTIONAL SCALE

1. Wild love, joy, passion, enthusiasm, freedom, empowerment, appreciation, gratitude, playfulness, optimism, trust, intuitive knowing.

2. Calmness, acceptance, contentment, inner peace, patience, hopefulness, forgiveness, compassion.

3. Boredom, pessimism, frustration, irritation, impatience.

4. Being overwhelmed, over-busyness, worry, concern, disappointment.

5. Blame, judgment, self-righteousness, stoicism, arrogance, anger, vengeance, hatred, jealousy, obsessiveness, need to control.

6. Guilt, insecurity, unworthiness, self-sacrifice, martyrdom, loneliness, feeling trapped or controlled.

7. Depression, grief, despair, fear, disempowerment.

Your emotions might not correspond exactly to this Emotional Scale; it is just a rough guide. But if you are becoming a conscious creator, then any negative emotion – any emotion in the bottom half, or even the middle of the scale – should prompt you to take urgent action. After all, your deep Self is sending you a message. What are the negative thoughts that are bringing up this emotion? And how might you shift to a slightly higher vibrational frequency?

A higher level on the Scale indicates a higher vibration – that is, greater alignment with Source. (Even within each level is a wide range of vibrations, so boredom tends to feel better than frustration or irritation, and blame or self-righteousness are a little higher than anger, which feels a bit better than hatred.) There is no point in trying to leap from abject despair to joy and bliss as this is too large a vibrational shift – rather like trying to change ice directly into steam without melting it to water first. This is where positive thinking and affirmations usually fail – by trying to do a massive pole-vault. It only leaves you feeling even more despairing, as you fail to make the jump.

However, as any psychotherapist knows, when a depressed or guilt-ridden person starts to feel *angry*, they start to feel better! Anger, rage and blame are higher on the vibrational scale than depression and guilt. There is more energy flowing through you when you are angry or blaming than when you feel depressed or guilty; even thoughts of revenge can feel sweet! (I'm certainly not suggesting you *actually* slash the tyres of your ex-lover or dump a bucket of water over your critical boss, but *imagining* it might lead you to smile! If so, then your energy is moving in the right direction.) If it feels better to be angry, it means it is a step towards reconnecting with Source *from where you are*. So it makes sense to choose to feel angry – to deliberately choose critical or angry or vengeful thoughts about a person or situation – to begin shifting out of a depressed, guilt-ridden or hopeless state of mind.

This might sound confusing. If we create our own reality, and there are no victims, how can we ever be 'justified' in feeling angry about how someone behaves towards us, or about events in the outside world? For those on a spiritual path, this can be a stumbling block. You might tell yourself that since you created the situation, you have no right to feel angry with anyone else – or that being spiritual means being kind and loving and accepting at all times, and denying your feelings. Or you might express your anger towards someone who is stuck in self-righteousness, who manages to convince you that they are right and you are wrong. Or you might talk to someone who is disapproving of your anger, or doesn't want you to be angry with *them*. (Most people would prefer you to be depressed or guilt-ridden, rather than angry!) Then you are at risk of tumbling back down the ladder into guilt, self-blame and disempowerment.

But the point is that your feelings do not have to be *justified*. Choosing to feel angry can be a conscious, deliberate way of *shifting your vibrations*, so that you move higher up the ladder, towards greater connection with Source, towards freedom and empowerment. It is not about 'what really happened' or who is in the right. It is all about taking charge of your own energy-consciousness.

If you are feeling guilt-ridden, depressed or inadequate, anger takes you a step closer to alignment with Source. It makes you feel less disempowered. More energy is flowing.

But you are still not connected to deep reality – beyond victimhood, beyond the illusion of 'You did this to me', or the idea that anyone can be bad or wrong. You are still a long way from love and compassion and wisdom and freedom. And your negative emotion is telling you that. Anger, criticism and blame are still low on the vibrational scale – so this is not a place to remain stuck for long. Nevertheless, countless people cycle back and forth endlessly between shame/guilt/unworthiness/insecurity and anger/blame/self-righteousness. And if you are aiming to be good, you are likely to remain ensnared here: in the duality of good-bad, right-wrong, blame-guilt. Trapped in the world of the ego.

Ideally, anger is only a temporary way-station as you leave behind fear or guilt or depression or insecurity *en route* to emotions in the mid-range of vibrations – such as disappointment, frustration, boredom, irritation and impatience. These are not yet positive emotions, but they are moving in the right direction. How do you know this? Because those new thoughts bring a feeling of relief from anger. The new thoughts feel soothing and reassuring. The tension in your solar plexus softens. You feel somehow freer, more able to breathe, more energised. You begin to see the bigger picture, to understand the dance of co-creation; or the situation simply bothers you less. You might have new insights or conversations, which give you a different perspective. And once you have stabilised your thoughts about the issue or situation so that you are feeling frustration or pessimism, for instance, it isn't too big a leap to start choosing new thoughts that make you feel contented or even hopeful. From there, you might be able to reach towards positive beliefs, and to the highest echelons of joy and unconditional love. Now you are truly back in the flow.

It might take minutes, hours or even days to shift your thoughts in this way – depending on how big the issue is, and how long you have been stuck – but once you *feel* good, or simply get a sense of relief, you know that your vibrational frequency is increasing. Resistance is being released. You are setting yourself free. Your ego is giving way to the deep Self. Soon enough, outside events will begin to mirror this higher vibration back to you. (In the meantime, feeling happy will be reward in itself.)

Your deep Self is constantly guiding you to align with Source – to raise your vibrations by trusting your emotional-intuitive guidance. Moving up the Emotional Scale, step by step, is all about remembering that we are vibrational beings who are learning to consciously shift our energy-consciousness, so that we can create our own heaven on earth. It is part of changing our lives from the inside out. It is crucial to becoming an apprentice god/goddess.

Despite what centuries of religious dogma would have us believe, whenever you try to be good, you are disconnecting yourself from Source energy. You are exiled from unconditional love and joy. (And just to keep you really trapped, your ego might suggest it is nice people – good people – who feel guilt-ridden, worthless and insecure!) It is only when you accept that *everyone is good and worthy*, and you aim to be happy rather than good, that you escape from these lower vibrations and move towards freedom and empowerment and well-being.

> In this life we are to become heaven so that God might find a home here.
>
> **Meister Eckhart**[7]

I recently saw a woman who was recovering from breast cancer. Like many women with this disease, Angela had always cared for others at her own expense, and had ignored her own need for nurturing, personal growth and creativity. Her illness had made her reassess her priorities, and begin to get her life into balance. While convalescing, she had discovered a natural talent for watercolour painting – something she had longed to do for many years, but never made time for. But she still dipped down into despair and hopelessness at times, and wanted to feel more empowered and positive about her future. We explored some of her usual thoughts about the situation:

✧ The cancer might come back. *(Anxiety/powerlessness)*

✧ I've caused my family so much stress and anxiety. *(Guilt)*

✧ Might there be another tumour that hasn't been noticed? *(Fear)*

✧ How much damage has the chemotherapy done to my body? *(Anxiety)*

✧ Am I really allowed to put myself first, and consider my own needs? *(Insecurity)*

Sometimes it can help to feel angry about an illness, especially if there is a feeling of disempowerment – and many doctors and hospitals are probably blamed for mistakes and inadequacies by people who need to feel anger and blame in order to find a sense of relief. Whenever we feel disempowered, we want someone else to blame! But Angela had taken full responsibility for having cancer, and for the decisions she had made about treatment. She knew that she often had difficulties in dealing with anger, but couldn't find any angry thoughts that she could resonate with – and there is no point in choosing thoughts that we cannot 'feel', since this is not shifting our vibration. However, she could find some new thoughts of overwhelm, disappointment and frustration about her illness, and those gave her a sense of relief. These might not sound like positive emotions, but they are a huge improvement on guilt, fear and powerlessness! So I encouraged her to stabilise her thoughts at this higher level. She was soon able to do this and, within an hour, Angela was in touch with even more positive thoughts as she reconnected with Source energy:

✧ My life is getting better and better now. Having cancer feels like a gift that has transformed my life. *(Optimism/appreciation)*

✧ I have learned so much from this experience. *(Empowerment)*

✧ I am discovering new talents and interests *(Joy/passion)*

✧ I am a much better role model for my children when I care for myself better. *(Love/happiness)*

✧ I can appreciate every day now, instead of life feeling like a treadmill. *(Joy/appreciation)*

✧ As long as I hang on to these positive lessons, I won't ever need to create having cancer again. My body is my friend. *(Empowerment/freedom)*

Angela knew that she might spiral down into negativity at times, but she now knew how to catch herself if she felt the warning signs – by tuning in to how she *felt* – and how to deliberately choose thoughts that would raise her vibration, ensuring that her energy flowed freely, and thus preventing any likelihood of cancer recurring.

As energy psychology is vividly demonstrating, *all physical illness stems from resistance.* Our natural state of being is glowing health, vitality and well-being – and it isn't possible to have any emotional distress or physical disorder when Source is flowing freely through us. When energy is not flowing freely, this resistance is signalled to us by negative emotion; and if we ignore negative emotion (or inner guidance) for a long time, we eventually become ill or depressed. And why do we ignore negative emotion? Because we have convinced ourselves that we have no choice, or that we are doing the right thing – that we are being good, or staying safe, or doing what others want us to do. In other words, we have somehow come to believe that it is good to feel bad.

THE SEARCH FOR APPROVAL

If we are biochemically 'hardwired for bliss', as neuroscientist Candace Pert[8] suggests, however did we come to imagine that it might be good to feel bad, and bad to feel good? How did we ever construe the world in such a crazy, upside-down way?

Since our cultural beliefs in ego-based gods have disconnected us from Source, it isn't hard to understand how good becomes twisted into bad at a psychological level. We begin life with emotions and intuition, which constantly coax us towards happiness and fulfilment, towards connection with Source. It is simple: good (connecting) feels good, and bad (disconnecting) feels bad. So far, so good.

The problem is that parents, teachers and others – while in a state of disconnection – urge us to make *them* happy by doing what *they* want. *Sit down. Keep still. Eat it up. Don't cry. Don't shout. Don't be cross. Be careful. Don't make a mess. Be nice. Work hard. Be quiet. Stop fussing. Smile for the camera. Do as you're told. Be good. Make us proud of you.* As children, we are totally dependent on these God-like 'big people' and want to please them, and it makes life easier and more pleasant if we gain their approval. Even if our parents are kind and loving, we soon get the message of conditional love: that is, you will receive love and approval *as long as you behave as we want you to*. Even the most loving of parents give their children more compliments, more smiles, more hugs, more warmth and affection when they are 'behaving well', getting good marks at school or being polite than when they are creating uproar, scribbling on the walls, teasing their little sister, or shouting and screaming.

Few parents realise that their children's behaviour is largely evoked by *their* vibrations. Children are highly attuned to the energy of their parents (and teachers). When we are happy and relaxed and positive, our children tend to be happy and relaxed and positive. When our children 'behave badly' it is usually because they are acting out unresolved tensions in the family, or because their needs (for love or joy or freedom or growth) are not being met, or because they are picking up our vibrations, or because they are mirroring our negative beliefs about them or about parenting, or simply because we have unreasonable expectations of how children 'should' behave at a given age. When we are disconnected, we tend to disconnect them.

Yet instead of taking responsibility for what we evoke from our children, and for our own reactions, we try to control our world from the outside in – by getting *them* to change *their* behaviour. And we usually do this by making them feel bad, and urging them to 'be good'. We try to tame them. (Or we pretend to be calm and happy, and smile when we are seething or depressed, thus teaching our children to be inauthentic.) Such patterns are then transferred to our adult relationships; that is, we try to resolve problems by wanting to control or 'fix' the other person, or by shaming ourselves and feeling guilty – or denying problems, and pretending everything is fine – rather than by changing our energy-consciousness, our vibrations, which are the origin of the problem.

Most of us were raised by parents who themselves grew up with 'shaming' as a method of controlling their children. Shaming includes any form of criticising, rejecting, demeaning, insulting or threatening someone verbally, or with an angry or disdainful or threatening look – based upon their behaviour. Whenever you call a child naughty or spoilt or selfish or clumsy or stupid or childish or a cry-baby or a nuisance, or use any other put-down ('Look what you've done!') you are shaming them. Whenever you are cross or disappointed with a child for not doing what you want, you are shaming them. Whenever you punish or withdraw from a child for being 'bad' or behaving inappropriately, you are shaming them. And every parent does it.

Shaming often brings a short-lived sense of relief. It is a way of expressing anger and seeing the badness as 'out there' – and it often coerces a child (or adult) into compliance. But if you assume that everyone is good and well intentioned at heart, you always try to *understand* 'bad' behaviour, rather than judge or control it. (Of course, in practice, we're all just muddling along as parents, and it's important not to shame ourselves for being disconnected at times. As I once told my son when he was less than delighted with me, 'I'm doing the best I can – and you did choose me as your mother!')

As a method of controlling behaviour, shaming often works. The child learns to behave well – to seek approval and to do what is expected – and the parent thinks that they are successfully teaching the child 'right from wrong' and 'good from bad'. But in fact, the child is being taught to live from the ego. After all, we only need to be shamed and punished into behaving well if we are inherently bad. If we are inherently good, then we are naturally kind and loving *unless we are disconnected from who we are.* And the more we are shamed, the more disconnected we become. Shaming sets up a vicious circle which disconnects us from our true, wild self.

The ego believes that people behave better if they are shamed, punished and 'shown the error of their ways' – that judging people as bad helps them to be good. Yet as we know from the penal system, imprisoning people and labelling them as criminals rarely has a positive impact; the recidivism rate is shockingly high. Judgment comes from the ego, and can only reinforce the ego. It disconnects us from Source – whether we are judging or being judged – and it is then that we might hurt or harm others, since we feel separate from love. The only way to 'reform' anyone is to help them remember who they are, to see the essential goodness within them, and help Source energy flow through them; that is, to offer unconditional love. Wild love.

Everyone pays a huge price for being shamed into

conformity. Shame is toxic. You internalise it, like an under-ground poison that seeps into your water supply. If you are shamed and tamed in childhood – and everyone is, to a greater or lesser extent – you grow up believing that your feelings and desires are bad and unacceptable. So you pretend to be happy, and become inhibited and repressed. When your emotions and needs are dismissed or trivialised, you come to feel unimportant and undeserving. And when your parents' happiness seems to depend upon your behav-iour, or you feel a need to 'make them proud of you', you begin to feel responsible for other people's feelings. Gradually you lose touch with your own emotions, your own inner guidance and impulses – the language of your soul – and learn to *be* good rather than to *feel* good. You stop daubing your fingers in the mud, and dancing in the rain, and giggling until you fall over in delight. You learn to conform to what others want. You are controlled and disem-powered. Your centre of gravity shifts outside yourself.

If you are frequently shamed as a child – or abandoned, emotionally or physically, for any length of time – you are likely to become an adult who either feels guilt-ridden and undeserving (that is, identified with the shamed child within), or is blaming and self-righteous (that is, identified with the judgmental parent within). This means that you will inevitably struggle with intimate relationships, and slip into patterns of controlling or sacrificing (see chapter 10). You will be trapped at the lower end of the Emotional Scale, mostly disconnected from Source. And when we cycle around these bottom-of-the-scale emotions, we tend to feel hollow and empty – since we are not 'filled' by Source energy – so we often look to roles or relationships to fill and define us, which disconnects us even further.

> *Allowing your world to be shaped by others,*
> *you sacrifice ourselves to false gods –*
> *to approval, to guilt, to conformity.*

Joyless gods of false love which diminish the soul.
Gods which render life paper-thin and worthless.
Weighted down, your wings cannot take flight;
your angel feathers start to moult.
Slowly, slowly, your bright colours fade,
the breath is crushed from your ribs,
your own Voice is hushed to a whisper –
and then to silence.[9]

By the time you are an adult, you no longer *need* others' approval, since you can take care of yourself, but it has become a habit. Since you have lost touch with your deep Self – which *knows* that you are safe and loved – you crave a sense of love, safety and belonging from 'out there'. You are no longer Self-centred. Your natural exuberance and self-expression have been crushed. Your emotions are muted and largely ignored. You have internalised a critical, controlling, undermining voice that keeps you (and others) in check. You become imprisoned by a need to please others, to become who they want you to be – or to satisfy an imaginary God who wants you to be dutiful, self-sacrificing and perfect. You feel numb. You have lost yourself. And deep down, you feel vulnerable, insecure and unworthy of love. Life becomes a pale shadow of what it might be.

The more conditional the love you receive in childhood (or adulthood), the more you become stuck in your ego, and the more you long to reconnect with unconditional love and authenticity. Then you develop patterns of addiction such as dependency on work, alcohol, drugs, food, TV, sex, exercise, shopping, frantic busyness or co-dependent relationships. When these are driven and compulsive, they are futile attempts to reconnect with Source energy through the outside world, of trying to fill your emptiness, to squash your painful sense of disconnection, or get a quick 'fix'.

Every addiction is about craving a lost connection with deep reality – and although it might give you the occasional high, it can never be a substitute for the real thing. It keeps you stuck in a vicious circle of loneliness, neediness and dependency, which blocks your freedom and growth. It means that you live a life based upon others' needs and expectations, a life driven by fear and insecurity, a life restricted to surface reality. You are imprisoned in a life that is not your own. And a caged bird might sing – but it is a desperate song of yearning.

SELFISHNESS AND RESPONSIBILITY

Let's look more closely at this question of selfishness and responsibility. You have probably been taught that it is good to be unselfish, to put others' needs first, to consider others' feelings before your own, to be dutiful and loyal, to sacrifice your own wishes. You might even have been taught that this is what love means. However, if you consider what is happening energetically, this makes little sense.

If you focus primarily on other people's feelings, you are disconnecting yourself from deep reality – which guides you through your *own* emotions – and this blocks your ability to love unconditionally, which comes from the deep Self. So then you are stuck in the ego, which can only love conditionally.

This contradicts most of what we have learned about love and relationships – but that is because our models are based upon the old paradigm of conditional love. A paradigm which separates us from love. A paradigm based upon surface reality. A paradigm which emerged from our limited ego – from fear, shame and insecurity.

Whenever you sacrifice your own needs or desires for another, you are inwardly saying 'Look how good I am being! Please love me for this!' Who are you saying this to? To the Other, whom you hope will love you for your self-denial. And to the judgmental God within, whom you pray will see you as worthy, and give you brownie points in heaven for being a martyr. In other words, you are feeling unloved and unworthy. You are disconnecting from the god or goddess that you really are, and giving in to your ego. The ego imagines that self-sacrifice will *make* you happy, because it will bring love, approval or admiration from others – or at least avoid the pain of guilt. However, it always backfires since we cannot *attract* love from the low vibrations of shame and unworthiness.

If you go into sacrifice – whether at home or at work – you will always feel negative emotion, because you are disconnecting from Source. *You are trying to be good.* You are short-circuiting your energy system – which contracts your awareness, and blocks your higher potential. This is different from loving, which always *feels* good. Society admires sacrifice and martyrdom, due to the painful legacy of patriarchal religion. But sacrifice is not love. Love does not split our energy, making us neurotic. Love does not feel heavy or dutiful or restrictive. Love always feels light and liberating and expansive.

'But surely if I do what my partner asks, if I put their needs first, I am being loving and giving, and that is good for our relationship?' Not necessarily. Imagine that your partner asks you for a back massage. It is a heart-centred and open request, and you feel uplifted and energised by the idea, and say yes. You both enjoy the experience, and it leaves you feeling closer and more intimate. All is well. But imagine instead that their request for a massage makes you feel heavy, or guilty, or suffocated, or gives you a sharp twinge in the solar plexus – yet you ignore your emotional guidance, and tell yourself you 'should' say 'Yes.' (You are trying to be good.) Now the massage is likely to make you feel tired and resentful, or self-righteous. Then your partner might complain you are not doing it right, you have an argument and both go to bed grumpy.

What is happening here? Well, you might be responding to your partner's energy. If he or she is disconnected from Source, their request might be a 'demand' that you meet their needs regardless of your own feelings (and if you don't, they will sulk or sigh or withdraw from you). If you say 'Yes' to this, you go into sacrifice – which means your vibrations are giving off shame and insecurity. Your partner gets a brief jolt of satisfaction from pulling your strings, then reacts to your vibration of 'unworthiness' and feeds it back to you. Then you are *both* disconnected from Source – and things are likely to spiral downwards. If you see the world in terms of energy and vibration, relationships look very different.

If your partner makes a heart-centred request, but you feel tired and depleted, or want to do something else, then you can honestly express your own needs: 'I'd like this and you would like that – so let's see how we can find a win–win solution.' Not a compromise, but a *higher* resolution that meets both your needs. Perhaps someone else could meet your partner's wish, or it would work well for you at another time. As long as you both stay centred, there will be no control and no sacrifice. Source energy can always harmonise everyone's needs for the higher good. And then you have *two whole people* in relationship – which means that love and intimacy can grow.

Sacrifice often means supporting the other's ego defences, and so keeping them stuck, or it means trying to please from a place of insecurity. Either way, you are both trapped in ego. It might seem as if you are being loving, but it is not love. And if this happens more and more, the relationship will be in trouble.

So how can you tell the difference between love and sacrifice? By how it *feels*. Love helps Source energy to flow. If it feels passionate, freeing, heart-expanding and joyful, it is love; if it makes you feel closed-down, defensive, insecure, resentful, trapped, virtuous or self-sacrificing, it is not love. It is as simple as that.

So it might seem paradoxical, but choosing to be happy – rather than trying to be good – is exactly what is needed to make our relationships work. From ego, we always fall into control or sacrifice. We try to control the other, or we sacrifice ourselves for the other. (In chapter 10, we shall see how this characterises dysfunctional relationships, and restricts our potential.)

When you believe in a God of unconditional love, you choose to be happy. This means you are 'doing God's will'. Not the will of the judgmental God within – your harsh superego – but the will of Source energy, of unconditional love, which is guiding you to align with joy and create your own heaven on earth. Choosing to be happy does not mean treading all over others, or being irresponsible. Nor does it mean just lying on a beach day after day, or ignoring your tax demands. It means loving yourself enough to honour your emotional guidance – to 'put no other God before' the god within – knowing that choosing joy and freedom and expansion will always lead you in the right direction for *everyone* involved.

When you are connected to Source, love pours out of you like an upturned honeypot. Not the self-sacrificing, constricted or needy pseudo-love of the ego, but the warm, giving, expansive, open-hearted and genuine love of the deep Self. If you nurture yourself, if you stay aligned with Source, you have so much more to give. You are whole and energised. You can give from a full honeypot, rather than an empty one. And your love will have no strings attached. Real love asks for nothing in return. You will not be asking for approval, or expecting gratitude, or wanting your own needs and demands to be met. You will be giving love from an open heart. When we love ourselves unconditionally, we can love others that way. We can set others free. We can love wildly.

If you have always been inclined towards duty and martyrdom, learning to follow your emotional guidance in this way is likely to rock the boat. You might find that Threshold Guardians of the old paradigm will accuse you of being selfish and irresponsible, and try to rein you in. They might say you're not as 'nice' as you used to be; in other words, you can't be guilt-tripped and controlled as easily! (Parents and partners can excel at this threshold role, as well as religious fundamentalists.) But if you persist, your uniqueness and creative potential will begin to blossom. You will become fuller, richer and more multi-dimensional. And it might have escaped their notice that wanting you to meet *their* needs, to fit into *their* model, was 'selfish' on their part! Not the healthy selfishness of aligning with Source above all else, but the ego-based selfishness of wanting to control others – that is, trying to control the world from the outside in.

Anyone who loves you unconditionally will want you to be happy, first and foremost. That is what loving someone means. And once you learn to be happy, you will hugely increase your ability to love. To really love. To love wildly.

Of course, it might feel easier and more comfortable to flow down your old riverbeds – to control, to make demands, to guilt-trip and shame others; or to give in, to please others, to do what is expected, to become who others want you to be. It is easier to follow our old habits, to fall asleep for another lifetime. But our deep Self is longing for us to wake up.

Joy and fulfilment come from our connectedness to Source, to the universal web of energy-consciousness – and from living from our authentic Self. Oneness *and* individuation. A well-known cosmetic brand uses the strapline 'Because you're worth it' in its advertising – cleverly, since this is a message that every human being needs to hear. After centuries of being told that we are bad, unworthy and must suffer and struggle our way to redemption – or that others are bad – we need to put the record straight. *We are good. We are worthy. We are loved.* We are gods-in-the-making. Our primary responsibility is not to be good — since loving others comes naturally when we are aligned with Source — but to be joyful. This means paying attention to our emotional guidance, and honouring our deepest desires. It means being true to ourselves. And *then* we can truly love.

 PRACTICAL SUGGESTIONS

1. Choose a problem or issue in your life, or a dream that has not yet come true. What are your usual thoughts about this? Talk to yourself about it, and notice how it makes you feel. This indicates your current vibrational state on that topic. If it feels wonderful, you are moving rapidly towards what you want. If not, you have some work to do. So, search for a thought about this issue that feels soothing or reassuring, calming or expansive, liberating or hopeful. Try out various thoughts until you find one that feels just a little better, that brings you a sense of relief and allows you to breathe more easily. It might help to look at the Emotional Scale (see page 115), and choose an emotion just a little higher than where you are (this might be on the same level of the Scale; only you can know whether it feels better). Choose more thoughts like that, to stabilise that new vibration. You are already beginning to attract a new reality towards you! It will feel easier to stick to your usual thoughts — they will reflect your old riverbeds — so you have to make an effort to choose new thoughts. Next time you think about this issue, make sure you haven't slipped back. Instead of focusing on 'what is', focus on what might be. Don't be realistic — be a visionary! Daydream, imagine, visualise. *Feel* your way into that new future. Keep choosing thoughts that feel even better.

2. Make a constant habit of tuning in to your emotions, knowing that how you feel is your direct link to your deep Self. Every time you choose happiness and joy, rather than trying to be 'good', you are honouring the God within you and allowing Source energy to flow. Choose thoughts that feel joyful. Choose actions that feel joyful. Only say 'Yes' to others when it feels good and uplifting and expansive to you, so that you know that their request aligns you with Source. If it feels good, it is good!

3. Notice what makes you feel wonderful. Choose at least three or four activities that help Source to flow through you – perhaps meditating, playing the piano, sketching, walking in nature, hugging your partner, stroking your cat, sitting in your garden, running or yoga – and make these a top priority in your daily life.

CHAPTER SEVEN

Reclaiming Your Authentic Self

You enter the forest at the darkest point, where there is no path. Where there's a way or path, it is someone else's path; each human being is a unique phenom-enon. The idea is to find your own pathway to bliss.

Joseph Campbell[1]

In the beautiful film *Whale Rider*, a young Maori girl is the grandchild of an elder who is a wisdom-keeper for the ancient lore. Although Pai is the direct descendant of a long line of chiefs, her grandfather refuses to see her as a future leader – because she is a girl. The traditional old order is collapsing, but he ignores the warning signs of separation, loss and fractured relationships, and clings to the age-old traditions of his clan. The girl's shining love and respect for her grandfather, despite his cold and harsh behaviour towards her, conflict with her deep yearning to fulfil her destiny as leader. But her passion and talents will not be subdued, and she listens to the voice within her. She trusts in her deep Self, and takes the hero's journey. When a whale is beached – an ancient symbol of her tribal lore – she rides the whale deep into the ocean. Eventually, Pai's striking courage opens her grandfather's heart, and he 'sees' her at last. He begins to melt, her natural leadership is allowed to emerge and wider relationships are healed. Her personal individuation serves the greater whole, since she is connected to deep reality.

In many ways, *Whale Rider* is a metaphor for our times. Our wild feminine energy is breaking free from the confines of the patriarchal past, from the straitjackets of fear, guilt and conformity, from the old world of duality and judgment. By refusing to give in to others' expectations, but instead being true to our own heartfelt desires, we die to our immature ego-self and give birth to our greater Self. And it is our authentic Self that can inspire others by example – through its inner strength and wisdom, through its radiant joy and love, through its vision and courage. By being true to ourselves, we might become a wayshower, a lightkeeper, a pioneer who points towards a new way of being in the world.

❤

On 11th August, 1999, I stood on the steep cliffs above Bedruthan Steps in Cornwall – its magnificent spiky boulders rising like giants from the golden sands – awaiting a total eclipse of the sun. After a few minutes of extraordinary light, darkness fell suddenly and a hush descended among the gathered crowd. Then there were gasps of surprise and awe, and everyone rushed towards the cliff edge as the moon's shadow approached across the water. Hundreds of flashbulbs sparkled like tiny stars on the darkening coastline. On the dusky beach, giant bubbles were blown in celebration. Then the eclipse came. A dark expanse like a vast black monster crept slowly across the Atlantic Ocean, while a reddish-orange glow lit the horizon, and a kaleidoscope of strange unearthly colours whirled in the sky. I found my whole body shaking, and had to catch my breath – overwhelmed by the primal energy and the sheer majesty of the spectacle.

At 11.11 am, total darkness fell; a deep and filling darkness, which I never wanted to end. I was still shaking, awestruck. Then there was an unexpected gift. While still gazing across the darkened ocean, a vibrant and electrifying energy swept through me in the wake of the eclipse. It brought me to tears, and almost to my knees. It felt like being brushed by the wings of God.

I did not merely *see* this eclipse. I was in the midst of it, participating, indivisibly part of it. It was like a holy baptism, a rebirth. Deeply primal yet also mystical, it later reminded me of the incredible experience of giving birth. It was an experience of total immersion, of the soul fully embodied, blissful, ecstatic. In the midst of it, I became deeply aware of the miracle of life. Here we are, spinning on a small blue-green planet in the middle of space, utterly dependent on a distant star for our daily existence. Why are we not on our knees in awe and wonder each day? How easy it is to fall asleep, to take this miracle for granted.

For me, the total eclipse was a global wake-up call – a powerful reminder of the need for us to reclaim what we have lost: our dreams and visions, our inner wisdom and power, our connection with deep reality. The moon blotting out the sun. The awakening of the divine feminine. The shadow of this eclipse fell across the birthplace of all the major world religions, and seemed to throw down a gauntlet. 'Let go willingly,' the eclipse seemed to murmur, 'or your old security blankets will be ripped from you.' It was a time of surrender, of letting go, of releasing the past and former certainties. Any wake-up call brings hope and promise, but it also carries a warning of what fate might befall us if we ignore its invitation.

The eclipse prefaced what so many prophets and visionaries, ancient and modern, have seen as an intense period of personal and global transformation – a time of spiritual awakening – of which we are now in the midst. For many, the eclipse was followed by unexpected and dramatic changes.

A week after the eclipse, a dear and close friend came to stay with us – a bright, caring and talented man. After 20 years of teaching, mostly at a boarding school where (by choice) he was rarely off-duty, he was emotionally and physically exhausted. His home had just been severely flooded when the nearby river had burst its banks, mirroring his feeling of being overwhelmed. He told us of his yearning to take a year off, to retreat to a Scottish isle and live on a tiny croft, grow vegetables and walk by the sea. Or to become a taxi driver. Or *anything*. We urged him to follow his dreams, to explore the possibilities, to step into the new life that was calling him. But his mother had died young – an alcoholic and martyr – and he believed, like her, that life was a struggle but you must do your duty. Alarm bells started to ring. He appreciated our concern, he said, but the children at school needed him. Anyway, he couldn't afford to lose his teaching salary. As we waved him off on his motorbike, we were still urging him to reconsider.

Two weeks later, his wife phoned me. A minibus had collided with his motorbike at high speed – 'It was not his fault,' she said – and he was alive, but seriously injured and in a coma. Broken ribs. Damaged spleen. Broken leg. Shattered arms. And worst of all, brain damage. Although I felt deeply shocked, part of me was not surprised. He had outgrown his old life long ago, and it was no longer sustainable. But he had refused to listen to his emotions and desires – he had chosen to be good rather than happy – and was catapulted into a crumpled life. He 'succeeded' in creating his year off, and spent it in hospital. Seven years on, he is still a shadow of his former self, and has never returned to work.

Joseph Campbell famously urged us to 'follow our bliss' – and this is one of the keys to reconnecting with our authentic Self. All too often, we fill our days with superficial and trivial tasks, with mundane duties and responsibilities that neither gladden the heart nor stir the soul. All too easily, the ego packs our diary with busyness and activities, often in response to the needs and demands and expectations of others. Then our lives are built up from the outside in, instead of from the inside out. We get lost in surface reality.

Following your bliss means reaching into your depths to unearth what brings you truly alive. Joseph Campbell defined bliss as 'that deep sense of being present, of doing what you absolutely must do to be yourself '.[2] Passion and enthusiasm ignite a flame within us. (The word enthusiasm comes from *en theos*, meaning 'the God within us'.) Whenever you focus on what feels most joyful and meaningful, you are aligning with your deep Self. You are being authentic, honouring your own truth, being uniquely yourself; and in doing this, you also help to change the world – not by teaching martyrdom and self-sacrifice, but by teaching joy.

In the inspiring true story of *Patch Adams*, the film opens with the eponymous hero admitting himself to a psychiatric hospital in a suicidal state. He has lost his way in life, and has no sense of meaning or purpose. He soon becomes disillusioned by the controlling and distancing of the pompous, humourless psychiatrists – but discovers that he himself has a gift for healing. He can truly *connect* with people, making them laugh and caring for them as individuals. He eventually leaves hospital with a vocation: a burning passion to become a doctor, and to make medicine more humane, more compassionate, more loving and more fun. His passion and vision transformed his own life, and have since touched thousands of other lives.

The pioneer of flower remedies, Edward Bach, grew up with a great love of nature. As a young adult, he trained as a physician in London, but always hated city life. However, he was afraid that his yearning for nature might distract him from his work, so he rarely left London for two decades, and avoided even going to the city parks. In 1917, after years of failing health and a severe haemorrhage, he was given just three months to live. But Bach had a vision. He believed there was a *gentle* way of healing physical and emotional disease – and instead of lying down to die, he devoted himself to his studies. He lost all track of time, and in the months that followed, his office became known as 'the light that never went out'. His health grew stronger and stronger, and he went on to live for another 20 years. When he paused to consider why he had recovered his health, he concluded that 'an absorbing interest, a great love, a definite purpose on earth was the deciding factor of [our] happiness on earth . . . '[3]

Edward Bach was undoubtedly a workaholic, and seemed driven by a need to 'redeem' himself through service to others. Yet it was only when he eventually followed his bliss, in the last seven years of his life – abandoning city life, and reclaiming his early passion for nature – that he discovered his unique gift to the world. His vision finally became a reality. He intuitively found a gentle, energy-based approach to healing, which aligns us with Source through resonance with flowers. The Bach Flower Remedies were born. By setting himself free, and doing what he had secretly longed to do for years, Bach's lifelong dream came true. Bliss and passion take us to the edge of the transcendent, reconnecting us with our deep Self.

Our higher purpose and creativity often emerge when we combine our unique interests, skills and experience. My own love of writing and public speaking, my professional training in clinical psychology, and my fascination with mysticism and spirituality led me to become a writer-teacher of spiritual psychology. Then my love of wild flowers and gardens, together with my background in therapy and interest in energy medicine, led – thanks to Edward Bach – to the joy of making and using flower essences.[4] More recently, I became a volunteer for an historical garden restoration scheme, which combines my passion for gardening and nature with my desire to be involved in a visionary project for the local community.

Your own pathway to bliss will constantly unfold – if only you sidestep doing whatever you feel you 'should' do, or what others expect, and do what you love. This might mean writing poetry, or carving wood, or growing herbs, or African drumming, or sailing the oceans, or rock-climbing, or playing the saxophone, or hanging out in a wine bar with close friends. Whatever it is, it will keep changing and evolving. It doesn't matter what it is, or where it is going, as long as it lights your fire. It might lead you towards making a living, or it might not – but if it fills you with delight, it is aligned with Source energy, so it will help release your potential for joy, freedom, love, creativity and growth in *every* area of your life. It helps you to find harmony with your deep Self.

> *There are hundreds of ways to kneel and kiss the ground.*
>
> *Rumi*[5]

When you reach for your dreams and desires, you are transcending any part of you that feels unworthy and undeserving. Following your bliss is an act of self-love. It means that you are flying high at the top of the Emotional Scale, connecting with the effervescent God-force within you. You are aligned with Source energy, attuned to your authentic Self. A magnificent fountain is bursting forth from your garden hose, and the tap is turned fully on. Everything flows. You will be in the right place at the right time, bump into the right people and say the right things. Miracles will abound. When your passion flows freely, you are a god in the making.

MAKING CHANGES

> *We must be willing to get rid of the life we've*
> *planned, so as to have the life that is waiting for us.*
> *The old skin has to be shed before the new one can*
> *come.*
>
> *Joseph Campbell[6]*

Most of us face dramatic turning points at some time in our lives. It might happen once, or a dozen times – but we come to a threshold, a choice-point between an unknown but tantalising new future or a life of stuckness, mediocrity or even tragedy. Perhaps we feel drawn towards something that has always scared yet attracted us – setting up our own business, travelling the world alone, public speaking, trekking in the Himalayas, running a marathon, going on stage, building our own home, creating a retreat centre, doing voluntary work in Africa . . . Perhaps we are being called away from the town we have always lived in, or out of the marriage that has become our security blanket, or away from the job or career which has become so easy and familiar.

The outer form it takes is perhaps irrelevant – but desire is calling us on the hero's journey. The tame voice of reason might urge us in one direction, while our feelings or intuition lead us the opposite way; and often there is a middle or alternative path that we have not yet seen. We might need to sit uncomfortably with our decision for weeks, months or even years. But how we deal with these turning points can mark the difference between living a half-life filled with regrets, lost dreams and unfulfilled potential, or an authentic life that is deeply passionate, rich and meaningful – a life which makes a difference.

At the age of 33 – while I was still single – I had faced a major turning point. I felt a deep longing to put my spiritual awareness at the centre of my life and work. So I resigned from my salaried clinical post in the Health Service, sold my much-loved house, left close friends and moved to London to start a freelance career as a spiritual writer-teacher. It was scary at times. I had to face anxiety, loss and uncertainty – but it was also exciting and stimulating. I wrote my first book, *Living Magically*, and found my true vocation at last. I learned to trust deeply in the Universe.

At such turning points, becoming authentic often means letting go of the life you have known. Your deep Self whispers to you to dream the impossible dream. It often asks you to break the rules, to do the unexpected – even the unthinkable. It pays no attention to the norms and inhibitions of society, family or religion. The deep Self is a non-conformist. The soul is wild and untamed. It soars above the crowd. It is not concerned with safety or security or predictability. It has no interest in pensions or mortgages or social status or what others might think. It does not mind rocking the boat. It offers no guarantees. And it is willing for you to face a dark night of the soul, if necessary, on your pathway towards bliss. It holds the power of the crucible. It longs for you to express your uniqueness, to release your potential. Its only concern is the inner-outer journey of your life: who you came here to be, whether you are being true to yourself, whether you are living your dreams, whether you are opening your heart to love and joy and passion.

Sometimes this means making sacrifices – sacrificing your old habits, your old ways of being – so that you might die to your ego-self and be reborn. The word 'sacrifice' comes from the Latin *sacer* (sacred) and *facere* (to make) – it is a letting go that turns you inwards towards the deep Self. The ego might hope that you can make minor, superficial changes – that you can 'try harder' to mend a relationship, or meditate occasionally to develop your spirituality, or work fewer hours if you are workaholic – that you can shuffle the deckchairs on the *Titanic*, and all will be well. But the Self knows that sometimes the ship needs to sink. Sometimes the unthinkable needs to happen, to throw you through an invisible wall into a new way of being.

In the film *Shirley Valentine*, a suburban housewife in a soul-destroying marriage seeks relief from her 'quiet desperation' on a Greek island holiday. Once she is free of others' demands and her clockwork routine, she feels new life stirring within her. First she takes on a Greek lover, releasing her lost passion and sensuality. Then she slowly begins to find her own centre again, after losing herself in others for so many years. As she queues for the flight home, she follows her heart and suddenly decides to stay on the island – forsaking her old life, her former identity, even letting go of her suitcase, stuffed with the unwanted baggage of her past. By the time her husband comes looking for her, he scarcely recognises the relaxed, confident and vibrant woman she has become. (And we are left to wonder whether they moved on together, or apart.)

When we lose our security blankets, when we can no longer rely upon the external world – the relationships, home, places, work or possessions on which we based our identity – we are forced to go within. We have to search for our inner resources, build our own strength and courage, tap into our inner guidance, clarify our values and priorities, find out who we really are. Through surrender, through letting go, we are sometimes stripped bare of our old ego: we are 'made sacred'.

At one of my workshops, a woman told me that, in the process of moving house, their removal truck had fallen over the edge of a cliff. Everything they owned had been lost in the sea. Once they had recovered from the initial shock, she said it was strangely liberating. She realised how few of their possessions were really necessary, and as she slowly let go of her attachment to their 'things', she felt a new and deeper sense of Self emerging.

> *Change is the constant, the signal for rebirth, the egg of the phoenix.*
>
> *Christina Baldwin*[7]

Change is natural. It is part of the ebb and flow of life. Nothing stays the same; the wheel is always turning. Even if you stay in the same job or relationship, its form is forever changing. It is when you cling to the status quo that life becomes uncomfortable. Unless you learn to go with the flow, and listen to your emotional guidance – especially in this era of rapid change – you risk being hit by a tidal wave.

If you're the kind of person who never throws anything away, whose house is full of clutter, you can be sure that you are resistant to change. As space-clearing expert Karen Kingston notes, 'Clutter accumulates when energy stagnates.' It begins as a symptom of what is happening in your life, but then it becomes part of the problem – since the more clutter you have, the more stagnant your energy becomes. Clutter blocks your life force energy, your chi; it stops your energy flowing. It keeps you stuck in the past, holding on to situations and energy habits that need to be released. It drags your energy down.

Yet many of us hang on to clutter because we intuitively know that it holds a lot of stuff to be dealt with. It reflects emotional baggage that we do not wish to face – such as fear, hurt, anger, pain, grief and regrets. According to Karen Kingston, 'People unconsciously keep clutter in order to suppress their own aliveness. They may want to change and improve their life, but their subconscious mind is afraid to journey into the unknown.'[8]

Change always means letting go, so loss and grief are an inevitable part of life. Poet David Whyte urges us to live at the frontier of our lives, at the cutting edge, to 'stay in intimate conversation with ourselves'. Yet he notes that we tend to retreat from the edge because *that is where the loss is.* Patrick Kavanagh, likewise, writes of the 'sticky self that clings adhesions on the wings to love and adventure'.[9] Most of us have a sticky self who wants to avoid change, who has a tendency to fall asleep and drift through the weeks, months and years. But change is where growth lies – and unless you allow for the dying away of winter, you make no room for the fresh growth of spring.

More than anything else, change means letting go of your old Self. It means shedding your old skin. It means giving up your old identity. It means giving up the stories you have been telling yourself for much of your life, giving up your old defences, and becoming someone new and unknown. And that is often what feels most scary. It might involve breaking free from your familiar ways of coping, and doing something different. If you are usually impulsive, this might be an opportunity to become deeper and more reflective. If you are timid or inhibited, it might be a chance to be more wild and spontaneous. If you are workaholic or busyaholic, the Call might be to slow down, to create more space and stillness in your life, and rethink your priorities. If you tend to be guilt-ridden and self-sacrificing, this might be a time to nurture yourself, express your own needs and emotions, make bold decisions or find your own centre.

Whenever life gets too comfortable, too secure, too predictable – or whenever you fall into the trap of trying to conform, or please others – you can be lulled into uncon-sciousness, and begin to sleepwalk through your days. You might distract yourself with busyness and activity to give the illusion of a full life, but as Elizabeth Lesser points out in *Broken Open*, 'If we don't go looking for what lies beneath the surface of our lives, the soul comes looking for us.'[10]

The Delphic Oracle at Greece offers a great pearl of wisdom:'This above all: To thine own self be true.' This means trusting your emotional-intuitive guidance – the gentle promptings of your soul – which tells you when it is time for change, and which direction to take.The authentic Self yearns for freedom and expression. Whenever you are not on your path, when you are not being true to yourself, when you are turning your back on your dreams and desires, 'divine discontent' creeps up on you. Your energy is split. Tension and uneasiness in the solar plexus warns you that something is amiss – perhaps for weeks or months, even for years. That 'something' gnaws away at you, troubling you, draining your energy, keeping you awake in the wee small hours, calling you to pay attention, softly shaking you by the shoulders. Perhaps it turns into physical symptoms. It is something you might prefer to ignore. Something you might wish would go away and leave you alone. After all, making authentic choices is not always easy – especially when your decisions involve other people, prior commitments and conflicting loyalties, and the path ahead seems strewn with boulders and fallen tree-trunks. But if you keep ignoring the whispers of your deep Self, it might eventually hurl down a bolt of lightning to jolt you into wakefulness. Which is what unexpectedly happened to me.

AWAKENING THE DIVINE FEMININE

Three years ago, I visited Mount La Verna in Italy, the remote mountain hermitage where St Francis received the stigmata. I had always loved St Francis for his reverence for nature and animals, and his celebration of the simple pleasures of life. Although he seemed deeply neurotic, St Francis also represented love and creation-centred spirituality during a particularly vengeful and bloodthirsty time for the Church. I was excited about visiting La Verna at last, and drank in every detail as we wandered around the chapels, caves and other buildings.

Just as we were about to leave, I spotted the door to another tiny chapel – the chapel of Mary Magdalene – almost hidden against the hillside. Inside was a beautiful statue of Mary, and I stood gazing at it while my son explored the chapel then ran outside. The apocryphal texts of the Bible suggest that Mary Magdalene might have been the loving consort of Jesus (rather than a prostitute), and as I looked at her statue, I wondered about their real-life relationship and the sacred marriage of masculine and feminine energy that they represent.

As I gazed at the statue, to my amazement it developed a gold-white aura and then seemed to become real. Mary transformed into flesh, and I 'saw' a milk-white tear roll down her cheek. I found myself praying: 'O Mary, Isis, Inanna, mother of God, divine Mother of all creation, please fill me with your energy and let me embody and express You to the best of my ability.' I closed my eyes – and when I opened them, the statue still looked fleshy. I kept watching as it now transfigured into countless different women – a Native American woman with plaits, an elderly Chinese woman, a young white girl, an olive-skinned Madonna and many others. She turned into a stone sarcophagus; then into flesh and blood, so real and soft that I gasped and half-expected her to move. The kaleidoscope of women of the world continued. The inner message I received during this transfiguration was: 'I am all women – as are you.' Eventually the vision faded. Before leaving the chapel, I touched the foot of the statue to offer gratitude – but the unusual energy had gone.

I'm sure it was no coincidence that around the time of this powerful experience at La Verna, I received my own wake-up call. The Call of the divine feminine. The Call of the deep Self. A Call to drink deep from the Elixir of Awakening – but first, to face my Road of Trials.

DIGGING DEEP

Let me share this personal turning point with you – a marital crisis that led me to question all I had taken for granted, and to make a life-changing decision. An unfolding journey that eventually led me to write this book. Your journey might be different from mine. Perhaps it is your work that is not in harmony with your deep Self; perhaps it is where you live, or who your friends are, or how you spend your leisure time. But there are likely to be some parallels in my journey, some pointers towards your own authenticity, some clues that might help you forge your own path, to give up your old energy habits and find greater harmony with who you really are.

Three years ago, everything in my life seemed rosy and settled. I had a beautiful detached home and garden, with stunning mountain views. I adored my work as a spiritual writer and psychologist. I was married to a man who had been a close and loving friend for 20 years, and we had a healthy, happy six-year-old son who looked like a blonde cherub. My dreams had come true, and my long-term future seemed secure and predictable.

One afternoon, a married friend turned up on my doorstep, deeply unhappy and in crisis. As we talked over the weeks and months that followed, I felt as if I was waking from a deep sleep. Many of the painful truths that my friend was uncovering seemed eerily familiar, and sometimes I felt that I was looking in a mirror. Much that I had taken for granted was being rocked at its foundations and crumbling around me, as I looked at my life afresh with searing honesty. Forgotten dreams and desires came up to haunt me. A slumbering part of me was awakening. I began to catch glimpses of my half-remembered wings.

Amidst all this new insight, something else was stirring – like a rare orchid blooming amidst the rubble. Like the song of a siren, it both enchanted and frightened me; and I kept hoping, even praying, that it would go away. Instead it continued to grow – and my personal life plunged into crisis.

You walked ticking, like a time-bomb,
into my neatly-ordered life.
I tried to close my ears.
I did not wish to hear my own voice.
I pretended it was only you who felt imprisoned –
a snared animal gnawing at its own paw.
Yet my heart cracked slowly open,
until I fell into a deep chasm
I hardly knew was there;
and I saw myself in your mirror,
tamed and locked away.[11]

After several years of marriage, it had never occurred to me
that I might face a dilemma over the future of our relationship. I was married – and that was that. Then I met the man
I'll call Matthew, whom I immediately recognised as a lover,
parent, child, colleague and friend from countless past lives,
and with whom I felt a deep and intuitive connection. I
quickly dismissed my feelings as coming from other life-
times, and gave it little thought, though as we came to know
each other better, I grew more and more fond of him – and
also more and more concerned.

A year or so later, he turned to me for help in circumstances which made it almost impossible for me to back off.
I wanted to be a supportive friend – yet it occasionally
flicked across my mind that I was sailing into troubled
waters. (Matthew and I would later laugh ruefully about
how carefully Spirit set us up for this unfolding drama.) We
began to meet regularly to talk – and I soon noticed that my
heart expanded whenever I met Matthew, or even thought
about him. Intuitively I knew I had loved this particular soul
for aeons; but as our relationship deepened, I slowly realised
I was probably falling in love with him.

I was well aware of the psychology of 'falling in love',

so I felt cautious about my growing feelings, knowing it might reveal more about my own unmet needs and projections than about the reality of our relationship. But I knew I was not prone to falling in love. (I had fallen in love only once before – 20 years earlier.) I also recognised there was no space for a third party until there was a gaping hole in a marital relationship – so I had to face the fact that my marriage was not as solid as I had fondly imagined. My apparently stable life was lurching into chaos.

My husband had been aware of my feelings for Matthew from the start; we had always agreed to be open and honest with each other. Eventually, as I realised my feelings were becoming more serious, I told my husband. The possibility of separation had not even occurred to me. In the weeks that followed, my husband and I talked endlessly about how I felt about Matthew, what it meant, what was therefore missing in our marriage, and how we might put it right. We had always been good at talking, and were hopeful we could find our way through, that the crisis might even strengthen us as a couple.

I knew it was time for some ruthless self-honesty. It felt like unwrapping layers of cellophane and bubble-wrap, searching through layers of defences, of half-truths I had told myself, determined to reach the deeper kernel of truth. What was the truth about my marriage?

Slowly and painfully, I began to admit to myself that I had probably married for the wrong reasons. I had wanted children, my biological clock was ticking away, and I had felt pressure to get married and have a 'perfect' life. Then my husband-to-be had persuaded me to turn our long-term friendship into a romance. I had married a close friend whom I loved, but was not in love with. Deep down, I had always known that – though I scarcely wanted to admit it, even to myself. I had married in good faith, hoping that commitment would help love to grow – but for years afterwards, I sometimes felt disbelief at whom I had married. After all, we had been friends for a decade before, and I had never seen my husband as a possible romantic partner.

TRYING TO BE PERFECT

How many of us pretend, even to ourselves, that everything is fine when it is not? Friends ask 'How are you?' and we reply brightly on auto-pilot, 'I'm fine. How are you?' – when the truth is that our job is under threat, a close friend is dying of cancer, our child is being bullied at school, a relationship is falling apart, deadlines and demands are driving us crazy, or we just have this 'unnameable discontent' that will not go away. I remember one social gathering where I noticed everyone being chatty and cheerful, yet I happened to know about ongoing serious crises in the life of every person present.

We need this thin veneer of happiness and normality at times. We need to maintain clear boundaries; if we spilled our guts to every passer-by, we would soon be swept off to a psychiatric unit. But I suspect that it often becomes a chronic habit, and we begin to believe in our own lies, failing to share the truth even with our close friends or partner, or privately worrying that everyone else seems fine, so what is *wrong* with us? Or we don't share what is going on because of a misguided sense of loyalty, or not wanting to burden others or seem negative, or from fear that our feelings are unacceptable (that *we* are unacceptable). And the more we pretend to be happy and content, the more lonely and isolated we feel, and the more cut-off we become from our true emotions and desires.

Looking back, I had always tried to be good. As a child, I was helpful and self-contained. I cared for my younger brother. I was academically bright. Like many too-good children, I rarely expressed anger, hurt, sadness or other negative emotions. Somehow I got the message that I must always be good, perfect and happy, and I did my best to succeed at that impossible task. At the age of 19, I became anorexic – aiming to be perfectly slim, perfectly in control, perfectly self-denying, perfectly free from any 'messy' needs or emotions.

As an adult, I chose professional roles as a therapist, writer and workshop facilitator in which I was often placed on a pedestal, and seen as wise, all-knowing and perfect. My role was to inspire and help others, to offer insights, to lead by example, to be a role model – so I felt under pressure to lead a perfect life. Perfect work, perfect marriage, perfect child, perfect home. But perfectionism exacts a heavy toll. It is not possible to be perfect while also being authentic and honest. Perfectionism leads us away from our emotional guidance – urging us to be good, rather than choosing to be happy.

THE GOLDEN CAGE

When I agreed to get married, everything seemed to be ideal. I loved my work. I'd made my home at last in the heart of the Lake District – a stunning landscape that I truly adore. And now I was to marry and have a family ... Yet by the time my child was a toddler, I had begun to feel the rumblings of 'divine discontent'. What was the problem? I wondered – perhaps even hoped – that it was my work. I decided to take a break from workshops, and try a change in direction. But I soon realised that my work was not the underlying problem. A year later, Matthew came into my life – and I began to wonder (with a sinking heart) whether the real issue was my marriage.

Looking back, something had gone badly wrong. My world had shrunk to the size of a tennis ball since I married, and I had lost my bounce. Somehow a whole year could pass without my spending a single night out alone. My husband was away a lot, but – as a once-ardent traveller – I rarely travelled any more. I no longer had any close male friends, and my women friends lived mostly at a distance. The rare hours I spent away from my child were devoted to work, and I had lost my creative fire and inspiration. My life didn't seem to belong to me any more. It belonged to other people and their needs. It looked good from the outside – but how did it really *feel*? I was daring to ask myself some big questions at last.

I realised that there was far more to my marital discontent than not being 'in love' with my husband. My marriage showed many classic signs of co-dependency – despite the fact that my husband and I were psychologists, and well aware of co-dependency as an issue. (See chapter 10.) I had felt lonely and trapped for years, though I hadn't realised it until Matthew woke me up. My husband and I were still good friends, but I often found myself pulling back, protecting myself, retreating from his rather harsh business-and-finance energy. Our marriage seemed to have suppressed so much of our richness and potential, and our lives had shrivelled up like prunes. We did not bring out the best in each other. Somehow we had shut down like telescopes, and lost touch with our former selves.

At last I understood the nameless discontent that had been with me for so long – the jangling friction within my energy system, caused by not being authentic, not being true to my dreams and desires, not honouring my own needs and emotions, being out of synch with my deep Self.

RECLAIMING LOST DREAMS

After weeks of talking, my husband and I consulted a well-known marital therapist – who wondered whether in years to come we might just be spiritual friends and co-parents. I was shocked to realise, for the first time, that this felt like an attractive idea *now*. I began to struggle over whether to stay in my marriage. Could I really risk everything for an unknown future? Couldn't I 'shuffle the deckchairs' without having to sink the *Titanic*? I had worked so hard to create this seemingly ideal life – and suddenly my marriage, my home, my child's stability, my financial security, not to mention my future happiness, were all at stake. And for what? Nothing else was on offer.

Yet what I had no longer felt like enough. I yearned for passion, warmth, affection, sensuality, magic, romance, emotional intimacy and unconditional love. I longed for the sheer delight in each other's company, the desire to touch and kiss and hold hands, and the shared perspective of a truly loving and soulful relationship. I wanted to make love with someone, to merge with someone, whom I desired with every cell in my body. I hungered for a relationship that made me dive into my depths, and reach for my highest potential. I knew that many couples settle for a friendly companionship based upon shared interests – a 'good enough' relationship that meets their basic needs – but I wanted more. I had recovered my lost dreams. I wanted to share my life with someone who made my heart sing and my spirit dance. Or perhaps I just wanted to feel deeply and fully and passionately alive – to open my heart, to reach out my arms to the whole world – with or without a partner.

In contrast to my marriage, I loved Matthew's softness, warmth and compassion, which brought out my natural gentleness, openness and vulnerability. I felt more heart-centred, more aware, more embodied, more loving, more inspired, more emotional, more alive with him. We seemed to wake each other up. Our differences and complementarity drew out my own undeveloped potential, making me feel more expansive and whole. I loved what he brought forth in me – and began to see the potential that might lie in other relationships.

I believe we are mutual angels –
restoring each other's broken wings.[12]

I felt hugely grateful that my husband never discouraged me
from seeing Matthew, despite his own anxiety. (He wanted
me to clarify my feelings – and we had both always agreed
that love meant setting someone free.) In the circumstances,
I assumed that Matthew was simply a catalyst, a wake-up
call, whose role was to lob a hand grenade into my marriage
– that he was a reminder that something more was possible,
that a greater love could be found; or perhaps my journey
was about recovering my passion for life, my sensuality and
embodiment, my authenticity, my creativity, my self-love and
connectedness. I talked openly with Matthew from the start
about my feelings and insights, what he mirrored in me, and
the impact of our relationship on my marriage – but he was
married with young children, and we were crystal-clear that
we just wanted to be friends.

I slowly realised that my love for Matthew was curiously
different from anything I had experienced before. Certainly
I had never loved my husband in that way. I wasn't sure it
was romantic love. *It was pure unconditional love.* It felt oceanic
and intoxicating. It felt expansive. It felt wild and free.
Somehow he connected me with Source – and, for me at
least, there was an intuitive connection between us that felt
like a magnet. Sometimes I could literally read his thoughts.
I believed there was room for many different kinds of love –
and whatever happened with my marriage, I hoped that
Matthew and I would be lifelong friends.

Weaving through each other's lives like threads of tapestry:
you are friend, lover, brother, sister, mother, child to me.
With you, my soul heaves a contented sigh and comes to
rest,
finding itself at home again, after so many moons in exile.[13]

S-L-O-W-I-N-G DOWN

All through that long winter, I felt in a state of limbo. What was I going to do? My husband and I continued to talk – but I spent a lot of time in silence and solitude. I kept a dream diary. I wrote reams in my journal. I went for long walks on my own. I gazed into a log fire into the small hours. I talked often and at length with a few close friends who were aware of what was going on. And I did a bare minimum of work. My priorities shifted dramatically. I spent hours staring out of the window across the landscape, reflecting on life, love, relationships – and the difficult choices that lay ahead. The unanswered correspondence, unfinished projects and unread books no longer seemed to matter. Instead I gazed from the window – doing sacred work.

In the months after I agreed to marry my husband, I now realised I had been superficially happy – but had kept myself ultra-busy with wedding plans, moving house, decorating and work projects. A few months later, I was pregnant. Looking back, I had been avoiding getting into 'intimate conversation' with myself.

Whenever you avoid stillness and solitude, or cannot find time to be alone (or cannot see the point), it is wise to ask yourself what you might be avoiding. We often get over-busy when we're running away from our authentic Self. After all, if we run fast enough, our emotions cannot catch up with us. Our ego-based society encourages us to be busy; but making no time to relax and reflect on life is often a warning sign that we are squashing down negative emotions that we'd rather not look at – emotions that are telling us that we are not aligned with our desires, and that (in all like-lihood) we are being swayed by others' needs and expectations, following pressures to conform, and wandering onto someone else's path.

One of the keys to staying on your own path is ensuring

that you spend enough time alone, making time to be still, centring yourself, slowing down the pace of life so that you can tune in to your emotions and listen to the intuitive voice of your deep Self.

THE POETIC VOICE

The poetic impulse is an expression of our inner voice. Good poems – whether we read them or write them – help us touch that space in which we ask those bigger questions we need to ask ourselves, and go within to find our own truth, our own path to wholeness. Stevie Smith says that 'All the poet has to do is listen',[14] and Mary Oliver likewise suggests that writing poetry is an 'act of slow and deep listening'. 'What I hear is almost a voice, almost a language,' she says. 'It is a second ocean, rising singing into one's ears, or deep inside the ears, whispering in the recesses where one is less oneself than a part of some single indivisible community.'[15] Poetry comes from the deepest space within us, and can be a wonderful way to access our authentic Self.

I've often uncovered hidden aspects of myself through writing poetry. Sometimes a phrase or an image comes to me – such as 'restoring each other's broken wings', or 'sweet warm ghost', or a 'red rose lying on bitter frost' – and I know that a poem will follow. So I take a notebook and pen, and wait in hushed expectancy. The poet Robert Frost says that 'a poem begins as a lump in the throat, a homesickness, a lovesickness', while John O'Donohue notes that 'For the poet, there is a sense of frightening vulnerability, for anything can come, anything can happen.'[16] I'm certainly no William Blake, taking dictation as if from the angels – yet there is often an element of surprise, of revelation, as words unfurl on to the page. I read and wrote a lot of poetry during this quiet winter of reflection – and I was struck by the pain, passion and longing revealed in my own poems.

I immersed myself in the work of David Whyte – an Anglo-Irish poet of the soul who suggests that poetry is 'a break for freedom'. I had invited a group of friends to a recital of his a few months earlier (an evening that Matthew described as 'devastating'). David Whyte is no namby-pamby poet. He believes that poetry should be dangerous, that it should change lives. His poetry urges us to live at the fierce edges of our existence, rather than conforming and staying safe. Instead of ploughing through our to-do lists each day, he implores us to live imaginatively and passionately, to be open to radical change. He observes that many of us will take a courageous step only when all the conditions are right, when no-one else will be affected, and when its outcome is guaranteed. And so, of course, we wait forever . . . Yet we have to make friends with the unknown, he says, if we are to cultivate a life that is truly our own.

As I pondered my own situation, one particular poem of David Whyte's echoed around my head, as sung out in his rich brown tones:

> . . . *You must learn one thing.*
> *The world was made to be free in.*
>
> *Give up all the other worlds*
> *except the one to which you belong.*
>
> . . . *anything or anyone*
> *that does not bring you alive*
>
> *is too small for you.*[17]

More than any other, this poem spoke to me in those dark winter months. It felt like an epiphany. Was I living in the world of freedom that I belonged in? I kept repeating that sentence to myself: '*Anything or anyone that does not bring you alive is too small for you.*' Did my marriage really bring me alive? This is a question which can illuminate any major aspect of our lives. Does *your* marriage bring you alive? Or is it a practical, convenient arrangement, based upon shared responsibilities and superficial conversation, which leaves your soul hungry and weeping? Does your work bring you alive, or does it feel too small and limited for you? Does your home bring you alive? Do your friends bring you alive? Does your leisure time bring you alive? Is your life big enough for you? Does it make you want to sing and dance? Do you feel wild and free? Are you living the life of your dreams?

As I faced my own turning point, Mary Oliver's stunning poetry also inspired me. Her poem 'The Journey'[18] is a dramatic description of what happens when we are given a major wake-up call, and set off into the dark and windswept night, ignoring the demands of those who urge us to stay and to put *their* needs first. As we leave their voices behind, she says, we begin to hear a new and authentic voice that we slowly recognise as our own. How many of us arrange our lives around the needs and expectations of other people? And what price do we pay for this? Gradually I knew that I was being called out into the woods, that I was being called to reclaim a life that was my own, to uncover all that had been tucked away.

One day, I wrote a poem called 'Wild Love' – a surprising and passionate poem in which I described my life as a golden cage, and myself as 'tamed and locked away'. I found myself yearning for what I had lost within myself, and for what might have been. Or perhaps might yet be.

LOVE AND FREEDOM

This period of seriously reconsidering my own marriage marked the start of two years of intense questioning and exploration of love, marriage and relationships. I began to study happy and not-so-happy partnerships among friends, clients and others, and noticed a pattern emerging. Happy relationships, in which both people blossomed and expanded, seemed to be marked by two qualities. Firstly, there was a sense of unconditional love that made the couple visibly bask in each other's presence, as if they reliably connected each other to Source. Secondly, they gave a high priority to each other's freedom and expression as individuals. Conversely, the unhappy (or even abusive) marriages I saw seemed to be based upon conditional love and restricted freedom.

I had not yet realised what 'wild love' was, or what my poem really meant. That would come much later. But from all I knew about energy and reality creation, I suspected that these two qualities – unconditional love and freedom – were crucial to our energy-consciousness; and that relationships that lacked these qualities somehow short-circuited our energy system, limited our growth, and made us 'fall asleep'. And I now realised that despite our shared commitment to spiritual growth, my marriage had sent me to sleep. I had lost so much of myself. The poet Rumi said that 'Love is for vanishing into the sky' – and I firmly believed that love is meant to expand and liberate us, to help us fulfil our potential, and never to restrict or diminish us.

I struggled over whether I had the right to put my own well-being first, whether I should stick to my marriage regardless, whether I should settle for what I had, whether we just needed to work harder at our relationship, whether I might be running away – and also how I felt about the prospect of divorce. I knew that my marriage was far better than most of those I saw around me; and in theory, one might create a perfect marriage with anyone, since we are all part of the same Whole. But in practice, I knew that different relationships evoke different dynamics and potential – they make us run along different riverbeds – and sometimes we need to move on in order to grow and evolve.

For many years, I had encouraged people to follow their heart and live their dreams, rather than following the well-worn paths of duty and martyrhood – and would always want my son to choose happiness rather than self-sacrifice. (Carl Jung suggested that nothing had a more disturbing influence on children than the unlived life of the parents.) I knew I had to love myself enough to honour my own feelings and desires, to choose to be happy rather than trying to be good. My own parents had a warm, loving and romantic relationship after more than 50 years of marriage – having 'fallen in love' at first sight – and I still held that romantic dream.

I had little doubt that we are meant to be happy and wild and free – not good and tame and perfect. I trusted that a Source of unconditional love makes no judgment about the choices we make, that there are no right or wrong decisions. Just different choices, with different futures. And I believed that when we are heart-centred and aligned with Source, our decisions are best for all concerned in the long term, that everyone's needs and desires are dovetailed for the highest good – that whatever is best for the individual has to be best for the whole, since Source energy runs inseparably through all that is.

Then I read Sarah Ban Breathnach's *Something More*, which reflects on marriage, relationships and authenticity. She quotes Carol Matthau: 'I don't think marriages break up because of what you do to each other. They break up because of what you must become in order to stay in them.'[19] That struck a chord with me. I could see now how much of my passion, creativity and freedom had been stifled, and how suffocated I had felt for years. (I even had allergic asthma.) Bit by bit, I was becoming sure of one thing: I did not want to reach my deathbed with lingering sorrow and regrets, after spending decades of my life in a marriage that fell far short of my hopes and dreams. Love was too important for that – and life was too precious.

Regret is the only wound from which the soul never recovers.

Sarah Ban Breathnach[20]

ASKING FOR SIGNS

In my kitchen is a small carved wooden angel that bears the inscription 'Sometimes you just need to take a leap, and build your wings on the way.' This is what the deep Self sometimes calls us to do. It calls us to cross the great ocean – without knowing what the outcome will be. It calls on us to have faith and courage, to love life with a passion, to open our hearts, to be honest and vulnerable, to be bold and visionary, to become the greater Self that we have kept hidden under wraps.

It was clear that the good, dutiful, safe thing to do was to stay in my marriage (and for someone else, this might have been a heartfelt and authentic choice). But as Mary Oliver says in 'The Journey', there comes a time when you know deep inside what you need to do, '*though the voices around you kept shouting their bad advice . . . and you felt the old tug at your ankles.*' Eventually a decision emerges from some deep place within, like a ripe peach falling from a tree. It seems inevitable and right. I knew I could not remain married, however reassuring and familiar it felt, while secretly longing for something more. Despite my husband's many positive qualities, I did not love him unconditionally – and now I knew that such love was possible, I could not settle for less. For both our sakes.

Whatever the risk, I had to be true to myself. I had spent too much of my life trying to be good. I didn't want to give in to that 'old tug at my ankles'. I wanted to be vibrantly happy and alive and free. A promising bud had opened within me, and I had to give it room to blossom and grow. I could not allow that emergent part of me to fade and wither. Although much of my life was wonderful, I felt as if

I had somehow been locked in a musty broom cupboard for years – and now I caught glimpses of a light, airy mansion with French windows leading out onto the lawn.

One weekend, I took a long walk alone in the hope of making a final decision about my marriage. I walked for hours over the fell-tops and into the next valley, pondering my question. I sat beside a mountain tarn and asked for guidance. I circled towards home, and lingered on a lakeshore. Towards the end of the day, I settled in my favourite place in the world – a bench overlooking the panorama of Rydal Water – and prayed. I silently said that I felt that my marriage was over, that it was time for us to let go and move on; but I asked for a sign such as a rainbow or a butterfly to affirm my decision.

Seemingly from nowhere, grey clouds gathered and a light rain began to fall. As I walked along the last mile of country lanes back to my car, I counted no less than *seven* rainbows! The next morning I took my son to Sunday school, and found a small tortoiseshell butterfly had somehow become trapped in the enclosed gallery above the church. I gently caught it – and set it free. Seven rainbows and one butterfly. I had my signs.

> *My path now looks fresh, unknown, uncharted.*
> *The future has opened up like a broken egg.*
> *This wild and beautiful love has plunged my soul,*
> *gasping, into a new life:*
> *an umbilical cord cut while still pulsating.*
> *And yet – already I breathe more fully than before,*
> *no longer held tight, no longer unborn.*[21]

PRACTICAL SUGGESTIONS

1. Do you strive to be good or perfect or special, or to fit in with social norms in an attempt to earn or deserve love? Are you being true to your deepest desires? If you followed your heart – without worrying what others might think or feel, or the possible impact upon them – what would you do?

   Commit yourself to aligning with Source energy from now on, to honouring the God within you – without ever beating yourself up when you 'fail' to do this. Keep asking yourself: 'If I was choosing to be happy, rather than trying to be good, what would I say or do right now?' or 'If I was being true to myself, what would I choose here?'

2. Write a free-flowing poem. Let yourself fall into a dreamy, relaxed state – perhaps while out in nature – then jot down any words or phrases that come to you. Let the poem write itself, rather than you trying to write it. You can tidy it up later if you want to, but start by letting it flow through you. Don't worry about rhyme or meter. Keep your critical, censorious, rational brain out of the way. It might help to write with the hand you do not normally write with, to access your intuitive side. This poem is for your eyes only (unless you later choose to share it). Allow yourself to be surprised by what your authentic, passionate, emotional Self has been longing to express.

CHAPTER EIGHT

A Foot In Both Worlds

Tell me, what is it you plan to do
with your one wild and precious life?

Mary Oliver[1]

Mary Oliver's question is a haunting one. It touches the heart of our deepest enigma: who am I and why am I here? So what *do* you plan to do with your wild and precious life? How much time do you devote to that ever-evolving question? Are you a potter carefully moulding the clay of your own creation? Or does your life just happen while you stand watching on the sidelines – trying to be good, aiming to stay safe, doing what is expected, getting through the days as best you can? Do you tell yourself you're a mere Muggle in a mundane and limited reality, or are you aware of being an apprentice god?

Abraham suggests that the basis of life is freedom, the purpose of life is joy, and the result of life is growth.[2] For me, this triad of freedom, joy and growth is the foundation of a grown-up spirituality based upon the new paradigm in science – a spirituality of unconditional love, in which we are sparks of an infinite and omnipresent Source of energy-consciousness. We are learning to be co-creators with Source energy – which means that we are constantly giving birth to new dreams and desires that we are finding out how to manifest in physical reality. And we chose to be here in order to have a delicious, glorious and wonderful time!

Life is like an ever-evolving garden, and each of us is a garden designer. We get to choose everything in our unique garden: the location and size, type of landscape, what to plant, special features, everything. We can create a squalid patch of lawn with a few scraggly and neglected plants, or a heavenly paradise with acres of flower beds, meandering paths, woodlands, lakes and waterfalls – or anything in between. We can tend, weed and water our garden with care, or allow it to become overgrown and neglected. We can design a new garden from time to time, or just enrich and improve upon our existing garden. And we can invite whomever we like into our garden. The garden is entirely our own creation.

Before we enter each lifetime, we pick our parents, our place of birth, and a few crucial experiences and relationships that will push us in our chosen direction. After that, the decisions are ours; we are free to choose. There are a few limitations, such as the human body and the law of gravity, but what we create in our lives is 100 per cent vibrational. It is governed by the universal Law of Attraction (see chapter 2), and that means we can create whatever we want. Source ensures that every desire we have *can* be fulfilled. After all, any heartfelt desire comes from unlimited Source. All that stands in the way is our own energy-consciousness. Not other people. Not our childhood. Not our karma. Not our bank balance. Not the government. Not our society. Just us.

Yet most of us create a life that is rather less than heavenly. Unless we are careful, we fall asleep and drift through the weeks and months and years – lost in consensus reality, in the busyness and roles and dramas of our ego, or the needs and expectations of others. Forgetting who we really are.

Forgetting that we are the artists. Then we might wake one day to find that our life is nearly over – and looking back, it was a life of muddy browns and greys rather than rich technicolour. It was not what we would have chosen for ourselves, had we woken up in time. It was a life that belonged to other people. If we are not Self-centred, then as Ezra Pound warns us, 'life slips by like a field mouse'.[3]

❤

So what are the secrets of aligning with your deep Self, and creating your own heaven on earth? How can you move beyond a self-destructive habit of trying to be good and worthy (or to remain safe and secure) instead of choosing to be happy? How can you live with a foot in both worlds – fully alive and present on the earth, while aware of your deeper multi-dimensional self?

Even when we wake up to the new paradigm, old habits die hard. Source energy wishes to make all our dreams come true, to send us miracles and blessings and wonders galore, but we keep throwing rocks and boulders in our path. 'No, I don't deserve it.' 'I'm not good enough.' 'I have to work really hard to earn it first.' 'Am I *allowed* to desire that?' 'I must do what others want.' 'It is more noble to suffer and deny myself.' 'It just isn't possible.'

Source patiently listens to all of this nonsense, aware of the challenges of being human, never judging us for getting in such a muddle, while quietly whispering in our ear: 'You *are* loved. You *are* good. You *are* worthy. None of that is in question. You are wondrous in my eyes. Go forth and create! You can have anything you want! Enjoy! Delight in the pleasures of the world!'

Every religion has its own version of the Golden Rule 'Love others as you love yourself.' The Golden Rule would be wonderful – indeed, it would be unnecessary – if we *did* love ourselves. Unfortunately, shame distorts this rule into loving others *instead* of ourselves: becoming a martyr, caring for others at our own expense, ignoring our own needs and desires, and therefore disconnecting from Source; or being as critical and judgmental towards others as we are towards ourselves. The Golden Rule urges us to *love ourselves first*, since all our relationships mirror this fundamental relationship with self, and that in turn mirrors our relationship with Source.

Self-love is a prerequisite for loving others. If we love ourselves conditionally, we can only love others conditionally. Self-sacrifice is not love; it is guilt in disguise, trying to deserve love. Dependency is not love; it is fear and insecurity in disguise, begging for love. Judgment and criticism is not love; it is shame in disguise, asking to be seen as worthy by comparison with others. When we do love ourselves – unconditionally, beyond duality – then truly loving others comes as naturally as a tree growing leaves.

Our lack of self-love – our disconnection from Love – is the core of almost all our problems. It is the root of all our neurosis. It is the root of our relationship problems. It is the root of settling for a life of bread-and-cheese rather than inviting ourselves to the banquet. It leads to mundane lives of 'quiet desperation', in the words of Thoreau – imprisoning ourselves in dull routines or stultifying relationships, or *needing* love (which means we won't get it), or caring for others at our own expense, or limiting ourselves to what we feel we deserve, or what others will 'allow' us. It leads to workaholism and over-busyness. It makes us believe that life is a struggle, and that the world is a tough place to be. It leads to self-righteousness, blaming and judging others, not listening to people, criticising others for making different choices or having different values, or for being less than perfect. Lack of self-love is also at the root of ignoring our own emotions and intuitive guidance. It is the root cause of not fulfilling our dreams and desires.

Without self-love, we cannot become conscious co-creators, since we will not *allow* ourselves to fulfil our dreams. Most of us love ourselves conditionally. It is part of the human condition. 'I'll love myself when ... ' or 'I could love myself if only ... ' or 'I love myself apart from this fault, and this part of my body, and this failure, and these mistakes, and this opportunity I missed, and this regret ... and this ... and this ... ' But conditional love is not love. It is merely approval. It is based on shame and judgment. Conditional love tells us we do not *deserve* a wonderful life, so we limit ourselves. We refuse to take too large a slice of the world's happiness, as if there is not enough joy to go round. We refuse to have too much money, as if there is not enough money to go round. We resign ourselves to a half-hearted or painful relationship, as if there is not enough love to go round. We prefer to add to the suffering and sacrifice in the world, just in case there *is* a judgmental God who is keeping score, and who *does* favour martyrdom! (I remember a client who shivered at home all day, only switching on the central heating in time for her partner arriving home. Apparently he was worth heating the house for, but she was not.) While we love ourselves conditionally, there *is* a judgmental God – inside us, disconnecting us from who we are, taming and limiting and controlling us.

At my workshops, I often ask people to complete a sentence such as: 'If I really loved myself, I would ... '; 'If I wasn't so focused on what others want and expect from me, I would ... ' or 'If I knew that life is an illusion that I am creating, and that none of the usual rules and limitations apply, I would ... '; or, 'If I knew that no-one would judge or disapprove of me, I would ... ' You might like to take a pen and paper, and do this right now. Such questions help you break free from the ego, and see how and where you restrict yourself. If you loved yourself as Source loves you (wildly, unconditionally), how would your life change? If you remembered that you *are* Source energy, having an adventure in human consciousness, and that the purpose of life is joy, how might your life be different? In response, many people say they would spend more time relaxing and doing what they enjoy, that they would choose work that they truly love, that they would devote time only to relationships that are warm, loving and supportive, that they wouldn't be so *afraid* and *guilt-ridden*, that they would believe in their dreams and stop beating themselves up.

> I don't know exactly what a prayer is.
> I do know how to pay attention, how to fall down
> into the grass, how to kneel down in the grass,
> how to be idle and blessed, how to stroll through the fields,
> which is what I have been doing all day.
> Tell me, what else should I have done?
>
> *Mary Oliver*[4]

Last week, I visited a sick friend who had been admitted to a hospice; she had aggressive breast cancer with secondary tumours, and a stark prognosis. 'What's going on? What are you *doing* to yourself?' I asked her, knowing that her first episode of cancer, many years earlier, had been triggered by workaholism and lack of self-nurturing. 'I abandoned myself,' she said grimly. 'No fun, no play, no relaxation. Just work, work, work. Total victimhood.' She had created a life that felt like a prison, so her body had kindly constructed an escape route for her.

Such a pattern of self-abandonment – lack of self-love – is associated with the classic 'cancer personality'. Cancer has long been linked with being people-pleasing, over-dutiful, over-compassionate, taking on others' burdens, suppressing toxic emotions, 'suffering in silence', and failing to resolve inner conflicts or openly express one's own needs.[5] Since cancer has reached epidemic proportions in Western society, perhaps our bodies are trying to tell us something? Denying our emotions and desires, trying to be good and responsible, and refusing to love and nurture ourselves – bowing down to the old gods – seems to be carcinogenic. It disconnects us from Source. It stops our energy flowing. It might make us feel virtuous, in our misguided attempts to be worthy of love – but it makes us sick.

Healthy spirituality is not about beating ourselves up; it is about falling in love with life. And we cannot fall in love with life unless we follow our bliss, and honour our emotions and desires. The patriarchal religions have denigrated the body, sensuality and the earth; heaven and earth have been split asunder, so our natural appetites for food, sex, physical comfort, sensual pleasures and even worldly success have long been seen as ungodly, and self-denial and martyrdom admired. Bliss revives the divine feminine.

Following our bliss is an act of self-love that overcomes the fear and shame, guilt and worthlessness that has tumbled down the generations in the name of religion. It embodies the soul. It aligns us with the true Source/God of unconditional love who wants us to be *happy*, rather than snivel and scrape at the feet of a cruel, imaginary God who sent us here in order to teach us lessons. To follow our bliss is a celebration of life, a celebration of love, a celebration of our divinity. It brings us fully present into the world. It is part of becoming a spiritual adult. It follows the Golden Rule: 'Love yourself, that you might love others.'

Following your bliss is not just about pursuing your dreams and desires. It is about putting joy at the very centre of your life. It is about creating your own heaven on earth, day by day. If you become too goal-focused, you lose your balance. You can slip into drivenness and sacrifice, which comes from a sense of unworthiness. But as you focus on bliss in *this* moment – delicious food, silken sheets, hot chocolate with marshmallows, walking barefoot on wet grass, licking honey from a lover's skin – you bring yourself back into balance. Sprinkling your days with sensual pleasures and fun-loving delights helps to balance your masculine energy of 'doing' with your feminine energy of 'being'. It reminds you that life is not about reaching your destination; it is about the never-ending journey. It is about *being here*. By taking time to savour the sunset, to stroke the cat, to smell the wild honeysuckle, to see the butterflies hover, to watch the clouds roll by, to gaze across the landscape in wonder, to laze beside a log fire, to dance and sing and laugh, you are inviting bliss into your everyday life. You're raising your vibrations. You're connecting with the God within.

> Before I scurry into the details of this day,
> let me touch that web of timeless peace
> and drape it gentle on my shoulders.
> Let me gaze from the leaded window
> and watch light dance upon the apple tree,
> and swell with tears of gratitude
> for the miracle of life.[6]

The purpose of life is joy. Your in-tray will never be empty. Your to-do lists will never get done. The jobs around the house will never be finished. The world will never be perfect. There will always be an excuse to stay busy. But if you are waiting to live, you will wait for ever. If you died tomorrow, would those tasks matter? Would the world keep on turning on its axis? Would the sun still come up the next morning? What *really* matters?

It is worth making a list of activities and people that bring you joy – then deliberately building those joy-bringers into your daily life, while jettisoning any time-wasters which feel deadening or negative (such as dealing with junk emails, or watching the TV news, or attending dull meetings), or anything you do because it makes you feel virtuous, or because you 'should' do it. If you observe how you *feel* during any activity, you'll soon notice whether it lifts you up the Emotional Scale, (see chapter 6) sends you tumbling down it, or just leaves you in neutral. If you're aiming to be happy, then your everyday life will be focused on whatever (and whomever) feels most pleasurable, loving, delightful, engaging, creative, meaningful, uplifting and joyful – that is, whoever and whatever makes Source energy flow through you. As Annie Dillard reminds us, 'How we spend our days is, of course, how we spend our lives.'[7] And it is all too easy to fill your days with joyless tasks and responsibilities, waiting hopefully for a mythical future when you will have time to live – rather than being here, and living for *now*. This is your life. Right now. Today.

CLARIFYING YOUR DREAMS

Once you have faith in a God/Source of unconditional love, you move beyond fear and shame and judgment, and into a new world of boundless love and freedom and joy. You begin to reach for your dreams and desires. You develop an intuitive knowing that anything is possible, that there are no limits other than your imagination, that life is meant to be heavenly – and you can create anything that you want. And you can always get there from here. Whatever choices you have made up to now, whatever your current situation, you can always get to where you want to be. All you have to do is align your energy with Source.

An essential step in becoming a conscious co-creator is to clarify what you really want. You might like to take a note-book and pen, and write down the major categories of life – such as relationships, work, home, money, health/body, personal growth/spirituality, creativity and leisure time, or whatever categories feel right to you. Then make yourself comfortable, light candles, play gentle music, relax or medi-tate for a short while until you feel calm, centred and peaceful. Then, under each heading in turn, imagine what you would do or have or be if your wildest dreams could come true. (And they can! There are no impossible dreams, unless you believe there are.) Or just make a list of everything you want to experience before you die. The only guideline is to be as heart-centred as you can, so that you are tapping into your authentic Self, which is your mature ego. Any heart-centred desire can be fulfilled, even if you cannot see how or when it might happen.

Perhaps you would like a job that is creative, fun, challenging, well paid, has flexible hours and makes use of your skills x, y and z. Or perhaps you love your current work, but wish that it involved more teamwork or collaboration. Perhaps you want friends who share your spiritual perspective on life, or who enjoy theatre, cinema and the arts. Perhaps you want an affectionate, fun-loving and intimate relationship with someone who loves you unconditionally and brings out your full potential. Perhaps you have been running too fast for too long, and you want to create a lifestyle that allows generous time for long walks, creative cookery, pottering in the garden, playing the piano or 'just being'. Perhaps you want more adventure and travel in your life. Or perhaps you long to make a difference in the world.

Once you have written down your dreams, choose a category that needs some improvement. Focus on what you desire in this area – and ask yourself *why* you want this. Asking the question 'Why?' starts to align your vibrations with what you want, so that you begin to attract it at an energy level, and it clarifies the essence of what you want. (Do you *really* want to win the lottery? Or is it that you long for a sense of freedom or prosperity or radical change or unlimited possibility?) It also helps to weed out any desires that do not belong to you, which are not authentic – any that come from fear or shame or unworthiness, or which reflect what your partner or family or boss expect, or what you 'should' want. (Perhaps you don't really want children. Perhaps you don't want an office job. Perhaps you don't really want a committed relationship.) Go beyond the duality of right or wrong, good or bad. No-one 'up there' is keeping score on your choices, or whether you are fulfilling your mission. We are gloriously free. The greatest guidance you have from your deep Self is that whatever feels most joyful – in any moment – is what you are meant to do.

The soul is here for its own joy.

Rumi[8]

BECOMING A LASER BEAM

Once you have clarified your desires, Source immediately says 'Yes, Yes, Yes!' The exact form and timing might be uncertain, but the essence of what you want is always possible. As soon as you ask, it is waiting for you. This is a magical reality, and Source energy is infinitely flexible and creative. But there is a catch! You have to align your vibrations with what you want – which means connecting with your deep Self. You have to shift your emotions, thoughts, attitudes, beliefs, desires and expectations until you *know* that what you want is coming. You might visualise it regularly – daydreaming about it, enjoying it, getting the 'feel' for the future you want to unfold. Or you can put in a request, a prayer, to Source, then just forget about it and get happy – that is, free up any resistance in your energy system. Either way, unless you are in resistance, your desire cannot fail to arrive. Deep and surface realities are interwoven through your energy-consciousness.

Needless to say, this isn't as simple as it sounds, otherwise life would be free of problems! Aligning our vibrations with Source energy – while in a physical body, in a physical reality, with a (necessary) human ego – is exactly what we are trying to get the hang of. It is the essence of living with a foot in both worlds. It is at the heart of spiritual awakening.

One paradox of reality creation is that you cannot create

what you want while focusing upon how things are. If you are worried about money, you cannot magnetise more of it. If you feel lonely, you cannot attract an intimate relationship. While you focus on your marital problems, you cannot heal your marriage. When you hate your current job, you cannot attract work you love. If you pray for good health while feeling trapped by your illness, you cannot get well. You get what you focus upon, so you have to joyfully focus upon what you *desire* – not upon what you lack, not upon the current situation.

The new paradigm tells us that *focus* and *intention* are crucial. Consciousness determines the collapse of quantum wave functions, which in turn determines what happens in the outside world. Our task, as conscious creators, is to align our vibrations with our *future* Self, with the Self that has already created what we desire. We have to start holding the thoughts, beliefs and emotions of that future Self. After all, reality has to match the signal we are giving off, not the signal we would like to be emitting. This is how the Law of Attraction works.

If you keep thinking and talking and worrying and fret-ting and complaining about *problems*, or what you long-for-and-don't-have, it is like constantly twisting the dial on a radio. You cannot hope to get a clear signal from a radio station unless you decide which station to listen to, then tune in to it. If you desire a close and loving relation-ship, but keep telling yourself that past relationships have turned out badly, or relationships are difficult, or perhaps you prefer being on your own, or there are no suitable part-ners around, then you are twisting the dial on your radio to and fro. The Universe tries to send a potential partner towards you, pulls him or her back, sends them towards you again and then pulls them back. Or it sends you a partner who will mirror the belief that relationships are painful. Reality *has* to match your vibrations, and if you are giving off contradictory signals, then reality will mirror that back.

It might feel as if you are stuck, or you might create confusing situations that mirror your signals: a promising first date is followed by a brush-off; an ideal job is advertised, but you are not offered an interview. Since every thought we have is like a magnet, you send the Universe into a tailspin as it yoyos back and forth, attempting to match your confusing vibes!

As soon as the ego sticks its little snub nose into your desires, you inevitably send out contradictory signals:

'I want this, but I can't have it.'

'I want this, but I do not deserve it.'

'I want this, but I can't see a way of getting it.'

'I want this, but it feels too risky.'

'I want this, but I shouldn't want it.'

'I want this, but sadly I don't have it.'

'I want this, but I can't afford it.'

'I want this, but this other person (*whom I'm giving my power away to*) doesn't want me to have it.'

'I want this, but I have these other responsibilities.'

'I want this, but I don't believe it is possible . . . '

'I want this, or perhaps I want that.'

You might feel caught between being good or being happy, or between being happy or staying safe, or between accepting the limitations of consensus reality or expanding your vision, or between feeling like a passive victim or accepting your power as a co-creator. You might feel stuck in the narrow 'either-or' possibilities of the immature ego, instead of seeing the expansive 'both-and' solutions of the deep Self.

Emotional pain is simply a sign of resistance – energy that is forcefully trying to flow, but is being blocked. The stronger the desire that you are blocking or resisting, the greater the emotional pain. So if you *really*, *really* want something that you *really*, *really* believe you cannot (or should not) have, it is *really*, *really* painful. At worst, you might even feel suicidal or lost in despair. Any extreme emotional or physical pain or dis-ease reveals huge and perhaps hidden potential or desires that are misaligned with your current thoughts and beliefs, or which apparently clash with others' needs and demands. This means that your energy system is agonisingly pulled apart, like two donkeys trying to pull a cart in opposite directions. There is a lot of conflict and wasted energy, but no forward movement.

Whenever we send out a clear, focused and heartfelt desire with no contradictory vibrations – expecting it to happen, without any question – reality quickly responds. Miracles happen. It is like the difference between a tungsten light-bulb and a laser beam. A typical 60-watt light-bulb gives off 1 watt/cm^2 of light. (By comparison, the sun's surface emits about 6000 watts per cm^2.) The vast majority of a light-bulb's energy is wasted because of destructive interference; that is, its waves cancel each other out, since they are not focused in the same direction at the same time. A laser beam, by contrast, has highly coherent light – which is why it is so powerful. If the light waves coming from a 60-watt light-bulb were coherent, their energy density would be thousands to millions times higher than that at the surface of the sun.[9] Imagine what this reflects in terms of our untapped human potential! The immature ego – with its fear, shame, judgment and belief in lack and limitation – is just a pathetic light-bulb; but if the deep Self and mature ego are aligned, we are invincible. If we can align our thoughts and desires in one direction, our consciousness is powerful beyond measure.

Don't keep focusing on 'what is'. (This is what most of us do, and it keeps life very stuck.) Be a dreamer. *Pretend* that life is as you want it to be, or that wonderful events and opportunities are on their way. Use your imagination. Daydream happily about what you desire. Focus on what you love and appreciate. Selectively focus on whatever supports your visions of the future. This changes your vibrations – and you begin to attract it. This is why the rich get richer, and the poor get poorer. It is why self-confident people tend to get what they want. It is why both pessimists and optimists tend to prove themselves right. You have to 'become' your future Self energetically, in order to attract a new future. It might sound crazy, but it is how our vibrational Universe works.

In writing this book, much of my time is spent aligning my energy with the book that is already written. I 'dream the book into being' by imagining the next chapter, or even the next paragraph, imagining the published book in my hands, feeling my way into its energy. It is like hearing a distant choir of tuning forks, then resonating with those harmonising notes. I align my energy with my future Self – with a feeling of joyful anticipation, and a clear intention to produce a book that will shift consciousness, expand the unconditional love and joy and freedom in the world, and reach as many people as possible. At times I feel like the sculptor; at other times, like the rough-hewn stone from which the statue of this book is being chipped and carved. At best, sculptor and stone become one, and I am simply the flowing movement which is giving birth to the new. As I align with Source energy, the book 'writes itself' through me.

ALIGNING WITH SOURCE ENERGY

How do we know whether we are aligned with Source? By how we feel. Feelings are vibrations. High and coherent vibrations feel good. Low and incoherent vibrations feel bad. It is as simple as that. In order to move towards what we desire, we need to feel good. We might be feeling good about a specific goal, project or desire, or just feeling good because we're having fun and following our bliss – but what matters most is *feeling good*. Perhaps your toes curl with delight, or you find yourself singing or dancing 'for no reason', or you laugh from deep down in your belly, or you feel like a child on Christmas Eve, bubbling over with joyful anticipation. Perhaps you feel heart-centred and loving. Perhaps you feel inspired and dreamy. Perhaps you feel wild and free. Any such good feelings indicate you are aligned with Source energy – and miracles are on their way.

As we focus upon any topic, our emotions indicate clearly whether we are moving towards or away from what we desire. Our emotions tell us – in any moment – how aligned we are with Source (which *wants* to fulfil our desires, and is offering guidance). Whenever we talk or think about a goal while feeling passionate and excited, or zappy and powerful, or hopeful and optimistic, or just calm and peaceful, we are pulling it towards us. If we feel over-whelmed or frustrated about it, we are stuck in neutral, in push-pull, in the middle of the Emotional Scale. When we feel sadness or yearning or guilt or fear or despair – whether we are thinking about a goal, a conversation with a friend, a news report, a physical illness or a memory – then we are definitely moving in the wrong direction; those thoughts are not aligned with Source energy. That tension, or feeling of suffocation, or sick feeling in the pit of the stomach is a gentle warning. At an energy level, we are pulling towards us what we do *not* want, and it is advisable to make a rapid U-turn.

Any negative emotion is an opportunity to grow. It is to be welcomed. It is grist for the mill. It is a sign from our deep Self that there is work to be done, that we are not currently aligned with our desires. We need to choose new thoughts that move us into more positive emotions – beyond fear, beyond judgment. Once we get as high as the vibration of frustration, at least we are moving – albeit s-l-o-w-l-y – towards our goals and desires. If we reach inner peace, we are attracting what we want much more easily. And if we are vibrating at the level of unconditional love and joy and freedom, the world is our oyster!

Unfortunately, the upside-down thinking of the ego tends to confuse and mislead us. We think that the cause of negative emotion lies 'out there' – so we want to fix, change or control the other person or situation (or even the world) so that we will feel better. Or we beat ourselves up, blaming and shaming ourselves for our circumstances in a way that leaves us feeling disempowered and inadequate. Characteristically, the ego goes round in circles, repeating the same thoughts, pushing against 'what is', getting more and more stuck in the mire. These repetitive thoughts act as radio signals, which – by the Law of Attraction – attract more thoughts along similar lines. If we are feeling irritable, we start getting irritated more and more easily; if we are feeling guilty, we sink deeper and deeper into self-deprecation. Then our negative thoughts begin to attract situations that match those thoughts – which confirm, for the ego, that it was right all along: 'Look, the world really is a dangerous place!' 'I really am guilty and shameful.' 'See, you can't trust anyone.' The world is a self-fulfilling prophecy, because that is how reality works. The ego sees itself as a victim of reality rather than as a co-creator. It thinks reality is really real, that it is solid stuff, that other people can 'do' things to us! So if it doesn't like what happens, it fights to change and control and fix it from the outside in.

I remember a gardening programme in which Alan Titchmarsh pointed at a rose bush with mildew. He explained that one approach to this problem would be spraying the mildew with herbicide. This might cure the problem for a while, he said, but it wouldn't sort out the *cause* – which is that the rose lies in the shade of a tree. By having mildew, the rose is 'saying' that its environment is not suitable, that it cannot thrive. Merely to kill the mildew is to mistake the symptom for the problem. To an organic gardener, the obvious solution is to transplant the rose to a sunny spot in good soil, so that it can maintain its own health.

Like gardening which relies upon chemical fertilisers, pesticides and herbicides, allopathic medicine mirrors our Muggle world view. It divides the world into good and bad, then tries to control or destroy what is bad. It beats up or excludes the bullies, instead of trying to *understand* what is going on within the bigger picture. It shoots the messenger by suppressing symptoms with drugs, slicing into diseased organs or blasting unhealthy cells with radiation, thereby *forcing* the body to stop sending its alarm signals. It focuses upon disease rather than health (and we get what we focus upon). It sees consciousness as a mere bit-part player in a solid physical reality, rather than as the prime creative force in the universe. In an emergency, this approach is necessary and can be life-saving, but as a general approach to dis-ease, it is limited and needs to be integrated into a broader perspective. It sees the world in an upside-down way.

In the same way, the ego shoots the messenger by suppressing, repressing or denying emotions, and trying to change reality from the outside – instead of using both emotions and reality as helpful *feedback* about your current vibrational state. The ego pours poisonous weedkiller over your garden, while seeds for dock and thistle are pouring out of your back pocket. It blames the sunflowers for failing to grow, while ignoring the fact that you planted them in the shade and forgot to water them. It complains that a neighbour has a bigger and better garden, instead of acknowledging that they simply made different choices, using their own energy-consciousness.

Reality is your garden, and you create every aspect of it. So you have to change it from the inside out, by shifting your consciousness. The outside world cannot change until you do! This is dramatically different from our usual view of the world – yet the cutting edge of the new paradigm does transform our way of seeing, flipping us like pancakes from dualism to holism. Instead of spraying pesticides, or trampling over other people's gardens, or deciding what *they* should be growing in *their* garden, you have to take responsibility for the beauty of your own garden, loving yourself enough to make it heavenly, and sharing this paradise with others. Then you make the world a more loving and beautiful place.

Shifting to a higher vibration not only makes you feel better; it changes your reality. And it only takes a minute or two to start making a shift. If you hold a new thought – at a new vibration – for just 15 seconds or so, really *feeling* it, it begins to attract more thoughts along similar lines. Then you begin to resonate with that new vibration, and stabilise at a higher frequency. Then you can reach for higher thoughts still – and in a matter of minutes, you can be attracting new realities towards you. This means searching around for thoughts that feel good, thoughts that feel soothing and comforting, thoughts that feel liberating, thoughts that release your resistance – perhaps shifting from frustration to hopefulness, or from guilt to anger, or from belief to intuitive knowing, or from irritation to acceptance. (You do not need to label the emotions; you simply need to focus on finding that sense of freedom and relief. This often means ignoring what *other people* might see as a 'positive' or 'negative' thought, and just noticing *how it feels* to you. Only *you* can tell whether it feels better, and is therefore a move in the right direction.)

Of course, it is much easier to carry on thinking the same old thoughts – which means that you keep on creating the same reality. Our thoughts tend to run along old riverbeds, so some people have frequent thoughts that mirror guilt and self-condemnation, while others feel most familiar with self-righteousness and blame, and yet others tend to feel overwhelmed much of the time. These energy habits feel 'easy' and comfortable, like any habit – even if the emotion feels negative – and they were generally set up in childhood (and often in past lives too). But we are never victims of our past. Our power is always in the present moment. It takes conscious determination to raise your vibrational frequency – and you might even create huge life challenges in order to motivate yourself to change. But in just a few minutes, hours or days of conscious focus and intent, you can begin to break your old habits. (And using energy psychology or flower essences can help to stabilise these new thoughts in your energy system.)

Sometimes your thoughts about an issue have become so stuck and circular that it is difficult to find relief. In this case, it can be wise to focus on something else – a project that requires your full attention, or anything which distracts you from the negative thoughts that are short-circuiting your energy. Scrubbing the kitchen floor, clearing out a cluttered cupboard or weeding the garden might do the trick. Or you can use some form of meditation, including active forms such as yoga or Qi gong. Or take a nap or daydream, linger over happy memories or soak in a hot bubble bath. Or you might listen to music, sketch or dance, or do whatever brings you joy. Or feel grateful for all the precious gifts in your life. Without judging your negative thoughts and emotions – which will keep you even more stuck – you need to find your way back to your natural state of free-flowing energy and well-being.

Learning how to follow our emotional guidance, how to raise our vibrational frequency in whatever way works for us, is what sets us free. It gives us true responsibility: that is, 'response-ability'. It gives us the power to respond in ways that are beyond fear and judgment, in ways that are aligned with love. Once we know that we can feel good whatever happens 'out there', we are no longer victims. We are no longer controlled by our past, or by other people. We no longer need to control others. We can stay aligned with Source – and therefore feel good – whatever. I believe this is the true meaning of 'Thou shalt have no other God before me.' It is about honouring the God within, which is an inseparable part of the oneness of creation. It is about being

Self-centred – about honouring the inner guidance from our deep Self.

When you are on your path, trusting your emotional guidance, life feels good. It feels joyful, easy, exciting and 'in the flow'. You feel energetic and free and powerful. Your energy feels coherent and whole. When you slip off your path, it feels heavy, sticky, difficult and uncomfortable. You feel limited and imprisoned. Your energy feels split and fractured. So your emotions are constantly letting you know whether your thoughts, words or actions are in harmony with your deep Self.

Choosing happiness, moment by moment, is a new energy habit to build for many of us. In a 'masculine' culture, which values rationality and thought, we are not used to trusting our 'feminine' emotions. We can become so used to ignoring how we feel that we consult our heads, rather than our gut feelings, before making any decision. A friend came round for a cup of tea, and we discussed *Wild Love*, and how we habitually disconnect ourselves from Source by trying to be good, thus putting our centre of gravity outside the Self. Hours passed, darkness fell, and I invited him to stay for supper. He immediately launched into a defensive barrage of 'too much trouble ... taking up your time ... being a nuisance ... didn't mean to stay so long ... ' – all focused on what he imagined *my* needs and wishes to be – until I laughingly had to say, 'Are you trying to be good, or choosing to be happy? *I* would like you to stay for dinner. Would *you* like to stay for dinner?' He stayed for dinner!

When we use any criterion for decision-making other than *what feels good* – what makes us happy, or brings a sense of relief or freedom or empowerment – we easily get out of alignment with Source. Our emotions constantly guide us towards connection, and once we are aligned, Source can effortlessly dovetail everyone's needs and desires, and bring us the people and events and inspiration that we need. If we are not in alignment, our decisions will come from fear or guilt or judgment, or we might force ourselves to 'be brave' or 'grit our teeth and get on with it'. From this place of disconnection, we inevitably head into problems.

For this reason – in contrast to what many self-help writers suggest – I don't advocate pushing beyond your comfort zone. (I never make 'brave' decisions myself!) Nor is it wise to make any big decisions while you are feeling trapped or guilt-ridden or inadequate, since you will be in self-sabotage. Instead you need to clarify your desires and intentions, then harmonise your energy with your future Self – by visualising and daydreaming, by choosing new thoughts and beliefs, by soothing and reassuring yourself – until any choice or action feels inevitable, easy and joyful. Then your actions will be well timed, and aligned with Source.

A friend tried to go freelance as a therapist and workshop facilitator some years ago. She worked long hours, slaved over her computer, sent out countless brochures – with very little response. After a year, she gratefully returned to a part-time salaried post, licking her wounds. Three years later, she decided to make the break again. This time, she had worked on her vibrations and was feeling relaxed and upbeat about her life. Going freelance was a breeze. She was offered regular work that was enjoyable and well paid, was sent more clients than she could reasonably cope with, and had plenty of free time to enjoy her life. Our ego tries to persuade us that rewards come from hard work and sacrifice, but if we are 'efforting', we are not yet in alignment with our goal – so we waste a lot of time and energy on busywork.

Similarly, our ego tries to persuade us that love means sacrifice, but if we put others' needs above our own emotional guidance, we step out of alignment – and we are setting up win–lose situations, instead of win–win. Sacrifice always comes from a place of duality, of separation from love. It is a form of self-abuse and self-loathing. It is shame and anger turned against the Self. It comes from a limiting belief that everyone's needs cannot be met, that someone has to compromise or override their own feelings and needs. It comes from believing that we have to pay a price for relationships, or for success, or for giving service to the planet. Bliss is our natural state of being. The truth is that if it doesn't feel good, it isn't good – and if we change our vibrations, reality can follow.

Dora consulted me about her elderly mother, who expected Dora to visit her every day, phoned her at work, and made constant demands. She loved her mother, she said, but the situation made her feel trapped and resentful. Could I send flower essences to 'sort her mother out'? Instead I suggested that Dora tune in to her own feelings, and begin to act only from (expansive) love rather than from (restrictive) duty – and ask Source to meet any other needs that her mother had. In the meantime, we explored ways of shifting Dora's energy habits of martyrdom and codependency. A year later, Dora emailed to say that, within a few weeks of seeing me, she had found her mother a companion-housekeeper, whom her mother had become very close to. (Previous attempts to find outside help had backfired miserably.) Dora now only visited her mother weekly, and their relationship was hugely improved.

We do not have to work out the steps to take in making our dreams come true. We do not have to struggle on our hands and knees to make it happen. We do not have to work so *hard* at it all. We can take the path of least resistance, and take the minimum amount of action. Source can co-ordinate whatever events and circumstances are necessary – if only we align our vibrations with our desires, and get out of our own way.

When my marriage ended, I decided I would like to return to the beautiful home near Rydal Water where my husband and I had lived previously for several years. However, some new tenants had recently moved in; and since I would have to support myself financially, I had fleeting doubts about paying the huge rent. Nevertheless, my heartfelt request had been made. A year later, I had to move out of the temporary house I was living in with my son. In the nick of time, a friend heard 'by coincidence' that the tenants were moving out of my old home in Rydal. I phoned the agents immediately, the tenancy was never advertised – and here I am. I soon discovered that the house had not only had a mysterious fire, but had also mildly electrocuted the previous tenants. I joked to friends that I felt slightly guilty about this. But who knows? Was the house evicting them? Was Source dovetailing everyone's needs in this situation, so that my desire could be met? It certainly seems to work that way. If we clarify our desires, put in a clear request, then let it go – that is, let go of our resistance – miracles often happen.

> To remember
> the other world
> in this world
> is to live in your
> true inheritance.
>
> David Whyte[10]

Taking action through joy is a crucial aspect of following our bliss. Whenever a task feels heavy, difficult, boring or a struggle, or we give in to pressures from others – our energy is not aligned with Source. If you search the internet for a new job while feeling downhearted and pessimistic, or when you would prefer to be listening to music or walking the dog, you will be wasting your time. You are pushing the river, pushing against the natural flow of your energy. You are not coherent with your desire. If you do whatever feels good, on the other hand, your vibrations begin to align with Source energy; then 'coincidences' occur that bring you closer to your desire. While walking the dog you meet someone who becomes a friend, and they have a friend who offers you your ideal job. Or you try the internet again while you are feeling joyful and optimistic, and within ten minutes you hit upon exactly what you were looking for. How you feel is a constant indicator of whether or not you are in synch with your desires. If you are not, then your task as an apprentice god is to change your thoughts, or follow your bliss, or get happy in any which way you can, so that you are in alignment. *Then* all you have to do is follow your impulses – and the Universe can deliver.

A friend whose mother died two years ago felt bereft after losing her only family. Sue had been adopted as a young child after both parents died; she had no family of her own, and felt a great yearning to 'belong'. Recently, after a long period of hard work, she decided to ease up on her work commitments and be kinder to herself. On impulse, she then booked a weekend retreat at a Quaker guest house. There she met a lovely woman who recognised her from early childhood, and who turned out to be her second cousin. Sue was overjoyed to have unexpectedly discovered a blood relative, who is now becoming a friend. Only Source energy could have magically arranged the many unlikely 'coincidences' that resulted in this meeting – which fulfilled her heart's desire. And it only happened after she freed up some resistance, and followed her bliss.

SURRENDERING TO THE FLOW

Some spiritual teachings urge us to aim for presence in the moment, surrendering, going with the flow, as the highest form of enlightenment. As I see it, being fully present and surrendering to 'what is' is all about letting go of resistance. What you resist persists, so when you accept whatever is happening, you allow energy to flow again. The paradox of change is that you cannot move on until you accept your starting point, loving yourself and your reality as it is right now. Saying 'No' to anything means that you focus upon it, and therefore hold it in your vibrations. You have to say 'Yes' to what is.

However, inner peace is only at level 2 on the Emotional Scale (see chapter 6). At the highest level, you move into joy, passion, enthusiasm, bliss and unconditional love. Such emotions *feel* even better than inner peace, which tells us they are a higher vibration. Contentment is a huge improvement on where most of us hang out emotionally (which is often around being overwhelmed, irritation or frustration, or might be as low as anger and blame, or even guilt and insecurity). Inner peace is a state of very low resistance; but it is not the end-point. And if you are stuck in the old paradigm, contentment can easily drift into passivity, resignation or victimhood – accepting 'what is' even when it feels uncomfortable, dull or disappointing (against what your divine discontent is telling you).

Buddhism sees desire as the source of all suffering or dissatisfaction (*dukkha*), and encourages us to relinquish desire. There is a half-truth in the notion that desire causes suffering – but suffering does not come from the desire itself, but from the pain and frustration caused by *resistance*. If you let go of the resistance, you can turn your dreams into reality. How much more satisfying this is than giving up the desire! You cannot become an apprentice god by simply accepting what is. If you squash your dreams and desires, you are pinching off your god-like potential.

We cannot have unfulfilled desires without feeling incomplete until those desires are realised. Desire is pure God-force flowing through us, and we are here to become conscious co-creators. That is where our bliss and ecstasy lies – in allowing Source to flow freely through us, and creating our own heaven on earth – and keeping this delicate balance between living in the moment and reaching for our future desires is what life is all about. Inner peace can only ever be a temporary state. It is not our destination. After all, there is no destination; there is only the journey towards ever-expanding joy and freedom and growth.

 PRACTICAL SUGGESTIONS

1. What are your dreams and desires? Spend time pondering what you really want from life. This is not a one-time list – it is just a list for now, perhaps projecting ahead for two or three years. You can change your mind at any time. (However, we get what we focus upon – so if you keep changing your mind, you will attract a seemingly stuck or muddled reality!) What do you want to do, or experience? What do you want to have? What do you want to be? What do you want to know? How do you want to feel?

   Choose any desire that feels really important to you right now, and list the reasons why you want this. This helps you to focus on desire – rather than on lack, blockages or resistance – and begins to pull it towards you.

2. Follow your bliss. Make a habit of always taking action from joy and desire, rather than from negative emotions such as fear, shame, guilt or drivenness. This avoids the endless struggle and 'efforting' of the ego, and helps you become an apprentice god. Wait until you feel a joyful or intuitive impulse to act; your timing will always be perfect. Avoid doing anything because you 'must' or 'should' or 'ought' to do it, since this is going against the flow. If it feels heavy, don't do it! (If there is anything you 'have' to do – such as filling in your income tax return – find positive thoughts about why you are *choosing* to do this, and wait for a time when you feel least resistance to doing it.) Make your life as heavenly as possible. Do whatever feels joyful.

3. Know that your desires are on their way! Others might tell you that you are being unrealistic, that you are a dreamer, that you are not facing the facts. But they do not know how reality-creation works! If you can consistently hold a vibration which is aligned with what you want – by joyfully anticipating it, by knowing beyond doubt that it is coming to you, by choosing thoughts that support your belief – then sooner or later, reality has to come into alignment. Even if there isn't a shred of evidence that it is coming, keep holding on to your vision. Be like a laser beam! It is coming. It is just around the corner. It is as sure as the sun coming up tomorrow. Don't let doubts creep in. Don't even try to reassure yourself. Just trust. And don't let anyone else burst your bubble. In the meantime, enjoy life in every way you can, appreciating every golden moment. Follow any joyful impulses. And watch the miracles arrive …

CHAPTER NINE

Turning Lead Into Gold

*When individuals change, the whole planetary
consciousness also evolves.*
As above, so below.

Richard Gerber[1]

If life is meant to be heaven on earth, how come there is
pain and suffering in the world? Is there any purpose to
suffering, or are we just stuck in our immature egos, making
a mess of things? The sky-god religions often revere
suffering as a path of martyrdom and self-sacrifice, or see it
as punishment from an angry and judgmental God, or
merely to be expected in a vale of tears. But what role might
suffering have in a heaven-on-earth spirituality based upon
unconditional love? Could it somehow be pointing the way
home towards Love?

In answer to these questions, let me take you on my own
unfolding path through wild and tame love – and towards
the chunks of gold that emerged as I journeyed through the
brightest light and the deepest dark ...

❤

In the months after deciding upon marital separation, I felt like a nascent phoenix flapping around in the ashes, struggling to take flight. On the one hand, I had an overwhelming sense of relief, and never doubted that I'd made the right decision. Parts of me that had been repressed for years began to re-surface. I felt more embodied and sensual; I threw out most of my dull wardrobe, buying brighter clothes that matched my emerging new self, had regular massages and spent more time fell-walking. I felt ten years younger, and an old friend commented that I seemed more like the vibrant, free-spirited woman she had known before my marriage. At the same time, I had found nowhere suitable to live with my son, and my husband and I – though on good terms – were still uneasily co-habiting our marital home. Everything felt uncertain, and I was overshadowed by a sense of loss, instability and confusion. Where was my life going? What were my dreams and desires now? What did I really want?

My friendship with Matthew faltered in the wake of my decision about my marriage – and he was occupied with major life changes of his own – so for a few months we rarely met. But eventually we spoke openly and honestly about our relationship, then agreed not to discuss it again for some time. We were both clear that we just wanted to be friends, and in the wake of my marital break-up, I felt delighted to have a close male friend whose company was so enriching, and whom I loved dearly.

That summer, Matthew and I met for a couple of hours each fortnight. Life felt challenging for us both. His long-term marital problems were still unresolved, and he and his wife had again discussed the possibility of separation. I encouraged him again to seek help for his marriage, and to keep trying; but looking back, we were both in a vulnerable state – and we grew much closer. We shared our hopes, our fears, our dreams, our regrets, our childhood memories, our secrets. We walked the fells, revelling in the wonder and beauty of the Lakeland landscape. We talked about books, films, poetry, travel, music, health, parenting and consciousness. We laughed a lot. We spoke of relationships, love and affairs. There never seemed enough time for all we had to discuss, yet our precious hours together seemed timeless and magical. There were no barriers between us; I could say anything at all to Matthew. I trusted him completely. Everything just tumbled out, and I found myself unfolding and expanding. Our conversations were so raw and honest, so rich and luminous – and I felt utterly present and alive when we were together.

> *Words cascade out*
> *like twin waterfalls, pooling*
> *in a secret garden.*
> *They reach out to each other –*
> *towards safety, towards danger –*
> *in search of something more:*
> *hidden treasures of the soul.*
> *For two hours, loneliness dissolves*
> *and the world is made whole again.*[2]

One afternoon I sat beside a lake with Matthew, reflecting sadly on my marriage and how, only a year ago, my life had seemed so perfect on the surface. Matthew was deeply unhappy too, filled with regrets about decisions he had made, and feeling lonely and imprisoned. But he trusted that, at a higher level, everything was unfolding perfectly. Most days, so did I. Then he admitted there was something he wasn't telling me. I joked that I thought he told me all his dark secrets, but I suspected I knew what it was – just as we were becoming real friends at last. That summer, in a handful of hours, we had both fallen in love.

Suddenly we were sailing into dangerous waters, and I had no idea how to return to harbour. Everything was spinning out of control. The rare and precious friendship that I trusted would last a lifetime now felt under threat – and I both did and didn't want to hear Matthew's secret. Once it was spoken out loud, we both knew that he would have to tell his wife that our friendship was wobbling. For someone who had spent his whole life trying to avoid hurting or upsetting anyone, this would be a nightmarish prospect. And what would happen to our intensely close and loving relationship? I felt as if I was living in a soap opera. We were both much too 'good and nice' to be in this awful situation. I just wanted to stabilise our friendship again, but I couldn't see a way through.

One glorious day, after a walk in the mountains, Matthew finally confessed that he was in love with me, and was in complete turmoil over what to do. Despite his unhappiness, it had not occurred to me that Matthew was seriously considering marital separation – much less that I might be a factor in that decision. But by now, he had become important to me beyond words. Like the ticking of a clock, I hadn't noticed my loneliness until it was suddenly gone, in the presence of someone with whom my soul felt at home, with whom I could share every aspect of myself. I loved everything about him – his light and his dark. I could gaze into his eyes and merge with the cosmos. His happiness meant at least as much to me as my own. I had never loved so wholeheartedly, never felt such unconditional love and trust and passion. And I had never felt so vulnerable. I told Matthew that I was so afraid of losing him that it felt like standing on the edge of a cliff, waiting to live or die. Whatever happened, he assured me, there would never come a time when he did not want me in his life. Likewise I told him that nothing could ever damage our relationship.

However, the dark shadow of impending separation now loomed over our time together. Matthew was married, devoted to his young children, and we knew that we had to clarify the boundaries of our relationship. We felt we could not carry on meeting with integrity, even as friends, without his wife knowing that we loved each other; and despite their problems, he loved her too. There seemed to be only one honourable option at the time. We had agreed that we wouldn't consider having an affair, or even kiss each other. After consulting with mutual friends, we decided we must put our friendship on hold, while Matthew did his utmost to sort out his marriage, and he and his wife came to a decision about their future together.

Soon after, we met for the last time. I told Matthew that, if they decided to separate, I would love to share my life with him. Whatever happened, we would remain close friends. Then we parted with a brief hug – and I fell off the edge of that cliff, and into an abyss.

JOURNEY OF THE SOUL

After many years of promoting growth through joy as a spiritual path,[3] it came as a shock when I created a prolonged and painful crisis in my own life. Where had I gone wrong? 'If we listen to the whispers, the Universe does not have to shout at us,' I had always taught. Had I been ignoring my feelings and intuitive guidance? Or was there a greater purpose to this experience?

Carl Jung wrote of the difference between soul and spirit. Spirit is light, inspiring and joyful; it is upward-moving, lifting us into higher realms, soaring towards the sun. The soul, by contrast, is deep, dark and downward-moving. It can thrust us into 'dark nights of the soul'. It yearns for wholeness, for holiness. It often works in mysterious ways, sending messages or puzzles or situations that might not make sense until months or years later. It asks us to surrender, to trust, to go with the flow, to allow greater forces to take over.

As I faced marital separation, then plunged into an even deeper emotional crisis over Matthew, I realised I was on a journey of the soul. A journey into the dark. A journey into the Shadow. A journey into our deepest wounds. A journey of reconnection and healing and growth. A hero's journey of separation-individuation and awakening. I now felt the vast, sweeping impact of greater forces in our lives – like the power of the eclipse. I began to look at things afresh.

As Thomas Moore points out in *Dark Nights of the Soul*,[4] psychology tends to be 'solar', seeking the light, trying to overcome the darkness. As a clinical psychologist, I could see this tendency in myself. But there are times when we need deepening and darkening, he says, when we need to step into the shadows in order to become more multi-dimensional. 'Your dark night is your own invitation to become a person of heart and soul,' Moore suggests – an initiation into spiritual adulthood. And sometimes we have to merge with the darkness, to sit in the belly of the whale, to sink into our depths, instead of trying to escape or run away. Instead of resisting, we must allow it to transform us, trusting that the alchemy will yield its own gold.

As part of my own journey, I moved beyond my former ideas of 'growth through joy' versus 'growth through suffering' into a non-dualistic perspective. This isn't to revere suffering, but rather – as we shall see – to realise that suffering and joy ultimately lead in the same direction. And it is crucial to wild love that we learn to accept *everything* in life – the light and the dark; that we say 'Yes' to it all, rather than splitting it into good and bad.

Being broken open can throw us into the crucible of transformation. Since problems cannot be resolved from the same level of consciousness that created them, major challenges force us to expand our awareness and clarify our desires. Breakdown can lead to breakthrough. And perhaps we sometimes *have* to be pushed against the wall – personally and globally – if we are to take a quantum leap, if we are to metamorphose into butterflies rather than merely becoming fatter caterpillars.

MY UNFOLDING JOURNEY

As the leaves turned to red and gold, Matthew and I parted
for an indefinite period, agreeing to avoid the places where
we might normally meet. A week later, my son and I finally
moved out of our family home into temporary accommo-
dation.

The winter that followed was the most anguished period
of my life. I soon heard from mutual friends that Matthew's
wife was enraged about our feelings for each other, but
wanted their marriage to continue – so I knew what the
eventual outcome was likely to be. I was committed to a
loving relationship with Matthew, whatever form it might
take; but I had foolishly promised to be there for him if they
eventually decided to separate, and my loyalty to that
promise kept me imprisoned in hope of a romantic relationship, and unable to move on emotionally until I heard
his decision. I respected their boundaries and gave them the
space they needed, but I was suspended in a tortured limbo
of despair, grief and powerlessness. I felt as if I had been
locked in a glass prison, totally exiled from the loving relationship that had become so precious to me.

The intensity of grief completely shattered me. As
Deepak Chopra notes, 'The complete disappearance of
someone you love is terrifying beyond words.'[5] Abandonment activates our deepest pain and terror. The pain of
it was astonishing; all I could do was sit with the wrenching
emotions. I wept rivers of grief, and seldom made it through
an hour without crying. I could barely eat or sleep for weeks
on end. I wrestled with guilt, feelings of worthlessness and
even suicidal impulses. I felt stripped bare of defences, like a
tree without bark, exposed to the whipping rain and wind.
At other times, I felt angry and bewildered at being so
utterly forsaken.

Yet there was still this deep love that would not go away, the
love that gave me a golden thread of hope that I might find my

way out of this terrifying labyrinth. 'You are always with me / your presence like a sweet warm ghost / inhabiting my every breath', I wrote in one poem[6] – and this deep sense of connectedness transcended our physical separation. More and more, I felt this 'sweet warm ghost' with me, wherever I went. And slowly, almost imperceptibly, this connection to Love began to restore a fragile sense of inner peace.

> Still we walk under the same sun,
> our bodies warmed by those golden rays,
> our feet treading the same scorched earth,
> incarnated from the one Light.
> Twin souls birthed together
> in the ancient of days:
> always connected, always One.[7]

As the intense emotions began to subside, I realised that Matthew had become my connection to Source – and since feeling separated from Love is the very definition of hell, I had been lost in Dante's inferno. Intellectually I knew that my connection to Source lay within, and was not dependent upon anyone else – but I had faced the agonies of withdrawal like an addict. And now, without denying that love, I had to reconnect with Source on my own. I wrote prose and poetry for much of the day, and with the support of close friends, somehow made it through that harsh winter. Month after month, my heart literally ached.

As the daffodils bloomed, Matthew arranged by letter to meet me again. We had not spoken for five months, but I had recently heard from friends that he and his wife were staying together. (I fired off an angry letter as a knee-jerk reaction, urging him to talk to me.) We met at last, walking and talking for a few hours. We were both tense, and both expressed superficial anger. ('Why wouldn't you even speak to me all that time, you rat-bag? I thought we were *friends*.')

But our relationship remained close, warm and loving. His marriage had been 'transformed' by the crisis, he said, and we both now regretted that our boundaries had become unclear. After all we had shared, we agreed it was hardly surprising that we loved each other – but in the circumstances, our love was clearly meant to be expressed as friendship.

Surprisingly, my love for him was untouched by those agonising months of silence. It was truly unconditional love. Whatever he said or did, whatever he felt or chose was fine with me. It made no difference to my feelings for him. It was love that asked nothing in return, that made no demands, that came with no expectations. A sweet and ancient soul love. Any hurt or anger towards him was always easily expressed and released, seeming like a pale, wispy cloud in the midst of that blue sky of Love. I just wanted him to be happy – and now felt relieved to have resolved the question of what form our relationship was meant to take. I simply wanted him to be part of my life, in whatever form was appropriate. Whatever happened, we had always said we would remain close friends, and perhaps also had work to do together.

However, Matthew was guilt-ridden over what had happened between us. His wife was still furious, he said, and he would do whatever she wished, since his loyalty to her was now 'absolute'. He felt it might take a few months to resolve the situation, but at least we could stop avoiding each other at last, and slowly normalise our relationship again. His wife had refused to speak to me from the start, but I wrote her another apologetic letter, hoping we could soon talk and clear the air.

Matthew and I hugged goodbye, arranging to meet in a social situation a few days later – but he did not turn up. Nor did he reply to a brief email. Before long, it became obvious that he was again avoiding me and not speaking. My sense of relief that the drama was over began to evaporate. We seemed to be back in our glass prison. I sent occasional letters asking for clarity about what was going on, asking for us all to meet and discuss the situation, but there was no response. I suggested a mutual friend as mediator – but the harrowing silence went on and on.

Several months later, Matthew sent a strangely cold and stilted letter, saying he had not read my previous two letters, and asking me not to write to him again. He was well and happy, he said, and 'trying to stop feeling guilty.' It was not possible for us to be friends now, he wrote, though he hoped eventually we could meet socially in the presence of others. It was clear there would be no discussion.

After that, Matthew continued to avoid me, and pretended not to know me if we bumped into each other socially. One day, he jogged straight past me with the weak smile of a passing stranger. It was the first time we had met alone in six months. It happened to be his birthday, and I was not even allowed to say hello. I felt numb and shocked, then went into another tailspin of despair. In the year since our abrupt and painful parting, he had spoken to me only once. Now he would not even open a letter from me. Our exile from each other was complete.

I had spent a whole painful year hoping to restore a loving friendship that was hugely precious to me – but it was now clear that Matthew no longer wanted this, or felt unable to do it. Someone who felt like part of my soul, whom I had expected to be a close and intimate friend for ever – or even to share my life with – now pretended that he had never known me.

DARK AND LIGHT LESSONS

Let me lead you through an analysis of this emotional journey, since a love triangle provides such fertile ground for exploring the themes of *Wild Love*. As I slowly integrated my emerging insights with my understanding of reality creation and energy psychology, it led me towards a fresh understanding of what love really means, and how relationships can block our spiritual growth and potential ...

During most of this year-long process, I was left baffled and bewildered – questioning, longing for answers, needing to talk – while also wanting to honour Matthew's wishes. How had our warm and loving relationship turned into this cold indifference and denial? Why would he no longer speak to me? My mind whirled round and round a maze of hurtful possibilities. I knew I was just caught up in a downward spiral of pain, but I could not find my way out. Had he blithely used me to make his wife jealous and sort out their marriage, holding me over her head like the sword of Damocles, while never intending to speak to me again? Had he never seen us as friends? Had it all been pretence and lies? Did he need to make it clear that he had never cared about me? Or had he turned his rage against me, transfiguring me into an evil, dangerous monster who must be barred and excluded from his life – crucifixes at the windows, garlic hung from the ceiling? Or had he simply found real happiness at home, and our friendship had become trivial and irrelevant, not worth the hassle, easier to pretend it had never happened? Or perhaps we were *both* being harshly punished for getting too close, being too honest, for loving each other – despite keeping clear boundaries, and doing our best to behave with integrity in a confusing and painful situation? If so, was love really meant to be so exclusive? Did he really 'belong' to one person? Could love *ever* be bad, wrong and dangerous? Wasn't there room for loving different people in different ways?

Whatever was going on, it felt strange to be so cruelly treated for loving and caring about someone. Something felt very screwy and twisted. When someone will not communicate, leaving unfinished business hanging in mid-air, it is hard *not* to speculate about what might be going on.

Unfinished business eats away at us, draining our energy and tying us in knots. I gathered glimmers from friends of what was happening behind the scenes – but whatever the truth was, neither of them would speak to me. Our friendship was over. Period.

I was used to open and honest communication, and had never been in such a bizarre scenario. Although I wanted to respect their decision, it felt like a win-lose situation – a sure sign of conflict not being resolved, of a pseudo-solution based upon sacrifice and control and compromise. Yet I knew that, in terms of reality creation, my intense focus on the stuckness was perpetuating it at an energy level. I was in strong and woeful resistance. I was saying 'No' to being exiled from a close and loving friendship. I was being guilt-tripped, and so felt controlled and disempowered. I was yearning for open communication – and yearning always means we are moving in the wrong direction. I was *battling against* the situation, and whatever we resist persists.

The temptation is to point a finger in such situations – to rail against how *others* are behaving, to 'shoot the messenger', to believe our hurt and pain is being caused by the outside world, and we would feel better if only *someone else* would change, disappear or get their act together! (It is tempting to sink into victimhood when we are in pain, and it can give us manipulative power.) Or we might shame ourselves as an abused child does – seeing ourselves as bad, unworthy of love, deserving to be punished. But either way, we are stuck in shame or blame, trapped in lower vibrations, imprisoned by the ego. Our energy collapses. We are being tamed. We are not allowing love to flow.

Instead of guessing what might be happening for Matthew, with my ego going round in circles, my task was to work out what was going on for *me*, and why. What was the bigger picture here? In a friendly and loving universe, there must be a positive reason for going through all this torment. As a writer on spiritual psychology, why was I creating this painful experience? Like the birth pangs of labour, I trusted that it would bear a priceless pearl.

The truth is that there are no victims. This ongoing situation had to be mirroring my relationship with myself, and with love. What was going on here? The bigger picture is that reality can only mirror the vibrations we are sending out. We evoke from others whatever matches our own radio signals. There can be no abandonment without self-abandonment. No betrayal without self-betrayal. No rejection without self-criticism. No cruelty and indifference unless there is a lack of self-compassion. No judgment from others unless there is shame and guilt. No separation from love unless we are lost in a world of duality. This must be an old riverbed of mine; so perhaps it was an old riverbed for humanity. *How do we keep ourselves separate from love?*

Whenever we face challenges, we can choose to learn what I call dark or light lessons. Dark lessons come from the negative stories we tell ourselves when we are stuck in our ego, and react to a stressful situation from an old riverbed, a long-practised habit of disconnection from Source. (eg. 'The world really is a dangerous place.' 'I am too trusting.' 'I'm not worthy of love.' 'I'm a failure.' 'I was betrayed again.' 'Men/women are so fickle.' 'I am a bad person.' 'My friends desert me.' 'It is safer to be alone.') Instead of seeing such beliefs as the *cause* of our current challenge – that we attracted a situation that mirrors a familiar riverbed of thoughts and emotions – we come to believe that we were 'right' all along. Dark lessons boost our feelings of insecurity, mistrust, bitterness, lack, guilt or unworthiness, or make us blame and rage at others, feel like a self-righteous victim, or want to control, fix or change others or the world. Dark lessons feel harsh and cutting and divisive. They reinforce our ego's defences, and put up barriers. They close us down, restrict our freedom, and increase our sense of powerlessness.

Our stories are the ways in which the immature ego

interprets events so that they fit with our negative beliefs and family patterns. If we believe in our false stories, we can deepen our wounds and defences. Instead of becoming an opportunity for growth, an outer event then becomes another knife in the belly, another scar that blocks us from deep reality. Our ego-stories often cast us as the innocent victims of a big, bad world – like the poor children in fairy-tales who have, tellingly, often been abandoned by their good, beautiful dead mother (the Goddess) and instead have a wicked stepmother (the Witch) and distant father (sky-God): stories of fear, guilt, blame, duality and separation from love.

'When something goes wrong,' says Rumi, 'accuse your-self first.' This does not mean blaming and shaming ourselves; nor does it mean passively lying back and taking whatever comes. It means lovingly taking responsibility for our lives, and keeping an open heart. After all, whatever happens in the outer world is a mirror of our inner world. Everything is interconnected. When we say 'Yes' to every-thing in our lives – whether an outer event or a person, or an inner feeling or impulse or desire – we soften our ego defences. We stop bracing ourselves against inner or outer 'enemies' and relax, which allows the deep Self to seep through into awareness. The deep Self takes us beyond duality, beyond judgment, beyond struggle, into that place of unconditional love that is our true home, our place of belonging.

Light lessons come from the deep Self, and increase our sense of love and trust and joy and gratitude. They help us understand the bigger picture. They increase our feeling of oneness, our freedom and empowerment. They open our heart, and make us want to reach out with love. Light lessons feel soft and soothing and expansive. They reassure us that everything is unfolding perfectly, that all is well.

Of course, if we choose dark lessons, that is okay too. We are free to cling to our familiar gods, to run along our old riverbeds. There is no right or wrong – but dark lessons will lead to a rockier road. Despite what many spiritual teachers say, I do not believe that there is a spiritual curriculum, or that anyone up there is awarding points of merit. (The idea of 'lessons' often comes from a false belief in our unworthiness and imperfection, as if we are playing catch-up with a perfect God.) We are not children who are being sent lessons. We are spiritual adults, co-creators, pioneers in consciousness. We choose our own lessons. But we do learn and grow from experience, expanding our wisdom and awareness. Ultimately, all roads lead in the same direction – towards joy and freedom and growth. Some roads are smooth, while others are strewn with rocks and boulders; some roads twist and meander more than others. But whatever path we choose, it is all part of our great adventure in consciousness.

LYING DOWN WITH RUMI

> ... we need our dross as well as our gold, because it is out of the dross that the gold comes; it is the blackness with the light that creates it and makes it not just light, but gold.
>
> *Jay Ramsay*[8]

This prolonged drama perfectly mirrored our personal and global suspension between two paradigms: the enticing, sparkling world of unconditional love and joy and freedom, and the old world of judgment, limitation, conformity, fear and struggle. For me, it was an alchemical journey into the greatest light of unconditional love and the deepest darkness of guilt, judgment, grief and despair.

Looking back, I had been in an emotionally vulnerable state – in the midst of marital separation – and was sending out muddy vibrations. My unresolved guilt over ending my good-enough marriage had led me into a hugely painful situation, since feelings of guilt tend to 'invite' pain and punishment. I had longed for a loving and intimate relationship – yet I also wanted time to myself after my marriage. I had been hooked into trying to rescue Matthew from his marital unhappiness, while also being horrified at the idea of him leaving his wife for me. I was full of contradictions; my energy was divided. On top of this, Matthew and I had both compounded the confusion by trying to be 'good', and putting his wife's needs first. Things had spiralled out of control – causing a lot of hurt for everyone – because we both focused on *others'* needs, and listened to *others'* well-meaning advice. We were both determined to do 'what was right', and so fell into judgment, into ego. We had both wanted a loving and lasting relationship, and simply wanted to clarify the form it should take – yet neither of us was Self-centred, which might have avoided the whole drama, and led to a win-win situation for everyone.

Trying to be good fed into the duality and judgment of the old paradigm. Duality always splits our energy, and creates win-lose situations – in which everyone loses. We only *try* to be good when we tell ourselves we are being bad, and are therefore disconnected from Source. When we try to do what is morally right (from the head), we lose touch with what feels good (from the heart). Then we lean on others' advice or the external rules of society to tell us how to behave, instead of being guided by our emotions, instead of trusting that everyone's needs and desires can be met. I created separation from love by trying to be 'good' within a dualistic world view. This is what humanity has been doing for thousands of years; and it is time for us to stop.

By trying to be good, Matthew and I falsely defined our loving and supportive relationship as bad and wrong, and his troubled marriage as good and right. And to be fair, I had done the same splitting in reverse. This good-bad splitting held the crisis in the bottom third of the Emotional Scale, where any higher resolution is impossible, and left us apparently forfeiting any right to our friendship. I had been 'banished to oblivion' – no doubt justifiably in their eyes – in a classic form of scapegoating.[9]

From the vantage point of unconditional love, Source would have defined both relationships as 'good' in different ways. Yet I had acquiesced to the old paradigm view (based on fear and judgment) that he 'belonged' to someone else, and that I could be rightfully excluded with no right of appeal – that our friendship must be curtailed and even invalidated because we had become too close, too fond of each other, were too honest with each other and (horror of horrors!) even found each other attractive.

I knew that Matthew was a deeply loving and caring man, who would not deliberately hurt or mistreat anyone – but he had spent his life trying to be good and loyal, and I guessed he was justifying his behaviour towards me in that context, regardless of his own feelings. I felt sure he saw himself as behaving honourably. Yet forever avoiding and ignoring me would be a drip-drip reminder of how 'badly' he had behaved, and how 'bad and wrong' our love was – an incessant form of guilt-tripping and denial which would painfully deplete him. More than ever, I saw how *trying to be good* means being lost in a world of duality, what a heavy price we pay for that, and how much chaos and distress it can cause. *We are separated from love whenever we are in judgment* – when we eat from the Tree of Good and Evil – which means we have lost sight of unconditional love. Our love has been tamed.

I finally stopped feeling so much pain over my exile from Matthew when I gave up defining what had happened between us as bad or wrong. Every fibre of my being protested at seeing loving and caring about someone – or even falling in love – as wrong and blameworthy. This idea created huge tension and resistance in my energy system, since my deep Self disagreed and refused to join me in my disconnection. Love can never be bad or wrong.

At the same time, I had to accept that Matthew and his wife had defined our relationship (or me, at least) as bad and wrong and dangerous, and not judge them for that. Everyone is always doing the best they can – doing what feels right from their own perspective, according to their own beliefs and values. Criticising anyone else disconnects us from Source; and in any case, we can never know what someone else's path is, or what they need to do and why. Also, I knew beyond doubt that Matthew and I had had a soul contract to go through this experience together – an agreement set up before we entered this lifetime – and that everyone had played their roles to perfection. I still missed him, acutely at times, but the terrible pain of judgment had gone. And my newly formed wings were unfurling.

> It is the paradox of spiritual growth that through such bleak winter journeys we eventually come through a hidden door into a bright field of springtime that we could never have discovered otherwise. This is the heart of the mystical.
>
> John O'Donohue[10]

This bitter-sweet alchemical process took me a whole year to move through – even with all the energy-healing tools at my disposal – but once I had fully transcended the good-bad duality, a huge layer of resistance dissolved. The love remained (for love is eternal), but the intense pain had finally gone. It was remarkable, like swimming out of a cold, shark-infested ocean into a calm, safe, warm lagoon. (I could still *generate* distress again, by choosing thoughts based on duality, since I cautiously experimented with this – but such thoughts no longer came unbidden.)

I realised I had created a situation that society offers many judgments about – falling in love with a married man – in order to *experience* the destructive power of guilt and judgment, to see the dynamics of tame love, and come to a fresh understanding of what love means. Theoretically I knew that judgment blocks our spiritual growth, yet part of me still believed that being spiritual meant being 'good'. (I had even been judgmental in the past about people having affairs, having seen friends badly hurt by this.) And though Matthew and I chose not to have an affair, I had still judged myself harshly for loving someone I 'should' not love, and allowed myself to be guilt-tripped for a whole year over it. My self-judgment was mirrored back by their lack of compassion and forgiveness. Yet I knew that everyone involved co-created this drama through their own vibrations – through their hidden longings or fear – and I came to see that it is our limiting definitions of love that make these situations so painful and conflictual.

Within the new paradigm, this is a blameless universe; and love is always good, always holy, always right. I realised that it is mostly judgment – of self or others – that stops love flowing where it will, splits our energy and drags us into the gutter of guilt, blame and 'control dramas' from which it is hard to escape.

Thomas Moore suggests that a dark night of the soul can 'torture the soul into a new level of awakening'.[11] I certainly felt as if I had been beaten up and pulverised for a year or so. (Nothing is more abusive than being ignored and invalidated – especially by someone you love.) Yet the violent succussion had thrust me into an awakening, a shattering of my old self. Death and rebirth. Everything looked so different. I felt so different.

One night, in an extraordinary waking dream, I found myself lying in the open air beside an olive-skinned man in Middle Eastern robes. The warm sun caressed my skin. Neither of us spoke, but I felt blissfully happy and at peace.

Suddenly I understood *in my heart* those mystical words of Rumi's, which I had long loved:

> *Out beyond ideas of wrongdoing and rightdoing,*
> *there is a field. I'll meet you there.*
>
> *When the soul lies down in that grass,*
> *The world is too full to talk about.*[12]

At long last, I had joined Rumi in that shimmering field. We lay together on our bellies in the sweet meadow grass – blowing dandelion clocks, and laughing.

ANAM CARAS – SOUL FRIENDS

John O'Donohue[13] writes beautifully about the ancient Celtic tradition of *anam caras*, or soul friends – a deeply loving and intense relationship which cuts across all convention, morality and category. This is a rare and precious friendship with an eternal and indissoluble bond, in which you feel fully accepted and understood, and can simply be who you are without any mask or pretence. A boundless soul love. I believe that Matthew and I were *anam caras,* which is why it felt so acutely painful to be severed from him. It felt like having part of my soul ripped out. It was a relationship that defied an 'either-or' classification, that went beyond duality. It was neither a romantic/sexual partnership, nor a simple friendship. It was simply love – and real love knows no boundary; it just seeks flow and expression.

Jay Ramsay[14] similarly suggests that there are 'erotic soul relationships' – which might or might not be sexual – which go beyond friendship in that they awaken and inspire us, and help us to unfold in new ways. Such relationships feel highly charged and passionate, since they stimulate the flow of Eros –

our life force, our vitality, Source energy – and illuminate whatever has been suppressed or denied within us. They release our hidden potential, and bring us alive. (Sexual energy and Source energy are the same energy, so we get 'turned on' by anyone who helps Source/love/joy/passion/vision to flow through us. But erotic feelings can simply be enjoyed, rather than being acted upon sexually.)

Relationships such as these challenge our usual strict boundaries. They are often judged, marginalised or invalidated in a society that promotes narrow co-dependency – especially when they do become sexual 'affairs' – yet they are immensely valuable relationships that can enrich our lives and help us discover more of our wholeness. And in a society that really honoured love, instead of trying to keep it in a box, these rich, soulful and yes, even erotic relationships, would be welcomed and nurtured (even if we still choose sexual monogamy). Wild love allows for the possibility of other loving relationships – including 'attractive' relationships – without catastrophising and falling into either-or dichotomies. It makes room for many kinds of love.

From my perspective, I was perplexed as to why Matthew could not have us *both* in his life, why he could not love us *both* in different ways, having established clear boundaries – and why we couldn't all simply talk about it. But judgment and fear took over, leading to a win–lose duality that excluded me totally from his life. Instead of being a loving and lifelong friend, I somehow became a dangerous 'enemy' who must be ruthlessly exiled.

Within a tame, conventional model of marriage, such behaviour is perhaps understandable. Our love was seen as bad and threatening. But when it is possible to see love as wrong, and to define 'behaving well' as pretending not to know someone we love, our culture is surely screwed up in its model of loving relationships. Something crazy-making is going on, and we have forgotten what love really means. Or perhaps we never knew.

TAME AND WILD LOVE

Throughout this long and intense emotional journey, I was reading and thinking and studying – feverishly searching for answers to my new questions about love and relationships. Why had my own marriage felt so restrictive and diminishing? Why had Matthew been so deeply unhappy? What made relationships work? What did it mean to be authentic? Why did some relationships bring out the worst in people, while others brought out the best? Why had my love for Matthew felt so 'different'? Why had our friendship plunged into crisis? What did it really mean to love someone? What was happening at an energy level in healthy, loving relationships? And how did love and relationships tie in with reality creation, and becoming apprentice gods?

I had lengthy discussions with friends about love and relationships, observed others' marriages closely and began to clarify different perspectives – which seemed to reflect the old and new paradigms. Since I can sense energy, I tuned in to people's energy during our conversations. 'Of course love means setting someone free,' said a friend in a happy marriage, her energy flowing and radiant. 'I wouldn't let *my* husband do that!' said another, as her energy short-circuited. 'I give in to her to keep the peace,' said a client, his aura shrinking. I watched a loving couple's energy fields expand and merge as they greeted each other with a delighted hug. I noticed how other couples seemed reduced and contracted in each other's presence. I monitored my own energy, and felt the impact of negative, critical or judgmental thoughts about others or myself. I listened to the recent teachings of Abraham about our emotional guidance system, and realised these were consistent with energy psychology and energy medicine. I re-visited all I knew about co-dependency and emotional abuse, considering them afresh from an energy-based perspective. I studied new developments in family therapy, approaches to the 'family soul', and how energetic patterns flow down the generations. I pondered the nature of love and freedom and quantum mechanics.

I felt like a detective searching for clues. I wasn't sure where it was all leading, but I had faith that my deep Self knew. Meanwhile the Universe helpfully sent me countless pointers – in the form of friends or clients in need of support, or the right books at the right time, or inspirational ideas or conversations, or the latest twists and turns in my own personal journey – which reassured me that, however painful it was, everything was unfolding perfectly.

Bit by bit, the pieces began to fit together like a jigsaw puzzle. Day after day, I wrestled with ideas. I woke each morning with my bedside table littered with notes made during the night. And I slowly realised that I was constructing an energy-based model of love and relationships. A philosophy of tame and wild love. A model that integrated reality creation, energy psychology and the divine feminine, and which offered some revolutionary insights into how relationships (as well as religious and social pressures to conform) can disconnect us from Source energy and keep us trapped in the ego. It also pointed towards how we might move beyond co-dependency, and free our human potential. By this time, through my passionate desire to make sense of my own personal journey, and deeply motivated by both love and pain, I had moved into a new level of awareness.

I could now see that relationships of any kind simply *cannot* work when we are in the lower half of the Emotional Scale (see chapter 6) especially while we are feeling either blame/rage or shame/guilt, which means we are trying to control (tame) others or allowing ourselves to be controlled (see chapter 10). And since we live in a vibrational universe in which separateness is an illusion, this means that *nothing* in our lives can really work until we shift beyond the duality of good-bad and right-wrong. From a place of duality, we are always stuck in ego – and will sabotage our own desires, and send out contradictory vibrations. We are tamed and disempowered. We cannot have loving, fulfilling relationships. We cannot create what we truly want. We cannot become apprentice gods.

Whenever we *try* to be good, or try to please others, *or* see anyone else as bad or dangerous, we disconnect ourselves from Source. We disconnect from who we truly are – which is love. It is only when we know that *everyone* is good and well-intentioned, that no-one can 'do' anything to us, that we just need to follow our bliss and everyone's needs and desires can be met – and that, whatever happens, all is well – that we enter a harmonious and peaceful world. We transcend duality. Then the sun shines radiantly upon a new heaven and a new earth.

BEYOND DUALITY

Anything that takes us beyond duality leads us towards wild love. Going beyond the idea of good and bad, right and wrong, safe and dangerous – which includes viewing suffering as 'bad', or the problems in the world as 'wrong', or any action we take as blameworthy – takes us home. It sets us free. It reunites us with Source. In order to get there, we need to look at the role of contrast in an evolving universe.[15] Understanding contrast is crucial to breaking down the barriers of duality and judgment.

If heaven on earth meant angels singing and harps playing and everyone wafting around in a state of permanent bliss, then we would not need contrast. However, perfection does not allow room for growth and change. The Universe is not aiming towards perfection (whatever that might be), but towards evolution and expansion. God/Source is ever-evolving – and exploring its own consciousness, in part, through us. We are aspects of God/Source in evolution.

Contrast is like the grain of sand in an oyster shell that

leads to the growth of the pearl. Contrast is a springboard for desire – and it is desire that leads to change. It stimulates growth and clarity and awareness. Pottering along in a mediocre life that is dull but tolerable is not going to light any fire of passionate desire within you; but suddenly discovering that you have a malignant lump, or that your partner is leaving you, or that your business is going bankrupt, might do so. When we are in emotional or physical pain, we badly want the pain to stop. It wakes us up. The contrast – the gap between 'what is' and how we want life to be – now seems like a chasm. This chasm launches huge desires, which can lead to enormous change and growth. It can therefore be a fast-track way to learn and grow.

Divine discontent might eventually lead to change, but a louder wake-up call is more likely to force us to ask big questions, and look seriously at our old riverbeds – and in time, we often look back with gratitude. Greater contrast leads to greater desires, which lead to greater growth. If life just offers a choice between strawberry and chocolate ice-cream, we might shrug our shoulders and pick either bowl. But if life offers either a plateful of pigswill or a bowl of ice-cream, our preference for the ice-cream is likely to be stronger. We are also likely to appreciate it more, by contrast. (I now *hugely* appreciate my beautiful home in the country after nine months in a small town-house with no garden.) The problem is that many of us become so mesmerised by having a plate of pigswill in front of us that we lose sight of the other option on the menu – which we could create if only we took our eyes *off* the pigswill, and instead focused on desiring and visualising and expecting the ice-cream!

Contrast is an inevitable part of an evolving universe. Contrast offers variety and choice, and it can bring spiritual awakening. When dark, chaotic forces enter our lives, they create depth and shadow. They throw us into a state of dis-equilibrium, which can overturn the complacent old order. From this high-energy state, we might take a quantum leap in consciousness.[16] The concept of contrast moves us beyond the idea of good or bad. It helps us knit together the light and dark to form a seamless tapestry – and, as everyone knows, darkness dissolves in the presence of light. *If we are looking through the eyes of wild love, there is no darkness.*

All of our experiences, without exception, are called forth from Source in response to questions we have asked, desires we have launched, or vibrations we have emitted. These include any people we've summoned into our lives for learning – perhaps through observing their riverbeds, which are easier to see clearly than our own, or as mirrors of our own beliefs or Shadow side, or in order to gain from their different perspectives, or to help clarify our own desires, or because their riverbeds will interlock with ours and – hopefully – stimulate growth. (Your experiences include reading this book, which *you* attracted into your life in answer to a request or question.) Whenever we invite contrast, it is because we want to grow. 'Here,' says Source, 'is an answer to your question.' So whatever happens is perfect. If it feels good, we can simply enjoy it. If it feels bad, we can learn and grow from it – and perhaps help others as a result. Whatever happens, all is well.

It is easy to transfer the psychopathology of the old paradigm into the new, and to shame ourselves for creating pain, suffering, illness or accidents. *Bad, shameful, worthless, stupid me for manifesting this!* But life is a journey of exploration and contrast – and contrast is designed to fuel our desire, which summons Source energy through us. There is no right or wrong. All is well.

Even if we die, all is well. The ego, in its illusion of separateness, sees life as good and death as bad (or occasionally vice versa, if life is hugely painful). News reports often tell gloomily of the 'death toll' in the latest accident or disaster – but life-death is another duality that we need to transcend. Death is not bad. It is not a tragedy. Every death is a suicide, at some level of consciousness, without exception. Death is always a positive choice. It is simply a decision to move on to another adventure, to merge back into Source for a while. No big deal. Death is merely a comma in the eternal journey of life–death–rebirth. It is stepping through a door, and being greeted by Love. As Henry Scott Holland, a canon of St Paul's Cathedral, famously put it, 'Death is nothing at all. I have only slipped away into the next room.' And now we can talk to the 'dead' person anytime, without building up huge phone bills! This isn't to deny the misery of grief – and tears help to release our painful resistance to loss – but taking death less seriously would make it seem far less fearful and negative.

> *All will be well, and all will be well and every manner of thing will be well.*
>
> *Julian of Norwich[17]*

If we move beyond duality, everything we have seen as 'bad' takes on a different hue.

Nothing is good or bad; it is merely a continuum of alignment with Source energy. The nearest thing to duality is *feeling* good versus *feeling* bad. Alignment feels better and attracts more joyful and pleasing experiences, even 'miracles'. But as we move out of alignment, it gives us contrast – in the form of negative emotions or painful experiences – which helps us to clarify our desires or expand our awareness. So it is okay to be in a place of disconnection. There is no judgment about this, no right or wrong. When someone is disconnected, they might be serving others by providing a contrasting example of what does *not* work, or how *not* to be. They might need to face deep unhappiness in order to wake up and explore their riverbeds. They might be delving into contrast to use it as a springboard for fresh desires. They might be stabilising society by clinging to the old paradigm, preventing change being too rapid and shocking for the rest of us, through their judgment and resistance. We cannot know what their path is. We can only trust that, in a friendly and loving universe, all paths lead back to Source.

If we move beyond duality, everything is okay. Negative emotions are okay; they are a vital indicator that our energy is not currently aligned with our desires. Extreme negative emotion can indicate enormous potential that is being blocked – so we can welcome that message. We just need to follow our emotional guidance, and move towards higher vibrations. If we move beyond duality, even suffering is okay; it helps us to clarify what we want, personally and globally – and this births a new future. If we move beyond duality, there is no fear, since we know that everything we attract comes through our own vibrations. We are never vulnerable. And if we attract *strong* contrast, it will launch *huge* desires. So all is well.

Moving beyond duality means that we no longer need to control others, or to change the world in ways that suit our own needs, values and beliefs. We know that you-and-I or us-and-them is a false duality, since everything we witness or experience comes from within. We set people free to create their own reality through their own vibrations – without judging what *they* are creating – while focusing on being in charge of our *own* vibrations, which create *our* reality.

Soon after my own expansion in awareness, I bumped into a rather pompous and overbearing man who creates tension and difficulties all around him – but I saw him with new eyes. I recognised how much awareness he triggered in others through running along his old riverbeds. My heart opened to him, and I felt that familiar feeling beyond duality: 'All is well.' We had a delightful conversation.

In a world beyond duality, there is such *freedom*. We can say 'Yes' to it all. Ah, such sweet relief! It allows us to breathe fully and completely. There is *nothing* that is not God/Source – and Source is unconditional love. So whatever is, is okay. Wild love is radical acceptance. It is a million miles beyond mere tolerance or passive resignation or *Que sera sera*. It is a heart-expanding love for all that is. It means seeing the beauty, the 'perfect imperfection' in everyone and everything.

This morning, I walked into the garden to feed my four white doves, who immediately swooped down from a chimney to the table beneath the dovecote. I was enjoying this beautiful and peaceful scene, with a low wintry sun melting into the blue sky, when a black low-flying air-force jet suddenly roared overhead, closely followed by another jet. Somewhat to my surprise, instead of feeling mildly irritated or judgmental, as I might have in the past, I found myself reverberating with *gratitude*. White doves, black jets. Symbols of peace, symbols of war. I held up my arms and mouthed into the sky, 'Thank you for the contrast!' Then I threw back my head and laughed. It would have looked crazy to an onlooker, but for me it was another sign of my inner metamorphosis. I could welcome the contrast, while allowing it to clarify my desire for a different world – a world of love and peace and harmony.

As I write this chapter, I am struck again by the exquisite and breathtaking perfection of my personal journey, at how carefully it was orchestrated, at how the strengths and weaknesses of those involved highlighted the emerging themes of *Wild Love* – and how humanity is grappling with these themes as we peep cautiously over the edge into the new paradigm, while clinging by the fingertips to our old world of duality. I can see how this two-year experience needed to be *exactly* as it was, so that I would gather together all the fragments that gradually led to a new awareness, which transmuted my own lead into gold.

If Matthew and I had simply become close friends again, once he resolved the question mark over his marriage, or if my love for him had been conditional, I would never have come to my fresh insights about tame and wild love, and how they affect our energy system – and this book would not have come into being. It had been a long and painful journey, yet it had delivered its precious bounty. I now felt profoundly grateful for it all. My heart had been burst open. I had walked through the flames. I had answered the Call, faced my road of trials, drunk deep from the chalice of the divine feminine – and could now return with an Elixir of Awakening.

TRANSFORMING THE WORLD

> *Today our personal crucifixions are particularly intense, as we take on the individual pieces of a huge and cosmic darkness.*
>
> *Marianne Williamson[18]*

At a recent conference in Florida, I listened to a remarkable woman[19] who was caught up in the genocide in Rwanda, in which a million people were slaughtered. Immaculee was a member of the minority Tutsis, whom the extremist government suddenly ordered to be exterminated by the ruling Hutus. (*Good Hutus. Bad Tutsis.*) For 91 days, she hid in a tiny bathroom with eight other women. They could not utter a single word for fear of being overheard. Murderers regularly searched the house with machetes, so again and again, she faced the gut-wrenching terror of being brutally raped then chopped into pieces. But she held on to love and prayer, constantly asking for help from God. Miraculously, she survived the massacre – and lived to tell the tale. The media reported the terrible genocide from its usual dualistic, victimhood perspective. (*Bad Hutus. Good Tutsis.*) But instead of feeling hatred and revenge, as might have been understandable, Immaculee emerged in a state of unconditional love. The alchemical contrast of love/prayer and unutterable fear had burnt her to ashes, then transformed her into gold.

The deepest darkness can elicit the greatest light. Since strong desire is launched by strong contrast, many of us are going through huge challenges right now. We are experiencing both ends of this polarity of tame and wild love. We are diving deep into darkness, so that we summon up contrasting desires which lead to new and visionary realities. We are shining a beacon into the future in order to forge new footpaths, to explore new territory – to give birth to the new paradigm. Our personal growth is a gift which goes hand in hand with changing the world. We are embodying the Goddess through our own awakening. We are weaving together the light and the dark. We are imaginal cells in Her re-emerging body. Our footprints become Her footprints upon the gentle earth.

Everyone reading this is part of the current paradigm shift. We are collectively helping the consciousness of humanity and the earth to take a quantum leap. We are becoming spiritual adults, which means shedding our old skins: letting go of our belief in separation from love; letting go of our shame, guilt and unworthiness; letting go of our fear and limitations; learning to trust our emotional and intuitive guidance; and remembering that there are no victims – that we create our world from the inside out, not from the outside in. We are finding out how to be conscious co-creators. We are learning to love unconditionally. We are learning to be wild and happy and free.

Whatever we learn from experience is what we came here to teach. This does not mean it is our 'mission' – that we must accomplish before we die, or else! But it does mean that we will feel drawn towards sharing our awareness with others – just as I am sharing my personal journey and insights with you – whether through conversation, art, poetry, books, teaching, film-making, music, social activism, in our chosen profession, or simply by being who we are within our own community; and we will gain huge satisfaction and fulfilment from doing so.

We are all part of the whole, so our personal and global journeys are inseparable. Each personal journey is a mirror of global issues, just as global issues mirror the current state of human consciousness. There is a saying in Sufism that God enters through a wound; in other words, our old energy habits and beliefs, which give rise to strong contrast, are exactly what creates powerful new desires for change – and these help to transform our world. We cannot embody our light without our shadow. We are all perfect in our imperfections, since our wounds become our gifts – to ourselves, and to the world – which give birth to a new future.

Each of us is a unique piece in a giant cosmic jigsaw. This cosmic jigsaw is double-sided, and we are now flipping it over. The old picture is based on fear, struggle, victimhood, judgment, separation, competition, lack and limitation; and on the flip-side is a new picture based on unconditional love, joy, freedom, creativity and unlimited potential – an intertwined and magical reality of energy-consciousness.

We are not on a mission to 'save' planet earth. We are here for a joyous adventure in expanding awareness. Despite what the doom-and-gloom merchants would have us believe, the world is not in a mess. That approach comes from shame and judgment. The world is doing just fine. In fact, it is doing better than fine! This is a thrilling time of personal and global awakening – hence the increasing signs of contrast right now – and many of us long to reach out and contribute our own piece of the jigsaw puzzle.

However, we can only help to change the world if we are aligned with Source energy. While we feel negative emotion about *any* situation, we are part of the problem rather than part of the solution. We are resonating with what is, rather than what might be. We cannot change the world by focusing on problems, or battling against what we see, since it means that we are not aligned vibrationally with what we *desire*. We cannot change the world from a place of blame, protest or self-righteousness, nor by trying to be virtuous or sacrificing ourselves. We cannot change the world by trying to control others, or by thinking we know what is best for them, nor by demanding change or making others feel guilty. And we cannot change the world while feeling disempowered, guilt-ridden or despairing. In other words, we cannot connect others from a place of disconnection – while we are trapped in conditional love, or the need to make an impact. Our love has to be unconditional. We cannot help shift the world into the holistic paradigm while we are stuck in the old dualistic paradigm. If we try to do so, any action we take will backfire, or merely lead to cosmetic or temporary change. Our muddy vibrations will produce mixed realities. Even 'peaceful protest' is only effective when it comes from *vision*, not when it stems from rage or self-righteousness. It is all about where we are holding our vibrations. *We can only transform the world from the inside out.*

We are not here to 'fix' the world, but we *can* make a difference – through aligning with Source energy. Like the Dalai Lama, like Gandhi, like Nelson Mandela, we can inspire people by remaining Self-centred – by being hopeful and visionary, by being loving and compassionate, by being understanding and non-judgmental, by following our bliss, by seeing the Light within others even when they act from a place of disconnection. Then we can make a positive difference in the world. Then we can deliver our gifts. Then we are moved to take inspired action – action that springs from Source energy, which knows what we envision for the planet. Following our bliss always takes us where we need to go. Passion helps us see solutions rather than problems. Passion takes us beyond duality and judgment. Passion takes us to the place where eagles fly.

My two-year journey into the light and dark launched intense personal and global desires within me. At a personal level, it fuelled a desire for the kind of loving, romantic, intimate, sensual, fun-loving, soulful and lasting relationship I had always dreamed of – and an equally strong desire to know that my connection to Source/love always lies within me.

At the same time, I did not want anyone else to suffer the unnecessary pain and torment I had endured over deeply loving and caring for someone. My experience birthed an overwhelming desire for a world of more expansive love, compassion and awareness. A world in which love means setting each other free. A world in which love is always celebrated, and never seen as a threat. A world of open and heart-centred communication. A world in which we reach out our arms to each other. A world in which we know that *everyone* is loved and good. A world in which we honour our differences. A world with no enemies. A world beyond fear. A world beyond victimhood and judgment. A world in which we release our old riverbeds of relating. A world of unconditional love, of wild love. This book is the result of that passionate desire to make a difference in the world.

 PRACTICAL SUGGESTIONS

1. Who or what pushes you into duality? What do you resist? What do you say No to? What aspects of yourself, or others, or your past or present life, or the world, do you find painful or unacceptable? Make a list. Then focus on any item on your list, and see whether you can breathe Love into that resistance. Relax into acceptance of 'how things are', knowing that whatever we resist persists. Feel your body relax as your resistance melts, as you stop short-circuiting your energy and allow Love to flow more freely. Allow your consciousness to expand, to move beyond the duality of good-bad or right-wrong into seeing everything

as a rich, multi-faceted expression of Source energy. Know that contrast is always giving birth to fresh desires. Know that we can never be bad or wrong – and we are always wholly loved by Source, just as we are. Relax deeply, choose another item from your list, then allow yourself to love that too – then another item, and another, and another – until you become an undivided ocean of Love for self, others and the world.

2. Is there anyone you need to make peace with? Or anyone you feel you need to forgive? If so, what aspect of you do they represent? What do you see in the Other which might (if you are honest) be a suppressed or devalued part of you? Can you allow your heart to soften towards them – and therefore towards yourself?

   If you are facing a difficult relationship – whether at work or in your personal life – try going beyond ideas of good and bad, right and wrong. Allow for the possibility that everyone can be right and good, if only you listen with an open heart. Instead of blaming others for your pain, judging them, or trying to work out what their 'problem' might be, the question is always: How are you keeping yourself separate from Love? How can you restore your own connection with Source? How does this relationship mirror your relationship with yourself? How might you reach out with love and openness? How can you listen to and understand the Other better? Focus patiently on what you wish to create here, instead of battling against 'what is'.

3. If there is any situation (past or present) that still troubles you, look for the light lessons. Once you understand the light lessons, you will move towards inner peace. What is the bigger picture here? Why might you have created this? What is the lead you are transmuting into gold – not just for yourself, but for our planet? Trust that everything is unfolding perfectly. Explore different ways of seeing this

situation until you find lessons that move you beyond duality, beyond fear and judgment. Choose lessons that feel soothing, reassuring, loving, awakening and expansive, that help you breathe more freely, that help you weave together the light and the dark.

CHAPTER TEN

Tame Love

Unless we are aflame
with passion's madness
will we ever reach for our dreams
with half-remembered wings, and
fly like Icarus –
and perhaps reach the sun?[1]

Love is the cosmic glue, the grand unified force, the deep substratum of reality. It is the still and eternal which lies beneath the fast-moving, choppy surface of everyday life. Love is our place of belonging, our true home. It reaches for our trembling hand when we are lost in the illusion of separateness. The soul hungers for unconditional love and passion, while the ego vainly seeks love as a place of safety, as an Elysian pool of healing for its fear and insecurity.

Intuitively we know that love holds enormous potential to release our authentic Self, to heal our wounds, to break through our defences, to set us free to be all that we can be. Yet all too often, it is our romantic relationships that deepen our wounds, reinforce our neurotic patterns and imprison us in a small and limited self. As W B Yeats says in a love poem, 'I have spread my dreams under your feet; Tread softly because you tread on my dreams.'[2] Romantic love has an overwhelming power to deliver us into transcendent realms, to transport us to higher levels of awareness, joy and ecstasy – but also to throw us harshly against the rocks, then abandon us like driftwood on the shore.

Throughout the ages, writers, poets and mystics have seen love as crucial to our search for unity, for wholeness, for 'holiness'. We often devalue Eros in our society – dismissing it as mere lust or infatuation, or being cynical about love – but love is a profound and sacred force that pulls us towards deep reality. In *Divine Beauty*, John O'Donohue describes the 'lovely disarray' that comes when we find ourselves deeply attracted to someone, and begin to lose our grip on the accustomed framework of our lives. 'A relentless magnet draws all your thoughts towards it ... You want to erase distance and become one with the flame. You grow innocent and careless ... .'[3] He notes that love might arrive suddenly, as if from nowhere, or emerge slowly and subtly, but it has no regard for social rules and niceties. 'It is always astonishing how love can strike. No context is love-proof, no convention or commitment impervious.' It can certainly explode like a fireball in our lives, and threaten the status quo, but love is always an opportunity for expansion and growth.

Love breaks down the ego's wall of separateness. It reconnects us with our deep Self. It returns us to a state of grace, of oneness – like stumbling with open-mouthed wonder into the Garden of Eden. Without love, we are like crabs without a sea, like gulls without the open sky, like a deadwood fire with no matches to light it. We are merely going through the motions of life.

Thomas Moore reminds us that 'Romantic love has a purpose, an enormous purpose. Its task is to free you from the bubble of practicality and ordinary busyness, to reveal

the fact that you have a soul and that life is far more mysterious than you imagined it to be.'[4] Love rescues us from the
illusion that life is mundane or repetitive, and restores its
sense of mystery and magic. Poet Mary Oliver urges us to
reach out towards love. If you catch even the faintest whiff
of love, she says, you must not hesitate – you must grab your
courage, take up your oars and 'row, row for your life toward
it.'[5]

> *There is life without love. It is not worth a bent penny,*
> *or a scuffed shoe.*
> *It is not worth the body of a dead dog nine days*
> *unburied.*
>
> *Mary Oliver*[6]

Love awakens our soul, swirling us into intense emotions,
fantasies, desire, longing, passion and sensuality. It gives us
renewed hope and vision. When we fall deeply in love, we
see the Beloved in the other. We see beyond the illusion of
their humanity to their 'unremembered wings', the spark of
God within them – and this also connects us with our *own*
divinity, our own wings, our own hidden potential. Our
longing is a holy longing. We sense intuitively that we might
blossom within this union, and become who we were always
meant to be. Love sprinkles everything with stardust. Love is
a million miles from mere friendship or companionship,
from marriages of convenience and practicality, or even from
lust. It sends us spinning into another galaxy. It is blissful and
exhilarating, numinous and mystical. When we fall in love,
we dive into an ocean with our beloved, becoming one with
the waves. We 'lose' the Self we once knew, while also
discovering ourselves anew. Together, we create a synergy
that neither could conjure up alone. In love, we become
mythical creatures who could dance until the end of time.

Yet love's bright and promising invitation also summons

us into the belly of the whale. Real love always calls for inner change, for letting go, for transformation, before it will deliver its gifts. The deeper the promise, the deeper the threat. In order to find true love, we must face our deepest resistance to growth. We must crumble our former ego-self to ashes.

In the film *Notting Hill*, a bookseller in London falls in love with a Hollywood film star. Despite their differences, Cupid has fired his arrows – and the two are pulled together. He belongs to a circle of close friends who show wild love for each other, accepting each other's quirkiness and vulnerabilities without question – whereas the female character has an abusive American boyfriend, and belongs to the superficial world of celebrity, the world of the ego, where authenticity is sacrificed at the altar of appearance, wealth and status. The two go through a period of separation, and the bookseller backs off and licks his wounds. Eventually she arrives at his bookshop and asks to see him again. By now, he has decided the relationship is too risky, that he is bound to be rejected and might never recover. He has fallen prey to his ego's fear and insecurity – and reluctantly says 'No' to her. However, clearly she has been through a period of transformation, and has come to a deeper space within. She assures him that celebrity is just a sham, that she hadn't realised before how much nonsense it is. Instead of responding defensively from her ego, she remains open-hearted, showing the fragile person behind the mask of fame. While accepting his refusal, she says with disarming honesty and vulnerability: 'I'm just a girl, standing in front of a boy, asking him to love her.' She has unpeeled her layers of defences, revealed her authentic Self, and opened herself to the possibility of real love.

Yet we know that the story did not really end there. Romantic love is often idealised love, which is temporarily blind to the human frailties of the other. It is rarely unconditional love, which goes beyond duality. All too often, romantic love turns sour, and fails to fulfil our happy-ever-after dreams. We begin to see 'imperfections' in the other, and want to change and control and fix them. Needs and demands and expectations sidle in. Old riverbeds of relating – patterns based on fear and shame and judgment – start to permeate the relationship, and make loving each other impossible. The passionate and liberating love of the deep Self is elbowed out by the limiting pseudo-love of the ego. Tame love creeps in at the side door with its rattling chains – and the glittering promise of wild love flies out of the window.

❤

The problem is that our habitual ways of relating are based upon surface reality, upon the fragmented world of the ego. We have learned to point the finger 'out there' whenever we feel uncomfortable. We have learned ways of controlling and manipulating others. We have learned to avoid the threat of intimacy. We have learned self-defeating ways of dealing with conflict. We have learned to be good or perfect or helpful or special in order to earn or deserve love. We have learned to hide behind roles and masks. We have learned to hold back. We have learned self-sacrifice and duty and martyrdom, patterns of tame love, energy habits that discon-nect us from Source. These patterns can affect all of our relationships, but if our *primary* relationship is based upon tame love, we are forever imprisoned within the limited ego. We are split off from the greater Love that is calling humanity to awaken.

The ego is only capable of conditional love. It lives in a world of duality. It seeks approval, control and security through its relationships with others – which makes real loving impossible. The ego lurks in the bottom half of the Emotional Scale, so it sabotages its own desires. It is invari-ably moving away from what it wants. Its attempted 'solutions' usually make problems worse. It tries to hold on to someone by clinging to them, or it criticises a partner for not being affectionate enough, so pushing them away, or it avoids facing up to whatever it fears might destroy a relationship. It gaily sows the seeds of self-destruction.

The ego can manage superficial relationships. It can handle buying a newspaper, or chatting with a friend or neighbour. No problem. It can also handle relationships based upon roles – especially unequal roles, such as teaching or nursing or parenting or helping others. But throw it in at the deep end with an intimate relationship, or any emotional conflict or challenge, and it hasn't a clue how to swim. It will throw its weight around and make demands, or use emotions as weapons, or run away and hide, or play a role, or try to please others – none of which can increase love and intimacy, or lead to any higher resolution of conflict. So let us look at what happens when the ego takes charge of our relationships ...

BLAMING, SHAMING AND TAMING

The fear and insecurity of the ego creates co-dependency in relationships. Co-dependency is characterised by COntrol and DEPENDENCY, and it is our biggest problem in personal relationships. It is probably the primary cause of marital breakdown and unhappiness, yet it also explains why so many couples stay together in 'quiet desperation', forsaking their higher dreams and visions. It is an addictive pattern of relating – that is, trying to connect with Source *through the other* – which means becoming over-dependent upon a relationship, then either controlling the other or allowing ourselves to be controlled.

Co-dependency blocks our personal and spiritual growth – yet like any addiction, it is self-perpetuating, trapping us in self-defeating circles from which there seems no escape. It allows no room to breathe. In effect, it says to the other: '*You* need to make me feel safe and secure. *You* need to make me feel special and loved. *You* need to make me feel whole. And I will tame you into doing that for me. And when this (inevitably) fails, I will blame and shame you – or withdraw and distance myself – while still hanging on to you tightly.' Or it says the converse, 'I am not worthy of love, so I will allow you to tame me. You need to tell me how to earn your love, and keep myself safe and secure – by pleasing you, and hiding whatever is bad or wrong with me.'

The ego offers pseudo-love, which comes with conditions, demands and expectations. Conditional love is an oxymoron, since real love simply is. The ego cannot love; it can only offer approval. Tame love. Controlling love. 'Do what I want, and I will love you.' 'Become who I want you to be, and I will love you.' 'Conform to this role, and I will love you.' Conditional love means that we receive love and approval only if we are good and well behaved by someone else's standards. It means that only the 'nice' parts of us are acceptable, or those aspects which fit with our partner's image of us – so we have to stuff away our Shadow side, our not-so-nice emotions, our secret dreams and desires, and either feel guilty about them or project them on to others. It also means squashing anything that is too bright and shiny, too different from the Other, anything which might threaten our partner – our light Shadow, our vast potential. So we become small, shallow and one-dimensional. We fret about what we can and cannot reveal, even to ourselves. Tame love splits us in two, and separates us from our wholeness.

The more conditional the love we receive, the more lonely and disconnected we feel, and the more we long to reconnect with Source. So people in co-dependent relationships often show other addictive behaviours – such as workaholism, alcoholism, eating disorders, compulsive housework or over-busyness. Their emotions – the language of the soul – are ignored or denied or invalidated, so they feel empty and soul-less; they might even feel as if they are dying. At its worst, co-dependency leads to suicidal impulses, since death is the ultimate way to reconnect with unconditional love.

The ego is ruled by judgment and fear – splitting the world into good and bad, right and wrong, safe and dangerous. So whenever we are relating from the ego, we fall into characteristic patterns of relating: namely, *blaming*, *shaming* and *taming*. (Or allowing ourselves to be tamed.)

Blaming: 'You did it to me – and you are in the wrong!' Blaming always comes from self-righteousness – or, as Rumi puts it, 'Anger rises when you are proud of yourself.'[7] The ego is unaware that we evoke behaviour from others according to the radio signals we are sending out, that no-one can 'do' anything to us. It cannot see the bigger picture, the universal dance of co-creation. It lives in a splintered world of duality – so it assumes that, when a situation feels painful, someone is in the right and someone is in the wrong. And it points the finger *out there*! It wants to be the one in the right. The good one. Which makes the other the bad one. The one it is allowed to judge and punish and control.

Blame is higher up the Emotional Scale than guilt – it feels better – so whenever possible, most of us try to blame rather than feel guilty. Blaming also protects us from facing our own sense of guilt. After all, if it's all *your* fault, it can't be *my* fault! *You* are the one who needs to change, and I can hold on to my (fragile) self-image of being perfect. 'You've given me a headache!' 'You've let me down.' 'You never *talk* to me.' Blame is an attempt to control and disempower the other; it is a form of emotional blackmail. Blamers tend to be convinced they are in the right, that their feelings or complaints are justified and reasonable – and will often persuade others of this too (including the one they blame). But right-wrong keeps us in duality, and prevents any higher resolution of conflict. It closes our heart to the inherent goodness in others. It stops us taking adult responsibility. It traps us in a mythical world of goodies and baddies, victims and perpetrators.

Blame says '*I'm* feeling bad, and it's *your* fault!' Of course, this is impossible – since no-one else can control our thoughts and vibrations, which is what our emotions give us feedback about. Instead of taking response-ability for our own feelings, we try to control someone else's behaviour. 'Something out there is making me feel bad – namely you – so I must change or control you.' This is trying to change the world from the outside in. Unless the other person is Self-centred, this guilt-tripping splits their energy. If we make someone else falsely responsible for our feelings, we imprison them. We diminish them. We sow mistrust and resentment. From there, the only likely direction is down-hill.

Anger can be useful as a conscious stepping stone towards higher vibrations – towards vision and passion and hope and love. And when any emotion is expressed cleanly and honestly – without blame – it quickly dissolves. But if anger becomes stuck for more than a few hours or days, it is always controlling and punishing and manipulative, and means we are projecting our falsely perceived 'badness' on to others, or transferring dusty old rage on to a new situation.

> *Anger is always an attempt to control the other through guilt.*
>
> *Chuck Spezzano*[8]

Shaming: 'You are bad and unworthy of love.' Shaming is any behaviour – verbal or non-verbal – which makes the other feel inherently bad, deficient, small or worthless. Like blaming, this can be an effective way of controlling someone else's behaviour, and it gives the Shamer a cheap shot of self-esteem. It tells the other that they are not getting it right, that they are defective (but you are kindly informing them how to change and reform themselves, so they might be worthy of love).

'You promised you'd do this, and you haven't. I can't trust you to do *anything*!'

'You know I can't bear the house being untidy, so why do you leave it like this?'

'Why can't you be more like Jack/Susan?'

'How could you be so selfish and irresponsible?'

'What do you mean, you want more time to yourself? What's *wrong* with you?'

'How can you behave like this, after all I've done for you?'

'Why do you *never* do anything I ask?'

Shaming can happen when a child spills a drink, or a partner comes in late from work, or the TV reports a violent crime or financial mismanagement. It is insecurity looking for a reason to feel 'better' than this other miserable earthworm, in an attempt to soothe your own pain. It comes from wanting to see badness and unworthiness as 'out there', so that you don't have to feel it within yourself.

When we are regularly shamed, our self-esteem is driven into the ground, and we feel more and more guilt-ridden, insecure and worthless. Then we are more and more inclined to cling to the other for security – which is why people often stay in highly abusive relationships. We might try harder and harder to please, but it is impossible to please someone who defends themselves from their own shame by criticising and shaming another. It is a vicious circle that can only be broken by going within, and reconnecting with the Truth of who we are.

Taming: 'Do what I want you to do.' Taming means controlling and manipulating another person through our needs, demands or expectations. (Blaming and shaming are therefore both forms of taming.) Taming says you 'should' or 'ought' to do this. It means feeling *entitled* to have the other behave as you want them to, regardless of their own feelings or needs – as if they were a possession rather than a human being.

'You went out last night, so I want you to stay in tonight.'

'You know it makes me jealous if you talk to other women/men, so don't do it.'

'If you really loved me, you would . . . '

'Do what you like – see if I care.' (*But you'll pay a price if you do.*)

Taming can be as apparently 'benign' as expecting a partner to follow your hobbies and interests, or as plainly abusive as marital rape. It can include telling a partner what to eat, or how and when to exercise, or always needing to know where they are, or wanting them to 'work on their issues', or to share your opinions and beliefs. Taming is quite different from an open and heart-centred request, which says 'I'd like you to do this, but there will be no consequences whatever if you choose otherwise. I want you to be free, and will love you exactly the same.' Tame love means there *are* consequences if you do not conform.

Common methods of taming include criticising, complaining, insulting, disapproving, sulking, sighing, accusing, coercing, bargaining, guilt-tripping, pleading, threatening, mocking, teasing, belittling, humiliating, invalidating, gaslighting,[9] withdrawing, freezing-out, going silent, or withholding affection or sex or money. These are distorted patterns of communication usually learned in childhood. Taming is often subtle and unspoken – but it always aims to control and disempower the other.

Taming means expecting the other to match up to your *image* of an ideal partner (or ideal child, employee or whatever). It says, 'You are not being the person *I* want you to be, and that feels uncomfortable. So I will try to control you, because blaming *you* for my discomfort feels easier than loving you as you are, and having to change myself.' Codependency blinds us to the unique individual with their own needs, feelings and potential; instead we see a cardboard cut-out who is there to meet our ego needs.

Whenever someone is motivated by fear, guilt, duty, obligation, loyalty, resentment, shame or insecurity – or resigns themselves to meeting your needs, or protecting your feelings, at their own expense – the relationship will suffer. (And if you love each other wildly, it simply won't happen.) Being motivated by the ego always leads you in the wrong direction. The voice of fear always leads you away from love. The deep Self will send you negative emotion to warn you that you are heading towards further pain – but you might have learned to live with the discomfort. You have learned to live in a box.

Any form of taming disconnects us from our deep Self, from who we are. A highly taming parent, for example, might say: 'I will love you as long as you follow my religion' or 'I will love you as long as you marry someone I approve of, or choose the career I want for you,' or 'I will love you as long as you are heterosexual.' Or they might expect to be phoned or visited every day or every week. Their children might not give in to such demands, but they know *there will be consequences* if they do not! This is love with strings attached. It is conditional love. Which is not love at all.

Shaming, blaming and taming often go hand in hand: 'You *made* me feel bad, and that makes you a bad person, so you have to make it up to me.' This is emotionally abusive behaviour which bears no relation to loving someone – yet it is inevitable when we are relating from the fearful, needy and shame-based ego. Such patterns sneak into even the most loving relationships occasionally, but if they become a routine occurrence, they build up bitterness and resentment, and begin to wreck whatever love there once was. And they can become a habitual way of relating in *other* relationships too – with colleagues, friends, relatives, neighbours and others.

We mistake so much for love –
neediness, dependence, mere familiarity.
And in reaching out for love, we vanish
into projections of who we should be,
and how our lives should appear.
One day, we wake to face a stranger in the looking-glass –
and know that we abandoned ourselves long ago.
Then, before it is too late, we must find our way home –
and learn the true meaning of love.[10]

CONTROL AND SACRIFICE

Co-dependency is an unequal style of relating in which one person is more in control – one-up, one-down – like parent and child, or professional and client. In personal relationships, this involves repeated cycles of Control-and-Sacrifice. Very often, one person *controls through anger* while the other *sacrifices through guilt*. Sometimes the control comes from hurt, jealousy, frustration, fear or other negative emotions, or simply from fixed roles or expectations, while the sacrifice comes from feelings of anxiety, weakness, shame, neediness or inadequacy. This destructive cycle – taming or being tamed – keeps both people stuck in ego.

Controlling comes from self-righteousness and perfectionism – 'I'm in the right and you're in the wrong,' or 'I'm perfect and you're faulty, imperfect, inadequate, guilty, bad, needy, hopeless or even crazy.' This taming method only works when the other person is willing to be controlled, which comes from old riverbeds of shame, unworthiness and insecurity – 'You're right and I'm wrong.' They give in to demands in order to seek love and approval, to 'redeem' themselves, or to keep the peace, or because they are so out of touch with their own emotions, desires and values that they need to be told who to be.

There is satisfaction for the ego in this toxic blame-shame cycle, so it can become a habitual routine in co-dependent relationships. The self-righteous Controller gets to prop up their fragile self-esteem, and gain some sense of power and control; whereas the guilt-ridden Sacrificer gets to feel virtuous through appeasement and self-denial. However, neither is aligned with Source energy, nor with their authentic Self. The control games of co-dependency disconnect us from the freedom and joy and unconditional love which are our natural birthright – and which are crucial for keeping relationships alive and healthy.

Guilt-tripping is a powerful weapon of control. Sometimes it is verbal – through expressions of rage or blame, or 'failure' to meet the other's expectations. But it is often subtle and non-verbal – a raised eyebrow, a cold shoulder, a stiff hug, walking away, looking hurt, being polite but distant. Just enough to create that twinge in the solar plexus that indicates that your meridians are short-circuiting – so that you feel disempowered, your awareness contracts and you cannot think so clearly. Even if you feel resentful about it, you are more likely to comply with their wishes.

If you grew up with parents (or caretakers) who were co-dependent, these kind of interactions will be familiar, and you will slip into that family-ar groove, however uncomfortable it feels. *You will feel responsible for other people's feelings.* You believe you are doing something wrong if they feel bad, and need to 'make them' feel better. This is a crucial component of the Control-Sacrifice cycle, which is built upon fear and insecurity.

If you are being tamed – even in a mild form – it creates a civil war within you. The ego sees duty, sacrifice and pleasing others as a way of expressing 'love'. But sacrifice is not love; it is an attempt to earn love from one who is not giving love. It means holding back, retreating, fitting in, not being who you are. Appeaser-Pleaser-Sacrificers say: 'If only I can be who he/she wants me to be, I will be loved – and then I will be happy.' They are only too willing to beat themselves up, to blame themselves for any problems in the relationship, or to contort themselves to fit into the (often well-meaning) Blamer-Controller-Fixer's image. However, being loved for pretending to be someone else does not feel like love – for the very good reason that it is not love.

Most taming goes unnoticed, since it is seen as perfectly normal or justifiable by the tamer (and often by the tamed). But whenever we control someone, however subtly, we pay a heavy price. If the other gives in, it leaves them resigned and diminished, or bitter and resentful. Prisoners are not happy people. Prisoners secretly long to escape, and often fantasise about it. They become deeply ambivalent about the relationship. We pick this up in their vibrations, which increases our sense of insecurity – which might make us even more controlling, so they feel even more imprisoned. The noose gets tighter and tighter. If we don't set someone free, we lose them. They might not run away physically, but their vibrations are held in shame, guilt and disempower-ment – so their bright, shining *potential* is locked away. Their energy is split. We lose who they might have become. Their self-esteem and creativity and aliveness are squashed. Their uniqueness is sacrificed. They might try to be good, but they are unable to love with wild abandon. They are only a shadow of the person they might be if we loved them unconditionally.

No-one feels truly loved within a co-dependent rela-tionship, since neither is being real. They are trying to fit the other's image of them, or expecting the other to fit their image – and no-one can *feel* loved if they are living from a false self, if they are trying to please, if they are trying to be good, if they are hiding whatever feels unacceptable to the other, if they feel unable to say No, if they are not being authentic and Self-centred.

Although co-dependency is usually associated with couples, it is common in many other relationships, especially where one person is needy or dependent – such as between an adult child and an elderly or sick relative, or a boss and employee, or a helping professional and a client/patient. (Not surprisingly, most helping professionals and 'carers' have highly co-dependent patterns of relating.)

Co-dependency often leads to an exaggerated sense of responsibility for others – feeling responsible for others' well-being, and even attracting 'lame dogs' to look after. It is common for one person to be depressed, ill, addictive, needy, stuck or inadequate in a co-dependent relationship, while the other might *seem* to be happy, robust and assertive (or the roles might swap around); but in fact, both people are equally trapped. Here, the cycle of Control-Sacrifice has taken the common form of Neediness-Rescuing. One person controls the other through being weak or needy, while the other gets to feel strong and good and worthy by caring for them, or trying to fix, protect or rescue them. But this often just reinforces the other's disconnection from who they are, and further disempowers them. (Even giving reassurance or advice is often a way of trying to 'fix' someone, instead of allowing them to feel what they feel, and be who they are right now. It can be a way of saying 'Don't bother me with your feelings,' or 'Fit my model of how you should think or feel or behave.')

Sometimes the underdog fights back over being controlled – but then often flips into the opposite role, becoming a self-righteous Controller-Fixer. They might criticise or blame the other for their behaviour, make demands, or angrily declare 'I'm not responsible for *your* feelings!' This new 'assertiveness' feels better to them than being controlled or guilt-tripped – it is a little higher up the Emotional Scale – but it is still trying to change relationships from the outside in. It might mark some progress, but it is the same co-dependent dynamic of Control-and-Sacrifice. It is tame love.

Whenever a relationship involves duty, guilt, sacrifice,

dependency, control, perceived inequality, trying to earn love or approval, being over-compassionate or over-giving, suppressing parts of the Self to accommodate the other, pretending, holding back, fulfilling a role, or striving to control or fix or rescue someone, it is co-dependent – which means it is limiting freedom and individuation for both people. And to the extent that any relationship is co-dependent, it will be dysfunctional. That is guaranteed.

> *Only when neither person feels like they're losing, giving in or giving up, do both people benefit from the action.*
>
> *Marshall B Rosenberg[11]*

BULLYING AND ABUSE

At one extreme, blaming, shaming and taming tip into bullying or serious abuse. Bullying is about as far away from love as a relationship can go, yet it is frighteningly common in intimate relationships – as well as at work, and between parents and children. This is the darkest face of tame love, often hidden behind closed doors and veiled in shame and secrecy.

Like Dr Jekyll and Mr Hyde, those who bully can seem charming and self-assured in public; in fact, they often have a strong need to appear wonderful, caring and perfect to others. Yet they can be relentlessly critical, fault-finding, nit-picking, cold, rejecting, mistrustful, evasive, controlling or punishing in private. They might swing between cold-shouldering or belittling the other, then idealising them – being nasty or aggressive, then super-nice or remorseful – as they flip between images of them as good or bad. Some bullies fly into a rage unpredictably, leaving the other reluctant to raise any difficult issues; or they twist and distort what the other says. If the other person reacts by closing down or withdrawing to protect themselves, this only draws further blame or criticism.

Bullying always comes from insecurity – wanting to be in control, wanting to feel safe, wanting to feel better than the other. A bully *wants* others to feel guilty, anxious, ashamed, remorseful or inadequate since – as religion discovered long ago – this allows them to be in control. It also makes them feel good and worthy by comparison. They might expect a partner to keep the house immaculate, or to have sex by the calendar, or put strict limits on how and when the other is permitted to meet others or go out alone. They might control their access to money, or block them from earning. They might threaten to cut off the children or kill themselves if a partner leaves. Or they might simply have fixed ideas about how a partner (or child, or employee) 'should' behave, think or even feel. Bullies often manage to convince the Other that they are right, and if challenged, will stoutly defend themselves – even when their own statements or demands border on craziness. (I remember one client whose controlling husband insisted she only wear white, offering 'spiritual' reasons for this strange demand.)

Last year, I saw a young woman whose boyfriend would not allow her to speak to other men, soon after they began dating. After a few months, he would not permit her to look at other men – and would control her in public with threatening glances. Soon after, he began hitting her in order to stay in control. By this time, she was becoming suicidal. Although this is an extreme example of abuse, emotional abuse can be even more damaging and insidious than violence, since it is more subtle and easily hidden, and often continues for years without being challenged.[12]

When women are controlling, it is often indirect and manipulative – such as looking hurt, sulking, sighing, shrugging, going silent, being cold and rejecting, making sarcastic comments and jibes, banging pots in the kitchen, refusing to discuss an issue, or bursting into tears. Men are often more directly abusive – making demands, throwing their weight around, shouting, accusing, threatening, or browbeating the other into submission.

Whenever someone tries to make another feel wrong, faulty or inadequate, holds them responsible for their own emotions, tries to control their behaviour or shape their thinking, or invalidates the other's feelings and desires, they are shaming, blaming and taming. And if this becomes frequent or extreme, then it is abusive. Abuse means controlling someone through fear, shame or guilt to conform to *your* expectations; or wanting them to protect *your* feelings; or trying to make them feel bad so that you can feel better.

Most bullies feel quite innocent, seeing their feelings, actions and demands as justified and acceptable: 'I'm doing it for the children's sake.' 'He behaved badly, so I have a right to punish him.' 'Of *course* she should put my feelings first. She's my wife.' 'He's just not pulling his weight.' 'It's for her own good.' 'He's lucky I put up with him.' People are always well intentioned from their own perspective, and genuinely believe that the Other is the problem. (Look at world governments who send in bombs, tanks and armies to 'protect' the world against evil!) Bullies often feel trapped and victimised themselves, and see the Other as the bad, defective or hopeless one; men or women who feel 'trapped' into a relationship by unexpected pregnancy, for example, often fall into bullying. And the roles of Controller and Sacrificer, or Bully and Victim, often do rotate; it becomes a vicious circle of mutual abuse, closed-down and self-defeating behaviour in which everyone feels stuck.

If you're being abused emotionally, you might try to convince yourself and others that all is well, but you feel increasingly anxious, shameful, guilt-ridden and powerless – and your own identity is slowly eroded. Abuse tends to remain secretive. You might be gagged through loyalty, cut off from anyone who might listen or be supportive, or even threatened; or the abuser might imply that the problems only occur because you are not yet up to scratch, or just deny that anything is amiss. You try harder and harder to 'get it right', to please or protect the other, to make excuses for them or pussyfoot around their feelings; but this merely makes the problem worse, since it reinforces the underlying pattern of Control–Sacrifice. Many 'victims' become more and more *self*-abusive – controlling themselves through fear, shame and guilt, or becoming depressed. In time, they often become virtually unable to make a decision for themselves, having squeezed themselves so tightly into someone else's mould that they have almost vanished from sight.

Such abusive patterns are only possible when we are stuck in surface reality – when we are trying to control the world from the outside in, and either trying to keep someone else in the 'one-down' position so that we can feel 'one-up', or trying to prove ourselves worthy of love. We are lost in fear, shame and judgment. We have forgotten that we are all gods and goddesses, that everyone is good and worthy and loved, that all is well.

I suggest you pause now and reflect on whether you control anyone, or allow yourself to be controlled. If you ever feel anxious about returning home, wondering what the atmosphere will be like, or are fearful about sharing your feelings or needs with your partner (or anyone else), or discussing a difficult issue, or get a sinking feeling at the thought of being alone with someone, or at the prospect of spending the rest of your life with your partner, then you are probably being severely tamed. And if *anything* happens in private that you would feel ashamed or reluctant to share with a close friend, or which it would feel 'disloyal' to talk about openly, it is quite likely that abuse is going on.

How does anyone come to tolerate abusive behaviour, and even confuse it with love? Because it is a family-ar riverbed of relating. If you come from a family in which blaming, shaming and taming was part of everyday life, then it becomes invisible to you. Your vibrations will attract someone who resonates with your patterns; and you will even attract friends or colleagues who mirror those patterns of relating. Your emotional guidance will warn you that something is wrong – but you have found ways of numbing yourself to the pain, as you did in childhood, or have learned to ignore your emotions. Or you see shame or guilt as a sign that you are 'getting it wrong', and must try even harder to please. You might believe you do not deserve any better, or that all relationships are the same and you just have to 'work' at them. Those who are bullied tend to be over-nice, over-tolerant and over-loyal; they often scuttle around trying to be supportive – perhaps following in the footsteps of an abused parent. Over time, their self-esteem might become too damaged for them to protest, seek help or make a break for freedom. Abuse splinters our energy, and makes our awareness contract.

Those who fall into controlling or bullying are not bad people. They have simply been shamed and tamed themselves, and often believe they are doing what is best, and are trying to 'improve' the Other, or to cope with a difficult relationship. In practice, they are struggling with their own fear, rage, pain and insecurity, which usually dates back to childhood (and to past generations).

There are no victims. Just as there are no villains. There cannot be any 'injustice' in a world which operates on the Law of Attraction. Bullies attract victims. The self-righteous attract guilt-ridden martyrs. Fear and insecurity attracts threat. Our relationships always mirror the vibrations we are emitting; we attract whatever we expect or feel we deserve. This is not about blaming bullies, or shaming anyone for putting up with it. It is all about awareness. Everything is unfolding perfectly. The pain and contrast of co-dependency launches huge desires for relationships to be truly loving – to feel warm and wonderful, to feel safe and relaxing, to feel liberating and joyful, to feel inspiring and stimulating. As they are meant to be. And it is through our fresh desires and visions that the world changes.

THE PRISON OF CO-DEPENDENCY

When we are co-dependent, we tend to become over-dependent upon one relationship – and insist on having a 'special' and exclusive relationship with that other person. (This is often an attempt to heal a childhood wound of not feeling loved enough.) 'You must love me to the exclusion of all others,' says the ego. 'You must prove your love to me. I must be your one-and-only. You must find no-one else attractive, and treat no-one else as special. You must have no space in your heart for anyone but me. And you must jump through all these hoops to satisfy me of your love.' The ego does not *feel* loved and secure, so it must 'get' love and security from the Other – which means taming them.

When we are self-centred – in an expansive state of awareness – we are connected to unconditional love for self and others. Then we give love freely, without demands, and create loving relationships from the inside out. We know that we can *never* be abandoned, rejected or unloved – whatever happens 'out there' – since our connection to Love is indissoluble. When we are self-centred in a small, fearful, egotistical way, on the other hand, we feel disconnected from Source – so we become needy and possessive and insecure. We try to change relationships from the outside in. ('Gimme, gimme, gimme,' says the ego.) We believe that there is not enough love to go round, so we must cling to it tightly, like a schoolchild who says 'You're *my* best friend,' and tries to exclude all others. And since our vibrations are saying '*You* don't love me enough,' we evoke behaviour from the Other that increases our fear of abandonment.

A Course in Miracles distinguishes clearly between a 'special relationship' based on the ego's fear and insecurity, and a 'holy relationship' that comes from two whole (holy) individuals who respect each other's freedom and individuality, and who reach out to the world with love. 'Love is freedom', says *A Course*, yet it notes that the ego always controls through guilt, keeping others bound and wanting love to be exclusive.

Our ego-based culture strongly supports this idea of love being exclusive and restrictive. In a materialistic culture that defines us by our possessions and roles, a partner can easily become another 'belonging' we own and display to the world, rather than a unique human being. And we can slip into playing this social role of partner/husband/wife, knuckling down to 'commitment' (with a heavy heart), and ignoring our divine discontent.

> You will be home tonight, you will park your body
> here and here only, you will deny yourself experiences
> that take you on a journey outside the box we
> live in, and you will pretend that this is what you
> really want. Most significantly, you will feel guilty
> if you find yourself thinking otherwise. And you
> will agree that I have every right to be outraged
> if I find you not toeing the line.
>
> *Marianne Williamson*[13]

Why do we still pretend that such limiting demands are acceptable? This tame, conventional model of marriage is not working any more, if ever it did. Our souls are longing to expand to a new level of freedom and awareness – and our definition of love has to expand, too. The 'security' of a co-dependent relationship comes to feel like a prison, since it locks out the deep Self. It feels shallow and unreal, and makes us small and child-like. It blocks our spiritual potential. It excludes anyone or anything that might be seen as a threat. It is like running in a three-legged race. The more it clings and demands, the more it excludes any possibility of real love. If we keep love under lock and key, it becomes thin, frail and splintered – and turns into bitterness and resentment, or resignation and despair. Co-dependency holds us spluttering beneath the waves. Not waving, but drowning.

At an energy level, tame love turns us into flickering light-bulbs with scattered energies cancelling each other out, instead of being brilliant laser beams. It constantly pulls us off-centre into meeting others' needs and demands. We become split internally into 'good' (what suits the Other) and 'bad' (what doesn't suit the Other). We stop trusting our emotional guidance, and so lose touch with our authentic Self. We might fall into rigid and obsessive routines. Life begins to feel mundane and humdrum. We are trapped in a broom cupboard instead of roaming the wide universe. Our freedom is left whimpering at the door. Caged animals show dysfunctional behaviour – becoming depressed, anxious or aggressive, or developing repetitive rituals – and so do we when we feel imprisoned. Our emotions send warning signals that something is wrong, but tension or guilt or in-security or depression or panic attacks (or even physical illness) might make us cling ever more tightly to the rela-tionship, rather than seeing it as the *cause* of our divine discontent.

No-one can really love you who is taming you, since you are giving off vibrations of neediness and insecurity – vibrations which say 'I am not lovable as I am, but if I jump through this hoop, will you love me? If I show you only my nice bits, will you love me? How about if I sacrifice myself in this way?' And the Other responds to your shame-based vibrations, and mirrors back your sense of unworthiness; or they lose respect for you since you are so easily controlled. Love slowly withers and dies. Taming someone is always a pyrrhic victory. It can only result in increased co-dependency, not love. It reinforces neediness, dependency and denial – and makes you both feel trapped and resentful.

Paradoxically, anyone we control becomes dull and unat-tractive to us. If it is a romantic relationship, we might cling to them for security, but we no longer feel passion and desire for them. When we control someone, it becomes like a parent-child or master-slave relationship, so attraction and romance fades. And if we *feel* controlled, the loss of control involved in sexual passion becomes too threatening. Passion is right at the top of the Emotional Scale (see chapter 6) alongside unconditional love – but co-dependency keeps us in the bottom half of the Scale. Tame love inevitably means tame and disappointing sex, or even an absence of sex. Sex becomes a 'performance' or habit or expectation – ego-based sexuality – instead of a blissful and intimate act of union, a heavenly merging of cosmic love and earthy sensuality.

Our culture sees such changes as 'normal' in a romantic partnership. ('Passion always fades after a while.' 'You can't expect romance to last.') Most marital counselling also sees it as normal and acceptable to make demands and expectations of someone who has taken on the role of partner, to feel 'entitled' to have them behave as we want them to, and to restrict their freedom in various ways. *But love does not mean controlling someone. And love does not mean having to sacrifice yourself for others.* That is taming, or being tamed. And tame love is not love at all.

Yet our society strongly reinforces tame love. Why? Because it mirrors the old paradigm, the limitations of surface reality, the fragmented world of the ego. And it is a useful agent of social control. Like traditional religion, it numbs and disempowers people. Tame love supports the status quo – placing an emphasis on conservative and head-based values such as loyalty, commitment, duty and conformity. It steers us away from the heart. It denies us mystery and magic. When we relate from the ego, we are trapped at the lower end of the Emotional Scale: in fear, blame, guilt, anger, resentment, loneliness, jealousy, possessiveness, insecurity, stoicism, martyrdom, addictions, feelings of unworthiness, numbness or despair. And we come to believe that love hurts.

Co-dependency stops us growing wild and free. It is creeping and insidious, like a weed which spreads from roots underground – and makes it impossible for us to thrive and blossom. When we try to tame love, we mangle it into a weak and crippled silhouette of itself. It often creates a public face of happy-togetherness and a private tragedy of pretence, distance, denial, struggle, shame, disappointment and stifled dreams. It can make people feel as if they are dying, since their true Self is being suffocated. Co-dependency drags us away from the depth and passion of the soul, and leaves us tiptoeing on the surface of life.

> *Strange how roles can mould us*
> *into certain shapes,*
> *limiting, distorting our growth, stripping us*
> *of depth and dimensionality,*
> *restricting us to thimble-sized pots.*

> *In becoming 'wife' or 'father', 'manager' or 'priest',*
> *an outer skin is formed with an empty smile –*
> *unlike the free spirit we once knew –*
> *a skin which grows thicker by the year, hemmed in*
> *by expectations, needs, demands,*
> *even ownership each of the other.*

> *Such roles may alight on our shoulders*
> *like an albatross –*
> *unseen, yet heavy and burdensome,*
> *taking all lightness from our step.*
> *Hardly daring to converse with ourselves any more.*
> *Knowing a precious world is lost to us,*
> *we secretly fear dying before we have lived.*[14]

AVOIDING INTIMACY

Co-dependency evokes our ego defences, which makes intimacy feel threatening, and conflict almost impossible to handle. As a result, we avoid intimacy through merging, distancing or triangulation.

Merging (or fusion, or enmeshment) means pretending to agree, denying any problems, avoiding in-depth discussions and lacking clear boundaries – becoming one person rather than two individuals. Couples who are merged rarely argue, and tend to say 'We' a lot. ('Anything for the sake of peace' is their motto.) They cling and smother and suffocate each other. Merging is a form of pseudo-intimacy which means suppressing parts of the self that are different from the other or do not fit their image of us, suppressing individuality and uniqueness, to avoid any risk of conflict. Another way to avoid intimacy is *distancing* – that is, busily focusing on work, parenting or other activities; perhaps occupying the same time and space while showing less and less closeness, emotional sharing or affection; or simply spending little time alone together; or even deliberately creating arguments to avoid the threat of intimacy.

Many couples swing between merging and distancing, never finding their way through their defences, locking each other into a lonely stalemate for years on end – like the sad long-married couples who sit in mournful silence in a café, not because they have nothing to say to each other, but because a wasteland of the unspoken stretches between them.

Co-dependency also leads to *triangulation* – in which a third party becomes the focus for concern or anger or hope, and any conflict between the couple is 'detoured' and avoided by focusing on a sick or troubled child, a difficult colleague, an elderly parent, financial worries, redecorating the house, serious illness or addiction, strife with an ex-partner or a love triangle. The unresolved conflicts between the couple are then swept under the carpet in favour of dealing with more manageable or pressing concerns, or their rage at each other is projected on to someone or something else, so that they can pull together against a common enemy (or scapegoat).

This often creates a classic 'drama triangle' in which people or situations take on the roles of Victim, Rescuer and Persecutor. These roles tend to swap around – so that someone who is pulled in to help with a situation ends up being blamed and persecuted. For example, a child becomes seriously ill and a hospital becomes the hero-rescuer, with the illness as the persecutor; then the child dies, and the hospital is accused of negligence. Drama triangles rely upon the good-bad splitting of the ego, and the false concept of victimhood – and they thrive on blame, guilt and judgment.

Whenever we try to help someone by seeing them as a helpless victim, or as inadequate, or feeling sorry for them, or believing we know better than them, or even wanting to make them happy (at our own expense), we are 'rescuing' rather than empowering them. We are not seeing them as the magnificent being of Light they are. Rescuing is not helping; it is not empowering. It always has a hidden agenda – such as wanting to be seen as good or loving or wise or heroic – and since it comes from ego, any attempt to 'help' is likely to backfire.

I remember an aunt of mine whose mother often threatened suicide. One day, after her mother said (yet again) that she wanted to throw herself in the nearby lake, something snapped. Instead of being sympathetic and trying to 'help', my aunt picked up their coats and led her mother towards the door. 'Where are we going?' asked her mother. 'To the lake,' said my aunt. Her mother suddenly changed her mind about wanting to die! My aunt was no longer playing the game of the drama triangle – with its rotating roles of Victim, Persecutor and Rescuer – but was instead giving her mother the responsibility of adult choice. This shifted them both (at least temporarily) out of the control games of co-dependency, and into a more mature style of relating.

DEALING WITH CONFLICT

In a healthy and loving relationship, conflict is seen as an expression of individuality, which can increase intimacy and help the relationship to deepen and mature – but the ego sees conflict or difference as a threat. Conflict rapidly activates the triple warmer (see chapter 4) – which blindly presses the emergency button, and sweeps into action. Danger! Red alert! We go into attack or defence mode – which leads to blaming, shaming and taming. Since these patterns are painful, the Other learns to tread on eggshells around us, not wanting to challenge or 'upset' us – so conversation remains polite, safe and superficial.

As a result, much of the emotional communication in co-dependent relationships is indirect, skewed or non-verbal – dropping hints, second-guessing, martyred sighs, grimaces, shrugs, silences, glances, frozen smiles and frowns, all of which have to be interpreted by 'mind-reading', or might be contradicted by what is said verbally. ('No, I don't mind,' with a mournful face. 'Whatever you say, dear,' with a sarcastic smile. 'Do whatever you like,' with an undertone of threat.) If you grew up with crazy-making no-win messages like this – which is likely if you choose a partner who communicates in this way – you are unlikely to ask openly 'What do you mean by that? It feels confusing.' You will probably just bend to the unspoken taming, as you did when you were a child.

Open and honest communication about our needs and emotions feels risky in the presence of tame love, since there is a constant threat of being controlled or guilt-tripped, or having our feelings or desires labelled as bad or inappropriate or even mad. This tends to block honest communication in *all* our relationships. It feels too dangerous to be vulnerable. Any hint of openness or intimacy feels threatening.

If we are cut off from the deep Self, our feelings are habitually suppressed or ignored or misinterpreted, so when they do eventually surface, we tend to over-react. We respond to current situations with over-blown fear, hurt or rage that belongs to the past. An unmade bed turns into complaints of utter selfishness and 'not loving me'. A glance at an attractive man or woman leads to enraged accusations about wanting to have an affair, or not being 'committed'. Failing to express admiration for a new outfit triggers fear and insecurity about whether the other really loves us any more. Our energy system gets short-circuited, and we go into a characteristic knee-jerk reaction.

The triple warmer is dualistic, like the ego. It sees the world as divided into good and bad, right and wrong, safe and dangerous. And if I am right, then you must be wrong. Or someone else must be wrong. The ego is always in a power struggle. Win-win solutions are nowhere in sight when the triple warmer is activated, since there is too much fear around. There has to be a winner and a loser – and that means someone being in control, and the other in sacrifice. Everyone is stuck in the bottom half of the Emotional Scale, where negative emotion is issuing a red alert that we are currently attracting what we do *not* want. But the triple warmer is too frightened to listen. It begins to short-circuit other meridians, cutting off more and more Source energy, and going into a downward spiral.

When faced with conflict, the triple warmer activates one of three reactions: fight, flight or freeze. It is easy to see how these lead to blaming, shaming and taming in relationships:

✧ **Fight** – Feeling righteous anger, blaming, shaming, seeing the Other as in the wrong, going into battle, controlling, manipulating, taming, complaining, criticising, making demands.

✧ **Flight** – Withdrawing, running away, hiding your feelings, avoiding the issue, pretending everything is fine, rationalising, defending or justifying yourself, sacrificing your own needs, being over-compassionate, giving in, merging, pretending to agree.

✧ **Freeze** – Feeling overwhelmed, paralysed, stuck, numb, guilty, anxious, panicky, depressed, unable to speak clearly or take positive action.

If someone goes into Fight mode – the typical response of our 'masculine' energy – it tends to activate corresponding defensive or offensive action from others. They might go into Fight themselves, resulting in a shouting match or a violent argument, perhaps culminating in Flight as one party exits and doors are slammed. Or the other might go into Flight – the more 'feminine' mode – agreeing that they are 'in the wrong', feeling guilt-ridden and inadequate, giving in, or trying to explain and justify themselves; or backing off and refusing to discuss the issue. Or they might panic and Freeze (also 'feminine') – silently withdrawing into themselves, or feeling unable to speak.

Fight, Flight or Freeze cannot possibly resolve a conflict, since everyone is locked into a dualistic world view, feeling threatened and unloved. One makes demands; the other withdraws. One complains and criticises; the other defends and justifies. One feels angry; the other feels guilty (and goes into sacrifice). The sad truth is that both people are asking for love – yet love is nowhere within reach. Since both are feeling negative emotion, self-sabotage is guaranteed. The relationship grows weaker and thinner – and the resulting insecurity often makes us cling even tighter. This creates a tragic but often lasting relationship.

Love brings out the best in us, whereas co-dependency brings out the worst in us. It makes us attack or defend. It closes the drawbridge to deep reality. It makes our awareness contract. If any resolution is reached, it will be an uneasy compromise based upon Control-Sacrifice, or Neediness-Caretaking. No wonder that co-dependent couples tend to avoid conflict through merging, distancing or triangulating.

Conflict resolution is almost impossible from the ego. There is no softening, no tenderness, no vulnerability, no authenticity, no depth, no mature response-ability, no real connection. We cannot resolve problems at the level at which they are created – so we cannot heal relationships while stuck in the immature ego.

Only the deep Self knows how to reach out and connect – how to be fully present. Only the deep Self can put itself in the other's shoes, and listen from the heart. Only the deep Self knows that there are no enemies, that everyone and everything is good and innocent. Only the deep Self knows that there is no Other, that we are all one, that any conflict with another symbolises an inner conflict which we need to resolve. Only the deep Self can find a way through conflict to higher resolution. Only the deep Self can offer a safe space for the mature ego to speak openly. Only the deep Self can offer unconditional love – which transcends fear and judgment, keeps Source energy flowing, and stops us going into a red-alert mode which blocks communication.

THE SACRED MARRIAGE

When two Self-centred people come into any kind of relationship, they neither control the other nor allow themselves to be controlled; they are equals who honour themselves as they honour each other. As I see it, control represents unbalanced (too-strong) masculine energy, while sacrifice is an expression of unbalanced (too-weak) feminine energy. Co-dependency reflects the imbalances in our patriarchal society, which suppress divine masculine and divine feminine energy. And when our energy is out of balance, we tread on each other's garden hose, and strangle each other's life force. In co-dependency, we cycle endlessly between anger and guilt, control and sacrifice, distancing and merging – trapped in the soul-destroying treadmills of the ego. This makes it impossible to really love each other, or create true intimacy.

Some people are so severely co-dependent that they are easily influenced by anyone and everyone, and might seem chameleon-like to others. They absorb the vibrations of other people like sponges. They take on others' beliefs, opinions and values as if they were their own, or say whatever they imagine the Other wants to hear, or whatever will avoid conflict or keep them 'out of trouble'. But inside, they feel empty and lost. They are in permanent Sacrifice mode, being tossed around on the rough seas of other people's needs and interests, and alienated from their true Self.

In any relationship, you will tend to go into Sacrifice if you feel 'not good enough' for the Other, or if you have less power, money, education or social status, or if you have more feminine energy (that is, you are more emotional, intuitive and relationship-oriented). If you have stronger masculine energy (which doesn't necessarily mean being male, but being more left-brained, logical, assertive or competitive than the Other), you will tend to go into Control. And whenever you slip into Control-Sacrifice, you are both in ego and the relationship becomes dysfunctional.

What can prevent a relationship (or any personal interaction) spiralling down into ego-based patterns?

✧ Firstly, the presence of unconditional love – which sees everyone as good, which makes no judgment; and which sees no inequality, no power differences, a love which sees the Other as equal in every way. (The ego readily labels others as 'better than' or 'less than' oneself, whereas the deep Self is blind to inequality. Whether it sees a street urchin or a princess, a monk or a mass murderer, it sees only Source energy expressing itself – or being resisted – in a myriad different forms.)

✧ Secondly, the utter commitment to trusting your emotional guidance – the God within – so that you stay connected to Source energy, and take 100 per cent responsibility for your own experience and feelings.

In other words, what heals any relationship is wild love: connecting to your deep Self. *Without the deep Self, without the divine feminine, there is only tame love.*

The mundane feminine – the weak, unbalanced feminine energy of a patriarchal society – either uses emotions as weapons to control and manipulate others, or sacrifices itself to others' feelings, needs and demands, since it feels small and disempowered. It has forgotten that you are an apprentice god, that everything 'out there' mirrors your own vibrations. The *divine* feminine, on the other hand, sends you wild dreams and desires – and uses emotions as inner guidance, as information about how aligned you are with Source.

The mundane masculine is ruled by fear and judgment; it tries to control through bludgeoning force and rational assertion and external power and exclusion, and it splits the world into good/bad and safe/dangerous. The *divine* masculine, by contrast – the mature ego – takes action which is inspired by the deep Self, based upon believing in your dreams, having clear boundaries, and moving towards what you desire as an individual, rather than pushing *against* what you do not want.

As you move towards a sacred marriage of the divine masculine and divine feminine *within you*, you can create truly loving relationships with everyone. Wildly loving. And your life is transformed.

FREEDOM AND COMMITMENT

> *Freedom is creation, because it is love.*
> *Whom you seek to imprison you do not love.*
>
> ***A Course In Miracles***[15]

'Fear of commitment' is often bandied around as if it were some strange disease – especially among men – but I believe this is a bogus issue. *Where there is real love, there is no fear.* The problem is that most romantic partnerships are not based upon a sacred marriage of the divine feminine and divine masculine, but upon looking for approval, control and security through the Other – and therefore falling into Control-Sacrifice.

Marriage is meant to be a romantic and sexual partnership with our most intimate, loving and supportive friend – the person we love and adore in every respect – yet all too often, it becomes 'a prison based on guilt and ownership'.[16] Not a wild and sacred marriage, but a tame and mundane marriage. Both partners sacrifice their own freedom, depth and potential for a sense of belonging, security and companionship. The walls might be invisible, but the feeling of emptiness, the holding back, the sense of resignation, is all too obvious. For many people, marriage means staying together however miserable and wretched you are, however shallow or disappointing it is, however little warmth and affection it offers, and however much it limits your freedom and growth. If we commit ourselves 'until death us do part', it seems to give us frightening licence to place demands and expectations upon the other which limit and ensnare us.

Commitment can be used as a weapon to guilt-trip someone into conformity. It leads to such absurdities as having a permanent and exclusive sexual relationship with someone who does not enjoy making love with you; or being *expected* to spend most of your free time with one person; or having to 'seek permission' to meet friends or have time to yourself. In past generations, such rules and restrictions were perhaps acceptable – but in the 21st century, we need to move beyond this prison of co-dependency into liberating, co-creative and loving relationships that meet our needs for emotional intimacy, passion, sensuality, sexuality, fun and romance, while also supporting our freedom, joy and spiritual growth.

Thomas Moore[17] even questions whether love is compatible with the idea of commitment – and if commitment means a fixed form, I certainly agree. Commitment can be just another word for co-dependency. Spiritual teacher Denise Linn[18] reports that her own marriage vows promised they would remain together 'for as long as it is good', which she felt content to agree to – and perhaps all marriage vows should be limited to this. If real love goes hand in hand with freedom, then it must be forever open to the possibility of changing its form. Our desires are ever-evolving, and our relationships must always be so. Nothing is static and fixed. Love is eternal, but it is always liberating and expansive; it can never imprison the Other. It must be constantly renewed and kept alive on the basis of how it *feels* to be together – rather than being frozen in time because you have made a 'commitment', or have a shared commitment to parenting, and will grit your teeth and carry on together regardless. (When children are used as the glue for dysfunctional relationships, *everyone* suffers – and the 'chain of pain' is passed on – as we shall see in the next chapter.)

This does not mean running away from issues or pain; nor does it mean giving up when you hit a difficult patch; but it does mean being committed to real *loving* – to being authentic with each other, fearlessly connecting at the deepest level, sharing your dreams and visions, being kind and caring (without sacrificing yourself), being warm and affectionate, having fun together, loving the other in all their darkness and light, and being committed to your own growth, individually and together. It means being on an ever-unfolding journey – and being willing to let go if unhealthy riverbeds run too deep, or you need to grow in different directions. Real love means living on the edge of adventure. Only the ego needs promises and guarantees and security. The soul needs to be wild and free – and if we really love someone, we want them to fly free.

 PRACTICAL SUGGESTIONS

1. Consider your primary relationship or other significant relationships in your life, past or present. Which emotions do these relationships tend to evoke in you? Love, freedom, expansion, relaxation, inspiration, warmth and joy? Or less positive emotions? Do you control or sacrifice? Do you tend to fall into blaming and criticising others, or trying to control others and make demands – however 'reasonable and justifiable' this seems to you? Or do you fall into guilt, insecurity and feelings of unworthiness, striving to please or rescue others at your own expense – allowing yourself to be tamed? Do you hold others responsible for your feelings? Do you ever deny problems and feign happiness? How do you handle conflict, especially when emotions run high? Do you avoid conflict altogether, withdraw when challenged, go into battle, defend and justify yourself, or take refuge in victimhood? Do you project your perceived badness on to the outside world, choosing 'enemies' whom you then criticise, avoid, or feel persecuted by? What are your riverbeds of relating?

2. Next time you are aware of repeating an old pattern, press

the 'pause' button – and make a new choice. Remind yourself that you are safe and loved, and that everyone is good and worthy. Imagine yourself expanding. Breathe deeply and relax. Move beyond fear and judgment. Now – how can you reach out with love? What would love say or do in this situation?

CHAPTER ELEVEN

Riverbeds of Relating

It is remarkable how often the family is experienced on two levels: the façade of happiness and normality, and the behind-the-scenes reality of craziness and abuse.

Thomas Moore[1]

In the film *Ordinary People*, a family is slowly disintegrating in the wake of a boating accident in which their elder son was drowned. The younger son, who blames himself for his brother's death, has attempted suicide. As he goes into therapy, it slowly becomes clear that the mother has split her feelings – that she idolised the 'perfect' son who died, while demonising her living son. She is lost in her projections and defences, which are blocking any possibility of intimacy or vulnerability. On the surface, the mother seems smiling and happy – but she is the family member who is most disturbed, most afraid, most alienated from herself and others. She blocks open and honest communication. She blocks the flowing expression of love. We learn that she didn't cry at her child's funeral. Her husband and son are both willing to face their intense emotions, to accept what has happened, to move on – and they courageously go

through their anguish to the warmth and love that reconnects them. But the mother suppresses her emotions or
blames them on others, refusing to grow and change. By
trying to 'protect' herself from pain, she has withdrawn from
love, and eventually isolates herself as the family breaks up.

How we learn to handle our emotions – either in childhood, or later in life – is a key to whether our relationships
are tame or wild. If we squash and deny our feelings, or
project our dark Shadow on to others, or sacrifice our own
emotions and desires, or hold others responsible for what we
feel or experience, our personal relationships are unlikely to
be loving and fulfilling. We will control and imprison others,
or allow ourselves to be tamed, or see intimacy as threatening and keep our distance. It is only when we reclaim the
divine feminine – when we trust our emotional and intuitive guidance, and restore faith in a Source of unconditional
love – that loving and authentic relationships become
possible. Without the divine feminine, all that remains is
tame love – the pseudo-love of the ego, which fractures and
divides us.

Yet the riverbeds of relating which have flowed down the
generations are based upon the old gods of conditional love.
Patriarchal gods. Gods of shame and unworthiness. Gods of
rage and judgment. Gods of guilt, control and conformity.
And these gods have built foundations for personal relationships which split and divide us, that support the ego at the
expense of the deep Self.

❤

It is a sad truism that *we mistake for love whatever we received in
childhood*. If we were neglected as children, we associate love
with neglect. If a parent was a martyr, we link love with guilt
and self-sacrifice. If a parent was critical or intolerant, we
expect to shame and control those we love, or to be
controlled. If a parent was absent, dead or withdrawn, we

associate love with distance or abandonment. If a parent smothered or over-protected us, love means lack of freedom. If a parent or caretaker was abusive, we confuse love with emotional or physical abuse. If a parent constantly worried and fretted over us, we link love with worry and anxiety.

As a result, we often choose relationships with those who will deepen our wounds, support our defences, numb and deaden us, and block us from deep reality. Many people ignore the warning bells which ring as they embark on such relationships, and even marry the person, perhaps only waking up after they have children (if at all). It feels 'comfortable' to live with what we are used to, even if it isn't love – and as children, we assume that whatever we see, hear and *feel* between our parents (or caretakers) is what is normal and healthy. So we often mimic our parents' marriage, or replicate our relationship with one parent, especially in an early or first marriage. (By the Law of Attraction, we also gather friends and acquaintances around us who mirror the same patterns and beliefs, so we can reassure ourselves that we are 'normal'.)

Research has shown that we can identify someone with similar family dynamics, in the midst of a crowded room, in a matter of minutes. We are unconsciously drawn towards them. We have energetic antennae that are attuned to those who 'feel' like our family of origin. The ego thinks, 'Great, I can use my usual defences with this person, and stay safe.' And the deep Self thinks, 'This person will bring up my old patterns, so that I have an opportunity for growth.' So the initial attraction that we feel towards a potential partner often arises from having similar or complementary defences. They feel family-ar, and will echo our childhood patterns. Then we project the same feelings on to them as we had towards a parent, and evoke the same behaviour from them. We keep on repeating the past.

The reality is that most parents want their children to be happy, and *not* to suffer their fate or repeat their mistakes. Yet family patterns, unfinished business and unresolved emotion are repeated through the generations – and often without any awareness of what we are doing. The 'survivor guilt' that afflicts the descendants of those who died in concentration camps is a well-known example of this. We feel guilty about being happy if parents or other relatives have suffered – so we invite misfortune or tragedy into our lives, or sabotage our own happiness; or we adopt the same dysfunctional patterns in our relationships. (Or we decide to adopt the *opposite* pattern – 'I will *not* be depressed like my mother', 'I *won't* allow my children to have divorced parents' – which is a sure way to imprison ourselves.) And so the suffering passes on down the generations.

> *Children unconsciously aspire to equal their parents in suffering.*
>
> Bert Hellinger[2]

Bert Hellinger was once a Catholic priest who served as a missionary with a Zulu tribe. He was transformed by the Zulus' approach to illness, which recognises that a sick person might be expressing disturbance – often in mysterious ways – on behalf of the whole family or community, including dead ancestors. When he later trained as a family therapist, he developed the concept of the 'family soul'. The family soul is a conscious energy field that extends across at least three or four generations – within which patterns are repeated as an act of 'misguided loyalty'. Any unresolved issue seems to be passed on to the next generation, or the next, as unfinished business for which our descendants pay the price. (Just as our descendants will benefit from any issues which we heal and resolve.)

For example, a lawyer came to see Bert Hellinger after researching his own family history.[3] The lawyer had discovered that his great-grandmother had been married and pregnant when she fell in love with another man. Her husband died at the age of 27 on 31st December, amidst suspicion that he had been murdered. The woman then married the man she loved. Since that time, three men in the family had committed suicide – all at the age of 27 on 31st December. The lawyer's cousin had just turned 27, and New Year's Eve was fast approaching, so the lawyer went to his cousin to warn him of the family history. He found that his cousin had already bought a gun, intending to shoot himself. This is systemic entanglement; in this case, it is *unresolved guilt* passing down the generations.

In another case, a woman with chronic asthma had been named after her older sister, who had died in infancy. Her parents never spoke about the dead child. The woman realised that she needed to honour her dead sister's place in the family – so she visited her sister's grave, talked to her, and told her that *she* was the first-born in the family – thus acknowledging that she herself was not her sister. Her asthma then vanished. The woman no longer had to 'identify' with her dead sister, and had permission to breathe at last.

Our ancestors seem to inhabit us like ghosts, sneaking into our thoughts, nudging us to worship their gods, imprisoning us behind the walls of the past, turning us into sleepwalkers, and weighing us down with their invisible luggage. Our energy field becomes 'entangled' with theirs. If mother was a martyr, we often adopt the same way of being in the world. If father was workaholic, so are we. If our parents merely tolerated each other, or stayed together 'for the sake of the children', we remain glued to a painful, shallow or loveless marriage. Our loyalty to family patterns can even extend to becoming chronically ill or dying young because a parent, grandparent or other relative did so. From our unconscious loyalty to the family soul, we try to be good instead of choosing to be happy – and the chain of pain continues. We follow the family rules, repeat the old patterns, and pass them down to our children.

At an energy level, these patterns are easy to understand (at least from one generation to the next). If children pick up parental vibrations of control and sacrifice – such as guilt and resentment, or rage and blame, or criticism and withdrawal, or neediness and rescuing – these are the energy patterns they come to associate with intimate relationships. They learn that 'this is what love means', regardless of what is *said* about love. (In fact, these vibrations are being stored in the subconscious before a child even understands what is being said.) Likewise, if a child senses that a parent's words do not match their vibrations – that is, their parents give mixed messages, or deny their emotions, or avoid discussion of painful issues – they learn those same distorted forms of communication. In later life, they will feel comfortable with those unspoken rules, and 'loyally' replicate them. They have learned patterns of tame love.

The irony is that, at a soul level, we might have chosen our parents in the hope of *healing* those family patterns, instead of passing them on. *And if we are following our emotional guidance, we will not repeat family patterns of tame love.* After all, negative emotion – such as guilt, anxiety, depression, resentment or even suicidal impulses – will warn us that we are not being true to our own path, that we are not listening to Source.

In co-dependent families, some of the most common 'rules' are:

✦ Don't rock the boat.

✦ Put others first.

✦ Be loyal.

✦ Don't express feelings openly. (Or even: don't feel.)

✦ Always be strong, perfect, good and happy.

✦ Don't discuss problems openly.

✧ Pretend everything is fine.

✧ Don't talk about these rules.

Such rules are perfectly designed to split our energy and to crush the soul – blocking the flow of unconditional love, blocking open and honest communication, suppressing emotions and authenticity, stifling growth and change, and making it almost impossible for real love to thrive. Since our culture strongly promotes co-dependency, it means that these rules are widespread – yet because they are unspoken, they often become invisible and unconscious. And pretending everything is fine does not fool our children; it simply teaches them to deny their emotions, and put on a false smile.

GUILT AND LOYALTY

Guilt and loyalty seem to be two systemic forces that keep these old patterns of tame love flowing down the genera-tions. Guilt and loyalty can both block the flow of love, and block open and honest communication – and so powerfully threaten our freedom, growth and authenticity. They repre-sent the 'old tug at the ankles' – the systemic entanglements – that imprison us in the ego.

For a child, the greatest fear is to be abandoned, to be exiled from the family. Guilt threatens us with disapproval or even exclusion if we break the family rules, if we are 'disloyal'. Yet Bert Hellinger comments that trying to avoid guilt is a childish need – symbolically, it is the need for our parents' approval (or social approval) – which prevents us listening to the guidance of our soul. 'Without guilt there can be no transformation,' he warns.[4]

From an energy-based paradigm, we see that guilt is always a symptom of split energy. Guilt is not a sign of doing something bad – as we have long been told – but rather of conflict between the desires, impulses or 'knowing' of our deep Self and the demands and expectations of other people or systems. As *A Course in Miracles* puts it, 'Guilt is more than merely not of God. It is the symbol of attack on God.'[5] Guilt is a sign of disconnecting from our deep Self, from our authenticity, from our innocence and grace. Guilt does not make us 'behave well'; it makes us behave as if our life does not belong to us. It is a form of self-abuse that imprisons us in a false self. *Guilt is the primary way in which we are controlled by other people or society.*

From the ego's viewpoint, loyalty – like guilt and self-sacrifice – is a good thing. But from an energy-based viewpoint, we see that loyalty always means entanglement. It means being virtuous in the eyes of others, meeting their needs and expectations at our own expense. Loyalty says 'This is what I must do to gain others' approval, or to think well of myself, so I will put my own feelings and needs aside.' This means ignoring what Source, who loves you unconditionally, is guiding you towards. It means lacking respect for yourself. It means splitting your energy. (After all, if it did not split our energy – if it did not create any inner conflict – we would not call it loyalty.)

One of the well-known characteristics of co-dependency is being 'over-loyal' – sacrificing oneself for others, or remaining too long in harmful situations or relationships, often while denying or minimising any problems. How many lies are told, or truths concealed, in the name of loyalty? How many people are hurt, dishonoured, judged or excluded in the name of loyalty? How much abusive behaviour is never revealed to others, in the name of loyalty?

Guilt and loyalty both call us into sacrifice; and no-one who calls us into sacrifice has our best interests at heart. Abraham even suggests[6] we should run for our lives if anyone asks for our loyalty, since they want to murder our soul. Loyalty can become a prison. It means putting what *others* think or feel first – or putting our loyalty to a religion, race or group first – instead of trusting our own emotional guidance, the Source of unconditional love within us. It keeps people stuck in dull jobs, dysfunctional relationships or family ties that they need to release. Even worse, loyalty is used to 'justify' most of the world's atrocities – such as war, suicide bombers, torture, genocide and family feuds. Loyalty stops love flowing where it will. It closes our heart to others, or blocks communication. It urges us to repeat old patterns in its name. It splits the world into good-and-bad, us-and-them. Love connects and heals, whereas loyalty tends to fragment and disconnect. It serves the divisive agenda of the ego. For the deep Self – as for St Francis – even a maple leaf or a frog is our sister or brother. Our deep Self sees no separation; it does not divide. *It simply loves.*

As Bert Hellinger notes, we subconsciously believe we will be rewarded for bending to guilt and loyalty – for being 'good' rather than choosing to be happy – or hope that our own suffering will somehow benefit someone else. However, guilt and misguided loyalty do not help anyone; they simply maintain the old vibrations of conditional love, of Control and Sacrifice. They strengthen the immature ego, and keep everyone disconnected from love.

Any system tends to resist change, and guilt and loyalty seem to be systemic forces that can block growth and transformation. They are conservative forces that maintain the old traditions, which urge conformity, which make us hang on to the status quo. (You can *feel* the heaviness and confinement of their vibrations.) Even visiting parents and relatives can pull us back into family-ar vibrations, which drag us into old patterns of relating. Yet overcoming this 'family loyalty' - or loyalty to any system, such as work or religion or peer groups – can be a crucial part of the hero's journey towards reconnecting with Source, and creating truly loving and authentic relationships. Real love is aligned with Source, so it can never split our energy. It can never call us into sacrifice. Love always sets us free.

LIGHT AND DARK CORDS

You are linked to everyone you know – past and present – by cords of energy, which are part of the inseparable web of energy-consciousness. Family patterns seem to be passed down the generations through these energy cords, which maintain our family-ar patterns of relating. These cords can be light or dark, healthy or unhealthy. The dark cords carry systemic entanglements such as guilt and martyrdom, which block our individuation, like a garden choked with brambles and bindweed; while the light cords of unconditional love strengthen and support us like the roots of a tree.

Barbara Ann Brennan, an energy healer and physicist, has observed that the energy cords of a healthy couple relationship look 'alive, bright, pulsating, and flexible'.[7] (I experience such cords as feeling warm, beating and heart-expanding, or as light, sparkling and energising.) These light cords characterise a relationship based on real love, intimacy, honesty, caring and trust, which supports the freedom and self-expression of the two individuals.

By contrast, the energy cords of a co-dependent relationship appear to Barbara as 'dark, unhealthy, stagnated, heavy, and slimy, or stiff, dim, and brittle'. (I sense these cords as heavy and sticky like thick cobwebs or black treacle, or sometimes jarring and discordant like clashing cymbals.) These dark cords – the energy patterns of tame love – hold insecure patterns of attachment formed in childhood. Through these energy cords, co-dependency binds people together in a needy, controlling and inflexible relationship that stifles growth and spontaneity. Over the years, these feelings of constriction can even make the body constrict, so that the shoulders hunch, the body becomes bowed down, the heart is protected, and the person looks smaller than they physically are.

Co-dependency is maintained at an energy level by these dark stagnant cords, so that even if one person tries to leave, the two often reunite like a stretched rubber band snapping back into place. Many never break free from these unhealthy patterns, forever sacrificing their bright aliveness and potential for the comfort and security of a twilight prison. At a subconscious level, we seem to fear that breaking the dark cords will disconnect us from love, or a sense of belonging – so we might endure having our wings clipped. But the light cords of love are eternal, and real love always sets us free.

Even if we do cut loose from a co-dependent relationship, these dark energy cords often remain. Some divorced couples remain locked in blame-guilt-control cycles for years afterwards, with their children and new partners caught up in the cross-fire. Often this is because the judgment of self and others around separation and divorce has not been released. Letting go of guilt and anger – by knowing that every situation is co-created by everyone involved, and that all is well – often releases the dark cords of tame love, and the twisted communication or control games can stop. (And it only takes one person to stop playing.)

Dark cords always support duality – fear, guilt, judgment, control, sacrifice, separation, us-and-them, broken or distorted communication, misguided loyalty. They block the natural flow of energy. What seems to heal our relationships is *not* repeating old patterns, punishing or sacrificing ourselves, remaining walled-up behind our defences, and bending to guilt and loyalty. What helps and heals is open and honest communication, compassion, forgiveness, honouring the Light within everyone, acknowledging whatever has happened and letting it be, allowing love to flow and be expressed freely – and walking the path of our *own* unique soul. Then everyone can breathe again. The feeling of relief is palpable.

In other words, what heals is allowing Source energy to flow. Releasing our resistance. Saying 'Yes' to life. Saying 'Yes' to love. Saying 'Yes' to freedom. Saying 'Yes' to the voice of our deep Self – which calls us out into the woods to find our own path, to follow our bliss, to be whoever we came here to be. That is wild love.

> *We have a moral imperative to use our freedom, to live at the fearsome edge of our consciousness when called upon to do so, because it is our very nature as conscious beings to be free …*
>
> *Danah Zohar*[8]

FORGING NEW RIVERBEDS

In the classic film *Brief Encounter*, Laura and Alec fall madly in love after meeting at a railway station. They awaken each other's dreams, and restore sparkle and magic to their routine lives. For a few short weeks, they bring each other alive. However, they are both married – and despite their love, they soon turn their back on the possibility of a future together, or even keeping in touch. A door briefly opens, but they do not walk through. As they prepare for a final farewell before their trains leave, a chattering acquaintance sits down at their table – a symbol of the superficial ego, blocking their loving intimacy – and they are forever parted. What haunts us is the sense of unfulfilled promise, of unlived potential, of 'quiet desperation' being chosen over passion, depth and vitality. More creative possibilities were not even considered. The film ends with Laura's dull, comfortable husband saying 'Thank you for coming back to me' – but one suspects that she never really did, that her soul slipped away to Africa along with the man she loved, and all that remained was an empty shell.

Back in the 1940s, *Brief Encounter* was hailed as a tale of moral strength and fortitude overcoming 'immoral love'; and guardians of the old paradigm might still nod their heads sagely in agreement. Yet we might also see Laura and Alec as succumbing to the voice of duty, guilt and conformity – flowing down riverbeds of tame love, and not honouring their own emotions and desires, not being authentic, not allowing themselves to grow and expand. Keeping themselves in a box. Trying to be good.

A marriage is a powerful archetypal energy. It is seductive to the ego since it implies security and belonging, so it easily lulls us into a trance. As I know from my own experience, we can find ourselves taking on the role of wife or husband or parent, as if we are slipping into a pre-made mould. The mould might cut and chafe and feel too small, yet we try to squeeze ourselves into it. We allow ourselves to fall asleep. We allow ourselves to be tamed. Then we become a pale and ghostly imitation of our true Self.

For most people, a marriage or partnership is our primary relationship. It is the human touchstone on which all our other relationships – with Self, with other people, with work, with Source, with the earth – are based. So it is crucial to how we live our lives, how we feel about ourselves, and how much of our potential we express. The problem is that we learned in childhood how to relate to others, especially within intimate relationships, and these old patterns are usually based upon tame love. And unless we change, these are the limiting patterns that will be passed on to the next generation.

We are connected energetically to our family soul, our race and culture, our karmic history and global consciousness in ways that would seem magical within the old paradigm. The web of energy-consciousness holds deeply embedded patterns based upon the false gods of conditional love; and those old riverbeds will only dry up when enough individuals 'wake up' and refuse to run mindlessly along those choked and toxic pathways of fear, shame and judgment – and instead dig healthy new riverbeds based upon unconditional love and freedom.

We are not helpless victims of our family and cultural patterns. We are constantly being guided from within to reconnect with love and joy, to allow Source energy to flow. *If we are paying attention to our emotional guidance – if we are Self-centred – we can raise our vibrations beyond the disturbed energy patterns that urge us to flow along old riverbeds.* We cannot get dragged into guilt or sacrifice or martyrdom or duty if we are listening to our emotional guidance. If we feel bad, it means that we are running along old riverbeds, or trying to please someone else. Our energy is split. We are bowing down to old gods. We are not listening to the ever-present voice of Love.

Am I suggesting you should leave a relationship that is less than wildly loving? Of course not. After all, that relationship is a perfect match to your current vibrations, and will bring up any issues that need to be resolved. If there was unconditional love and intimacy between you at one time, then perhaps it can be restored. Or perhaps it can even be built from scratch. Or perhaps this relationship is just designed to bring up your old patterns, so you can see them clearly before moving on. If you clarify your desires, courageously tackle unresolved issues, break through patterns of Control-and-Sacrifice, trust your emotional guidance and raise your vibrations, then any relationship has to change – either flowing into a deeper and more loving form together, or a new form apart. But in the long term, if you resign yourself to a taming relationship that falls far short of your dreams and desires – or restrict yourself to loving one person tamely and exclusively – you betray your deep Self, and disconnect from Source.

So why might you end a relationship?

✧ Because you bring out the worst in each other – that is, your habitual energy patterns lock together in unhealthy ways – which means you are short-circuiting each other's energy, getting stuck in ego and squashing your potential.

✧ Because the depth and quality of love between you is not appropriate to the form of the relationship – perhaps it feels too conditional, or too limiting, or too lacking in warmth and affection, or you cannot be truly intimate with each other.

✧ Because you feel lonely, frustrated, trapped or suffocated – you do not feel free – and 'working on your relationship' does not resolve this.

✧ Because your values, needs and desires have drifted apart, and you need to move in different directions; or because your shared interests feel too narrow and restrictive.

✧ Or because you just know, deep down, that this relationship is not good or right for you, that it is not bringing out what is best and highest in you.

But before you give up on a relationship, you might like to try out the principles in chapter 12 – and see whether you *can* love each other more wildly. The best solution *might* be a new relationship, but you cannot jump overnight from tame love to wild love. You have to build bridges. You have to deliberately change your vibrations, which takes time. You have to look honestly at your patterns (without shaming yourself). You have to take responsibility for all that you create. And above all, you have to learn to trust your emotions and intuition, knowing that choosing what feels joyful and expansive – rather than trying to be good – always leads you in the right direction. You have to start making choices based upon your emotional guidance, rather than upon the demands and expectations of other people or society. Paradoxically, this helps to heal your relationships – or allows them to change their form – since you are moving beyond fear and insecurity, and towards real love.

BECOMING BUTTERFLIES

As we shift towards an energy-based paradigm, we are in transition from ego-based co-dependency to more authentic, loving and co-creative relationships – from tame love to wild love. Friends or relatives or colleagues can get along happily enough with conditional love; but a marriage can only thrive in the presence of unconditional love. Inevitably this means that many of us are experiencing chaos in our personal relationships, as we break free from our old riverbeds – as we shift from dualism to holism, and allow Source energy to flow.

In *Broken Open*, Elizabeth Lesser writes of her year-long secret affair with a wild and wounded man who ignited her passion, but led her into furtiveness, deceit, infidelity, neglect, irrationality and darkness. To an outsider, it might have seemed a disastrous love affair with a man who was definitely bad news. But it was Elizabeth's way of walking through fire, of confronting the lost parts of herself, of discovering who she was. It was a rite of passage, an initiation. Her lover dragged her into the underworld. He forced her to dance with her Shadow. He opened her heart. He helped her to break the rules, to become more imperfect and whole, to move beyond judgment. Like Persephone, she eventually emerged into the light as a different woman: more alive, more passionate, more real. Ultimately she chose to end both the affair *and* her marriage – which liberated her into a new life, and eventually led to a fulfilling second marriage. She had risked everything, but reaped rich rewards.

Love triangles often mirror this contrast between old riverbeds of co-dependency and our unmet needs, hidden desires and potential for real love. (They also tend to arise when there was a longing for more closeness with one parent during childhood, or a feeling of exclusion or abandonment; in other words, where there was felt separation from love.) A love affair can offer the opportunity to transform tame love – if the current partners are willing to explore their own patterns, take their own responsibility for what happened, have the courage to love more wildly, and treat everyone involved with caring and compassion. Or it can merely deepen old blame-guilt patterns of Control-and-Sacrifice, papering over the cracks and leaving both partners hurt and diminished by the crisis. In other cases, a love triangle opens the door to new relationships, which evoke different behaviour and potential – relationships based upon a deep intuitive and emotional connection, which help us build fresh riverbeds of wild love.

Tame love is based on conformity – and we have outgrown that old riverbed. Humanity is ready to chart new waters, to sail into the great ocean of unconditional love. Beyond fear. Beyond judgment. Beyond lack and limitation. Beyond possessiveness and exclusiveness. Beyond the old forms. Towards truly loving, joyful and co-creative relationships that help us create our own heaven on earth.

> Yet perhaps we needed that dark winter.
> Perhaps our dormancy was part of the Plan –
> for lifetimes, even aeons, to ponder
> our heart's desires, and whether God
> favours love and freedom,
> or erects prison bars?
> Until true love arises with the fresh light of spring
> and we make our fierce break above ground –
> arms reaching for the sky –
> our Self uncrushed, indomitable.[9]

Co-dependency is not bad and wrong – any more than it is bad and wrong for a baby to be unable to walk. 'How things are' is exactly how they need to be. This is simply a stage we are going through on our journey. *We are always on our way*

to where we want to be. However, co-dependency is an immature and unequal style of relating which blocks us from
spiritual adulthood – and the underlying patterns of ego
defence create immense personal, social and global problems. (Just watch any soap opera, drama or the TV news,
listen to almost any politician, or attend any emotionally
laden local meeting or activist group to watch 'blaming,
shaming and taming' in action – with splitting, projection,
victimhood, self-righteousness, complaining, scapegoating
and beliefs in lack or scarcity.) Co-dependency strengthens
the fearful and insecure ego at the expense of the deep Self
– constricting our awareness, and placing real love and
authenticity beyond reach – and it is time for us to expand
our consciousness.

For many, this will mean facing the pain, discomfort and
restrictions of co-dependency – whether in a couple relationship, or with a relative or business partner – until the
contrast between what we have and what we desire is so
great that we break free and give birth to new realities. Deep
contrast gives birth to deep desire, and increased clarity,
focus, wisdom and understanding – so whatever happens, all
is well.

Countless signs point towards us making this transition
towards co-creative relationships, as we shift into the new
paradigm. Our old structures are collapsing and dying. We
are experimenting with new kinds of relationships, new
definitions of love and commitment, new styles of parenting
and richly complex 'blended families' . We are letting go of
negative family ties, and discovering the importance of close
friendships. Many people are making a positive choice to
live alone. As we let go of judgment, we recognise that there
is no right or wrong form for relationships – no way that
things are meant to be.

Having a stable first marriage and two-point-four children is not necessarily what is best. In fact, it might simply
support our old riverbeds of relating. Children are often

used to 'justify' staying in a dysfunctional marriage, but co-dependency seems to flourish best when we mimic the family we grew up in – so perhaps we often *need* new forms of relationships to wake us up, to break our old patterns and energy habits. For children to grow up sharing a home with both parents is not *necessarily* what is best for them; after all, it limits them to one style of relating and a restricted set of family patterns. Within the bigger picture, souls choose their parents knowing what the likely outcome of that partnership will be. Children want to know they are loved; but during this time of personal and global awakening, they need freedom and flexibility far more than stability and tradition. And ideally – unless we *want* them to be ruled by the old values of conformity, duty and self-sacrifice – they will have parents who choose to be happy, rather than trying to be good.

In these times of rapid change, we need to let go of our old blueprints and ideas of what is best, or trying to provide a 'perfect childhood' for our children, and instead follow our emotional guidance. We need to develop new models. We need to break the rules. We need to build unique and ever-evolving relationships. Mother Theresa said that we need to see the whole world as our family – and perhaps a complex, extended family, which includes intimate friendships and a supportive community, can be a step in that direction. Above all, we need more models of relationships based upon wild love.

Stalwarts of the conservative old order might argue that co-dependency supports traditional family values and social stability. The ego believes that we *need* fear, guilt and external rules to keep people under control, and to prevent society collapsing into chaos. ('Where would we be if everyone tried to be happy, and didn't do their duty?') But fear and guilt split our energy, dividing us from each other and from our authentic Selves. There is little merit in a long-lasting marriage or partnership if it stifles the dreams and desires of those involved, and blocks their freedom, joy and growth. In fact, such a relationship becomes a living tragedy. It keeps both people trapped in their limited egos – sleepwalking through life, denying their deeper creativity and potential, and often suffering mental or physical health problems as a result – and it passes on these family-ar vibrations of tameness and mediocrity to their children.

Wild love is the *natural* glue of society. It allows the dark cords to dissolve, and builds light cords which connect us in positive and healthy ways, while allowing flow and freedom and flexibility and openness. Through the eyes of the new paradigm, then, the current pattern of marital breakdown and relationship crisis might not be a negative sign of society breaking down, but a healthy sign of challenging the old norms and pressures to conform. Chaos is a necessary precursor to transformation. We are the imaginal cells in society, dreaming of what might be, with our visions pulsing in our incipient wings. We are the pathfinders of a new heaven and a new earth – dreaming of becoming butterflies.

THE JOURNEY TOWARDS WILD LOVE

Let us recap on the journey so far … We have seen that the ego lives in the small, limited world of surface reality. Since it is disconnected from the deep Self, it feels unsafe and unloved. It is ruled by fear, judgment and insecurity – and is only capable of tame love.

Tame love means accepting what is seen as good or safe, and rejecting what is seen as bad or dangerous – within yourself, others or the world. It means being guided from *outside* the Self – by others' needs and demands and expectations, or by conforming to social norms or religious traditions, or by playing roles instead of being authentic. The problem is that 'trying to be good' splits your energy. Every time you give in to fear, guilt or insecurity, you bow down to your ego – you bow to the imaginary God of conditional love – and turn your back on your deep Self. You shrink a little. You block the flow of Source energy, so that you fall asleep and your awareness contracts. Then your soul is imprisoned. Your dreams fade into the distance. You project your perceived shame or 'badness' into the outside world. You flow down old riverbeds of relating – patterns which are family-ar from childhood, or promoted by our culture. Riverbeds of fear and guilt and blame and misguided loyalty. Riverbeds of conformity. Your relationships will show co-dependent cycles of Control-and-Sacrifice. Taming or being tamed. Then real love and intimacy become impossible.

Your emotions will send warning signals – ranging from divine discontent to rage, guilt, anxiety, resignation, despair or even suicidal impulses – but all too often, this makes you cling even more tightly to the status quo. You try harder to be 'good' and to earn love, or try harder to control the person or circumstances that you believe are causing your pain or discomfort, or just resign yourself to 'what is'. And this leads you further and further away from love, and away from your deep Self.

The real solution lies within – in reconnecting with Source energy, with unconditional love. Then you *know* you are safe, you are loved, and you are worthy. You do not need to 'get' those feelings from anyone else. And you *know* you are creating it all, that it is all a dance of co-creation, that the world simply mirrors back your own vibrations. Then you can reclaim your power – and your consciousness expands.

Wild love means knowing that everyone is good, that everything within you is good, and everything that happens is unfolding perfectly. Then you love yourself enough to trust in your emotions, and to reawaken your dreams and desires. You choose to be happy, rather than trying to be good. You stop driving yourself so hard, or keeping yourself in a cage, or sacrificing yourself to please others. You become wild and free. You can be authentic with yourself and others.

You follow your bliss, using your emotions to guide you towards love and joy and freedom. You reconnect with Source, and become an apprentice god or goddess. You move beyond duality – no longer splitting the world into good and bad, right and wrong, safe and dangerous. You begin to love wildly.

Now you can truly *love* others – with an open heart – instead of expecting them to be who you want them to be, or trying to 'earn' love and approval, or holding back. You can breathe more easily. Your relationships become truly loving, joyful and liberating. You grow and expand. Your self-love is mirrored back to you by others. You become a whole person within a rich network of loving relationships – choosing to share your journey with others in whatever form, and for however long, feels good. You might not 'conform' any more – you might be a maverick – but your energy becomes coherent. By choosing to be happy instead of trying to be good, you release your true potential as a loving, co-creative and unique spark of Source energy. A spark of God. A spark of the creative energy of the Universe. Your mature ego merges with your deep Self. Now you can live with a foot in both worlds. You become a conscious co-creator, and can help to create heaven on earth. This is the hero's journey. This is the gift of wild love. It is the future of humanity in this time of global awakening.

We pay a huge price for flowing down riverbeds of tame love. Tame love disconnects us from our deep Self, and makes us fall asleep. Wild love connects us to our deep Self, and wakes us up. And it is time for humanity to wake up.

PRACTICAL SUGGESTIONS

1. Research your family tree, noting anyone in the past three or four generations who was forgotten, dishonoured, rejected or excluded, was 'illegitimate', committed suicide, suffered an awful fate, or died young (before age 45–50) – including abortions, miscarriages and stillbirths. Honour these 'lost' ancestors by framing a photograph (if you have one), planting a tree or shrub for them, saying prayers or holding a ceremony of remembrance. Or make contact with anyone alive who has been seen as a 'black sheep', or excluded from anyone's heart. Allowing blocked love to flow freely helps to heal the family soul – freeing the current generation from 'entanglement' with troubled ancestors.[10]

2. Have you slipped into old family riverbeds of tame love? Have you repeated any patterns in your parents' marriage, or identified yourself with one parent, or been attracted to partners who remind you of your mother or father? Do you find yourself getting stuck in the same old emotions? If you were not flowing down those old riverbeds, how might your life be different? What are your hidden longings and desires? How do you really want to feel? How do you want your relationships to be? Wherever you are now, know that you can always get to where you want to be. (Source loves you wildly, and is always calling you towards happiness and joy!) If you were wild and free, how might you re-design your life?

CHAPTER TWELVE

Wild Love

Feel nothing separate then,
we have translated each other into light
and into love go streaming.

Brian Patten[1]

Waking up means radical change – turning our world upside down and inside out. It means overthrowing our common-sense assumptions about love and relationships, about thoughts and emotions, about the material world – and seeing everything as energy-consciousness. It means throwing out much of what traditional religion has taught in its attempt to shame, frighten and disempower us. It means reconnecting with Source. It means letting go of fear and victimhood, and allowing ourselves to become apprentice gods.

Once we *know* that God/Source is unconditional love – and is both immanent and transcendent – we move beyond duality. We know that we are inseparable from Source, that Source energy flows through us, that we are sparks of God in human clothing and that everything that happens is what we have summoned forth. *Everything.* This transforms our relationships – with Self, with others, with life itself.

The truth is that real love scares us. It ruffles our feathers. It messes up our neat suburban lives and well-trimmed lawns. It calls us into the wild. Real love has no boundaries, no certainty, no limitations. Wild love does not follow the old riverbeds of relating. It leaves behind the dusty relics of fear, shame and judgment. It breaks into fresh new land-scapes in which no paths have yet been laid. We have to find our own way – guided constantly by our emotions and desires, which are always leading us towards our deep Self, towards the magic of being a conscious co-creator, towards being an apprentice god, towards unconditional love.

❤

So how do we practise wild love? Here are ten (intertwined) principles for everyday life:

1. No-one and nothing 'out there' is responsible for what you experience, or how you feel

You create your life from the inside out. Everything that happens perfectly matches the radio signals you are emitting. Whether you win the lottery or get burgled, whether you are made redundant or offered a promotion, whether someone shouts at you or gives you a hug, every single event is co-created through the interconnected web of energy-consciousness. This can feel like a huge and weighty responsibility, or it can feel liberating and empowering.

The Law of Attraction says that there are no coinci-dences, no accidents, no good or bad luck, no unavoidable fate or destiny. It is not possible to 'do' anything to anyone. You cannot fall prey to wicked people with bad intentions. You are not at the helpless mercy of viruses and bacteria and faulty genes. There are no victims. The ego wriggles and squiggles and squirms at this idea – ('Oh, please, please, let me have someone else to blame!') – but it is what the energy-based paradigm, ancient mystics and modern channelled sources have consistently been telling us. This is spiritual adulthood.

The ego can distort this idea into *blaming* ourselves for what we create. 'Bad me for creating heart disease, or a car accident, or a dysfunctional marriage!' 'Bad me for thinking negative thoughts, or for feeling anxious or depressed!' Or it can even twist it into blaming others: 'Well, *you* evoked that behaviour from me! I don't behave like that with other people. Go change yourself!' But blame always comes from the old paradigm. This is a blameless universe. It is all a dance of co-creation, in which everyone has 100 per cent responsibility, yet no-one takes any blame. Blame arises from judgment, which shuts us down like a telescope. Understanding the Law of Attraction means using reality as *feedback* – and simply empowering ourselves to create what we want, to become conscious creators.

A crucial consequence of the Law of Attraction is that *no-one else can be held responsible for what we feel*. Our feelings mirror our vibrations, which depend upon our thoughts and beliefs; no-one else can control our vibrations. Imagine that your partner borrows your car and crashes it into a wall. You might respond by being furious that he or she was so stupid and careless; you might simply be relieved that they were not hurt; you might (rightly) wonder whether they were secretly angry with you; or you might be pleased because you wanted to change your car and now have no choice. Your partner cannot control how you react. Yet someone who responds with rage will often imagine that 'anyone would feel that way in my situation' (and they will gather friends who agree with them). Not so. The higher truth is that *you* co-created that accident – perhaps because *you* were angry and wanted an excuse to express it, or because you disliked your car, or because you wanted to punish yourself – and then *you* chose how to think and feel about the incident. You can respond with love and responsibility, or you can respond with blame and judgment – and that will probably depend upon the energy habits between you and your partner.

Wild love means that our emotions and needs are expressed without blaming or shaming or taming – always within the wider context of unconditional love and acceptance, and honouring the freedom of others. We never blame anyone else for our feelings. We know that we evoke their behaviour from our own vibrations, and that how we *interpret* anyone's behaviour is up to us. We can only change the world from the inside out. We share our feelings openly and honestly, but without ever expecting the other to change or adapt in order to 'make us feel better'. We know that our connection to Source, to feeling good, never depends upon external conditions. On the contrary, in our looking-glass world, what happens 'out there' depends upon on our thoughts and vibrations. Likewise, we cannot be responsible for anyone else's happiness, since we cannot control their inner world.

Whenever we hold someone else responsible for our feelings, we imprison them. Conversely, if the Other knows that they *cannot* hurt your feelings, that you *cannot* be offended or upset by what they do or how they feel – since you take full responsibility for what you experience, and how you interpret it, and you do not expect them to fit *your* image – then they are free to be whoever they are. And they will deeply love you for that.

> True love has no trappings or consequences.
> Love simply is:
> generous and roomy,
> welcoming and accepting,
> freely holding out its arms
> and allowing the soul to breathe.
> Love does not thrive in a thimble.[2]

2. Any relationship problem mirrors your relationship with yourself

At a deeper level, what we are searching for in a relationship is a wonderful, loving relationship with Self. If we truly loved every aspect of ourselves – no ifs and buts, no reservations, no preferring some bits to others, no limiting ourselves to what is 'reasonable', no pretence or denial – we would have no need to please others, no need to conform, no need to prove ourselves good and worthy, no inner conflict, no problems in open communication. We would simply be deciding which delicious and joyful experience to choose or create next, and next, and next.

Instead we often hope that someone else will give us the unconditional love and respect that we are not giving ourselves, or at least trigger the possibility of loving ourselves. The problem is that we cannot get from others what we are not giving ourselves. We might get a whiff of it, if it is a strong desire. But ultimately we have to see ourselves as good, lovable and worthy before our relationships will mirror back our self-love. This means not hiding our 'unacceptable' feelings, thoughts and desires but embracing them, and not trying to be good or special, but being gentle and compassionate towards ourselves.

The Other is never the problem. If you imagine the Other *is* the problem – that you would feel fine if only they would change their behaviour or go away – you disempower yourself, since you cannot change anyone else. (You can try – but it will always backfire.) When you are disconnected from Source, you have negative thoughts about yourself and others, or feel needy and insecure, and the outside world mirrors back those discordant vibrations. Whatever 'badness' you see in another is what you reject, or dare not face, in yourself. Whenever you 'take something personally', it is because it resonates with your own vibrations – otherwise it would have no impact on you. Whatever you accuse anyone of doing to you, you are usually doing to yourself.

How have you neglected yourself? How have you abandoned or betrayed yourself? How do you criticise or guilt-trip yourself? What unreasonable demands do you make of yourself? How have you shown a lack of respect for yourself? How do you ignore your own feelings and needs? How have you been dishonest with yourself? How do you control or imprison yourself? How are you abusing yourself? How do you punish yourself? Or perhaps you are doing it to the Other? How might you have criticised, or controlled, or betrayed, or lied to them? And more importantly, how can you love and accept and nurture yourself more? How can you treat yourself as you wish to be treated by others?

Any problem in a relationship comes from splitting or dualism, from judging some part of self or other as bad or wrong. If we feel guilt or remorse about *anything* we have done in the past, or about *any* of our feelings and desires, our self-judgment depletes us – and our tame self-love will be reflected back by others. The more we love ourselves unconditionally, the more others will mirror that back (though paradoxically, we no longer need them to do so). And those who cannot offer wild love will simply back off or disappear from our reality, or their behaviour will no longer bother us.

3. Say Yes to everything

Whenever we see anything as bad, wrong, inappropriate, destructive or dangerous, we fall into duality and disconnect from Source. Even experiences of deep contrast are ways of springboarding into the Light, or reclaiming more of our wholeness. Contrast is an essential launching pad for fresh visions for the future. (A painful or taming relationship, for example, helps to birth a huge desire for real love.) Seeing everything as good does not mean seeing everything as perfect. It means understanding that everything is in evolution – and in an ever-expanding universe which includes free will, there has to be contrast.

When we say 'No' to any experience, or to any aspect of

self or other, it creates short-circuits in our energy system; we split off whatever we have rejected. By the Law of Attraction, this split in our energy attracts similar wounds, again and again, until we resolve the conflict and heal ourselves. By saying a deep and sincere 'Yes' to everything that happens, and to everything in ourselves and others, we keep our energy flowing – and so free ourselves from the need to repeat suffering.

Whenever others behave in ways that seem hurtful, unloving or destructive, we can see their behaviour as arising from disconnection from Source, without seeing the other person as bad or wrong. Perhaps we haven't listened with an open heart to the other's point of view. Perhaps it is our *interpretation* of their behaviour – our 'story' about it – that is the problem. Perhaps they just have different values and priorities. Perhaps they are expressing their need for freedom and individuality, in the face of pressures to conform. Perhaps they are lost in pain and fear – and trying to control others in an effort to solve the problem. (And if we try to control or fix *them*, because their behaviour disturbs us, we are falling into the same trap!) And if we are disturbed by someone else, how did we evoke that behaviour from them? If we are judging them, we are disconnected, and cannot help them to reconnect. Despite the ego's attempts to 'correct' and fix people – that is, to feel superior to them – judgment can only ever do harm. It is understanding, compassion, warmth, acceptance, honesty and heart-centred listening which helps and heals – and those only become possible when we know that everyone is good.

Wild love means that there is nothing to forgive. After all, forgiveness implies there has been wrongdoing; it comes from duality. The ego always forgives from self-righteousness. ('You did something *bad* to me, but I am big enough to forgive you!') It forgives but does not forget, so that it can control through guilt. It learns dark lessons, which will attract more of the same. When we love wildly, we see the dance of co-creation – so there is nothing to forgive.

Wild love means saying 'Yes' to *everything* in someone we love. Their feelings. Their needs. Their values. Their beliefs. Their patterns. Their dreams and desires. Through the eyes of wild love, we see the 'faults and imperfections' in the other – their ego defences, their old riverbeds, their bumps and cragginess – but with the same soft eyes with which we see their strengths, qualities and potential. We do not merely tolerate or accept their 'faults'; *we love every aspect of them equally*, as part of their unique wholeness. The light and dark are interwoven into this beautiful human tapestry that we call our Beloved. As I know from my own experience, wild love means we look at the Other with the eyes of God – who sees us as perfect in every way.

> Love is the power within us that affirms and values
> another human being as he or she is.
>
> **Robert A Johnson**[3]

When we love unconditionally, we long to know the deepest truth about the Other – rather than wanting to hear what suits our needs, or matches our image of them. It is wild love that allows us to have authentic conversations – not just at times of conflict, but on a daily basis. Wanting to hear what is true for the Other, and loving and accepting them, *whatever* it is. Digging deeper and deeper for the truth of what we are feeling ourselves right now. Knowing it can change, but wanting our words to match our vibrations. Wanting to be true to ourselves. Knowing that whatever we feel – and whatever the Other feels – is fine. The authentic Self has nothing to hide.

William Tiller[4] suggests that the rate of growth of consciousness is dependent upon 'meaningful communication' with others. If we are trying to be good and perfect, or to fit in with someone else's expectations, we can never be authentic. If we worry that we might be judged or criticised, or that the Other might feel hurt or affronted by our feelings and desires, we hold back our truth – and our growth is blocked. Only when we know that *everything* within us is good can we have open and honest conversations which help us to unfold, to knit together the light and dark, to become who we truly are. Instead of listening to the inner voices of fear or judgment, we listen only to the voice of love.

Open and honest communication – which builds intimacy and trust – is only possible in the presence of Love. This does not mean romantic love, which sees only the light. It does not mean conditional (tame) love, which splits the world into good and bad, right and wrong, safe and dangerous. It means real love, wild love – a love that says that everything within you and me is good. Everything within others is good. Everything that happens is good. Even when there is contrast. Even when it means letting go. Even when we do get lost for a while in fear or judgment. And nothing can threaten me, since all that happens and everything I feel mirrors my own vibrations. So whatever comes is giving me helpful feedback about the signals I am giving out. And in this deep awareness of goodness and safety, I can speak my own truth and listen with an open heart.

4. The Golden Rule: to thine own Self be true

If you care more about what anyone else might think or feel than about how *you* feel, you might congratulate yourself on being virtuous – but you are tamed and locked away. Your wild, creative dreams are smothered and slowly dying. You are a puppet on a string, dancing endlessly to the tune of others.

In *Unravelled*, Maria Housden writes of her own difficult journey out of a sticky, controlling, co-dependent yet sometimes loving marriage, and her struggle to stop being good and unselfish, and conforming to others' expectations. As she freed her own authentic Self, it released her creative energy, which led to a bestselling book about the death of her wise and courageous young daughter, Hannah.[5] Maria's new-found self-love and willingness to 'break the rules' also attracted a loving and co-creative second marriage.

The paradox is that we are only capable of real love if we remain Self-centred. We can only truly love when we stop *trying* to be good and caring. If we are trying to please someone else, or to meet their needs and expectations – or needing them to meet ours – we are in neurotic conflict. We are seeking love from outside the self. We are imprisoned in a false self. We are stuck in the fear and judgment of the ego, which makes our relationships dysfunctional. We are being co-dependent rather than loving, and therefore expecting something in return for our love. Only the deep Self is capable of real love – unconditional love, wild love.

The problem is that whenever we care about someone, or spend a lot of time with them, we begin to resonate with *their* thoughts and beliefs and vibrations. Our energy system becomes entangled with theirs – especially if we are open and sensitive, or when we are tired or otherwise vulnerable. If they are aligned with Source, with unconditional love, this raises our vibrations – and simply being in their presence will feel wonderful. If they are not aligned with Source, however, entanglement creates problems. Unless we remain firmly Self-centred, their shame or fear or guilt-tripping splits our energy – which means we tumble down the emotional ladder, and lose our sense of self.

This energetic resonance can even occur at a distance – for example, in the phenomenon known as 'telosomatic disease'. When a friend of mine discovered a breast lump, which thankfully turned out to be benign, she discovered that her mother – who lived hundreds of miles away – had found a malignant lump in the same week, on the same side of the same breast. From the mindset of surface reality, this would be dismissed as mere 'coincidence'; but from the perspective of deep reality, we would say that mother and daughter were in resonance. Their energy fields were entangled.

The new Golden Rule for loving relationships has to be: 'To thine own Self be true'. In other words, we have to put our own alignment with Source above all else. The paradox is that this releases unconditional love, since it allows our energy to be coherent and flowing. As you raise your own vibrational frequency, you become capable of real love – and also evoke what is best and highest in others. Real love can only emerge from unconditional self-love. If you try to love another *at your own expense* – that is, at the expense of your emotional guidance – you split your energy and fall into ego. And the ego cannot love; it can only sacrifice.

Being true to ourselves means being who we are. It means being authentic – ensuring that our words match our vibrations, that we are speaking with wholeness and integrity. This requires taking enough time alone, on a daily or regular basis, to disentangle ourselves from others' energy. It might mean meditating, or walking alone, or keeping a journal or dream diary, or just sitting and reflecting. It means being honest and intimate with ourselves, so that we can be honest and intimate with others. It means facing our truth, even when it is difficult. It means blending together the light and the dark – until light is all there is.

As nuns, monks and hermits know, it is easier to remain Self-centred when we spend a lot of time in silence or isolation; it is far more challenging in the midst of close personal relationships. Some couples I know choose to have separate bedrooms, or even separate houses, so that sharing a bed or spending time together is an active choice, and they can have their own space whenever they wish. Others go on separate retreats or holidays at least once or twice a year, ensure that they respect each other's privacy, and have generous time and space alone. It is also crucial to have other intimate friends who know the 'whole truth' about our lives, so that we do not become over-dependent on one relationship.

Wild love involves finding a healthy balance between intimacy and togetherness, on the one hand, and freedom and individuality, on the other hand. This does not mean either merging or distancing, but becoming our authentic Selves within an ever-evolving set of loving relationships.

> *To dance, to step into the fray of daily life and to keep true to our soul's intention to live who we really are, we have to be willing to live both the reality of our separate individuality and the reality of our unity in something greater.*
>
> Oriah Mountain Dreamer[6]

The key to remaining Self-centred is paying attention to your emotions – knowing that any negative emotion (or feeling numb) means you are disconnecting from who you are, and moving away from what you desire. A helpful technique which I learned from the Sedona Method[7] is to keep going within, and asking yourself how you feel right now – then to let it be, and let it go. In other words, accept the emotion – then release it (which means letting go of the resistance). You can also ask: 'Am I seeking approval, control or security in this situation?' Then again, accept that – without self-judgment, just allowing it to be – and let it go. If you can get your ego out of the way, all that remains is the Self.

'But I was honouring my feelings when I asked my partner not to flirt with other women/men because I find it hurtful.' No, no, no! This is not being true to yourself. It is making the Other *responsible* for your feelings and – worst of all – asking them to shore up your ego defences. If you feel negative emotion, *you* are the problem! Your thoughts. Your patterns. Your vibrations. Whenever you try to control someone else in order to protect your ego, you damage that relationship. Stronger ego, weaker relationship. Always. You might get a moment of triumph or satisfaction if they give in, but the underlying issue of your fear and insecurity is not resolved by controlling someone else. And they are not doing you any favours. Giving in – sacrificing yourself – always undermines a relationship. It leaves you both in ego. Instead you need to take responsibility for your own emotions. Then you empower yourself, and will neither try to control others nor allow yourself to be tamed.

My client Kay told me that her mother's first reaction, on hearing that Kay was leaving her husband, was 'How could you do this *to me*?' But Kay was just emerging from a marriage in which she had been relentlessly guilt-tripped, so she recognised the pattern! She felt a brief twinge of guilt, then let it go. If her mother chose to feel hurt about her decision – rather than being delighted that Kay was taking charge of her own life – it was none of her business. Kay was learning to love herself, and was not going to be controlled by other people's feelings any more. Her life felt as if it belonged to her at last. She was dancing to her own tune.

As you become committed to self-love and authenticity, you are less vulnerable to guilt-tripping and manipulation. You are more likely to say (gently) 'Are you trying to make me feel guilty? This feels like an old pattern of ours that we need to break.' Or 'Can we both talk honestly about how we're feeling right now?' You still show caring and compassion for others' feelings – but not at the expense of your own needs, and not if it means being coerced by *their* fear or judgment or insecurity, which short-circuits your energy and collapses you into ego. (A friend of mine who abruptly left her marriage soon learned to say to others, 'If you cannot say anything positive, loving and supportive about my choice, I would prefer you to say nothing.')

It is only when you put aside what others might think or feel – or what social norms or ancient scriptures might dictate – and listen to the God within, your emotional guidance, that you find your true path. If you remain Self-centred, you will be guided by Source towards joy and freedom and unconditional love. You will be guided to become who you truly are. New and expanded horizons will open up to you. You will become open to a wildly loving relationship – since you love yourself wildly.

If you remain Self-centred, the dark cords of entanglement no longer tug at you. Your vibrations remain stable, whatever others think. You no longer seek approval, control or security from 'out there'. You are no longer pulled into being 'loyal' or accommodating to others at your own expense, needing to be needed, or trying to be who others want you to be. You no longer blame or control others. You are no longer vulnerable to fear and guilt and rage and revenge and sacrifice and martyrhood and despair. You might tumble down there occasionally, but you know how to pull yourself up again. And you know that all of that stuff is just illusion – laughable little clouds in a vast blue sky – and that only Love is real.

What if you now recognise that your primary relationship is based upon tame love? Remember that the Other is not the problem. It only takes one person to change. No-one can control or mould or guilt-trip you unless you are succumbing to fear and self-judgment. If you love yourself more wildly, your relationship has to change. The other might complain that you have become more selfish and wayward; that is, you are less easy to control! But they will either grow to love the new person, the authentic you, who is emerging, or carry on trying to clip your wings. And if you keep following your emotional guidance, and asking for signs, it will become clear whether it is time to separate and let your love flow into a new form, or whether you can grow together and love each other more wildly. Either way, you will begin to fly free – with them, or without them.

5. Love means setting someone free

As well as being 'hard-wired for bliss', we are hard-wired for freedom. Freedom is our spiritual birthright. This means we have a natural and healthy resistance to being told what we 'must', 'should' or 'ought' to do – which includes telling *ourselves* what we should do. (Even if we tell ourselves we 'should' do something we *enjoy* – perhaps meditating, or going for a run – it sets up friction in our energy system. Whenever we feel forced or trapped, it short-circuits our energy, and diminishes us. Allowing it to be a free choice releases our resistance.) The ego is readily motivated by fear or guilt – it is easily imprisoned – but the deep Self longs for joy and freedom and wildness. In some old languages such as Celtic, the word for love meant the same as 'setting free'.

Wild love means that we avoid splitting anyone's energy. We avoid blaming, shaming or taming – that is, trying to mould anyone into what we want them to be, or losing sight of their divinity. We encourage others to follow their own emotional guidance, to stay in touch with their deep Self. (And if we truly love someone, this comes naturally. It is the very nature of wild love to want the Other to choose to be happy.) We split someone's energy whenever we make demands that conflict with *their* needs, feelings and desires. We split energy whenever we judge or criticise, or try to make someone feel ashamed, guilty or inadequate. We split energy whenever we hold anyone responsible for our feelings, and ask them to control *their* behaviour in order to make *us* feel better. 'If you really cared about me, you would … ' When we try to control others from the outside in, it only increases our fear and insecurity, while suppressing the other's freedom and growth and ability to love.

As authors Hal Stone and Sidra Winkelman put it, 'The price we pay for total security and well-being in a relationship is, generally speaking, an increasing loss of vitality, romance, sexuality, and general creativity in the relationship.'[9] Why? Because we only seek security 'out there' when we have thoughts based on insecurity. Those thoughts make us close down any parts of self or other which feel at all risky. We become smaller and smaller, and expect our partner to become smaller and smaller. Eventually a third party might well be drawn into this diminishing relationship, as a representative of all we are disowning and longing for. The 'betrayed' partner then says, 'See, I was right to feel insecure! I was right to be jealous!' Yet it was their own insecurity – resulting in controlling, distancing and lack of authenticity – which pushed their partner away. People only want to escape if they feel imprisoned.

When we split someone's energy, we lose what is highest in them. Split energy feels uncomfortable, and it throws people into conflict. They become small and ungodly. They lose their passion and 'inspiration'; literally, they no longer 'breathe in spirit'. Their energy is not coherent, so they become flickering light-bulbs with scattered energies locked in destructive interference. At an energy level, co-dependency crushes us – despite its illusory gift of a golden cage. By splitting our energy, it makes us 'fall asleep' and lose access to our wild potential. Life becomes small and limited – a predictable, conformist life that does not belong to us.

'What about my son refusing to make his bed, and leaving his room in such a mess? That affects me! He is being selfish and not considering my needs!' But your son cannot be responsible for your feelings – and it wouldn't bother you if you loved him unconditionally. Only the ego gets lost in the surface details of life, and loses sight of the bigger picture. Real love makes no demands. 'But what about him not doing his homework? I have to nag him about that, or it would never get done. *Then* where might he end up?' Well, perhaps he might end up being guided by his innate need for freedom and self-empowerment.

In any case, if you say to a child 'Let's tidy up your room', you will get a different response from saying 'Tidy up your room!' The first is a request; the second is a demand. The first is based upon love and harmony; the second on control and sacrifice. The first comes from high vibrations that will evoke the best from your child, whereas the second comes from lower vibrations, which will split their energy and throw them into resistance. And if they still choose to have an untidy room, is that such a problem? It is so easy to slip into taming our children.

The new children of this generation – the Indigo children, Crystal children and others[9] – are freedom-seekers. They are highly attuned to energy. They are right-brained and intuitive. They demand honesty and integrity, and can *feel* it when we are not being authentic. They also have an inherent sense of worthiness, and do not take kindly to being tamed or shamed. They arrive with the new paradigm pulsing in their veins. *We* are the ones who need to catch up! (I recently heard of a young child being diagnosed with 'Oppositional Defiant Disorder'! For heaven's sake! This is a child who has a healthy disregard for being told what to do by big people who do not know *what feels good to her.* Yet she was being drugged into submission.) Do you want your children to be tame conformists who follow the well-trodden path, and fit in with others' expectations (including yours)? Or do you want them to be wild and free, to take responsibility for their own lives, to express their own creativity and uniqueness, to be passionate visionaries for a new future?

Author Byron Katie[10] suggests that we ask ourselves 'Whose business is that?' whenever we are caught up in painful thoughts about someone else's behaviour. All too often, it means we are trying to control how other people handle their lives – our partner, our children, our parents, our colleagues, even our friends. And it is rarely any of our business. 'But surely it *is* my business if my partner is flirting with someone, or my teenager is taking drugs?' Well, perhaps not – at least in the sense that you are not 'entitled' to judge or control anyone else's behaviour, nor to have them fulfil *your* needs in *your* way. Whenever you believe you have that right, you risk damaging the relationship. You have your own feelings and needs, which are perfectly valid – but they have their needs too, and their own reasons for behaving as they do (if only you listen with love). And perhaps you need to take responsibility for what *you* are creating in this relationship. Then hold a steady and positive vision of what you *really* want – instead of looking at what you see as bad and wrong in them, and trying to change it from the outside-in. The Universe can only mirror back your vibrations – which is why criticising and complaining (even silently) always brings you more of the same.

Wild love means making no judgments about others' journeys. I certainly find it helpful to remind myself 'That's none of my business', whenever I find myself disturbed by other people's choices. Wanting to control or fix others (or the world) can be a deeply engrained habit, especially among those of us who are helper-rescuers – and this includes expecting others to love more wildly! Trusting that everything is unfolding perfectly – even when there is deep contrast – is remarkably liberating.

Wild love means setting others free to make their own decisions – even if we imagine that different choices might make them happier, or make *us* happier, or might be a less circuitous or rocky path. We are centred on our own journey, and allow others to be on their own journey – including our partner, and our children – knowing that we can never see the whole picture, trusting they are doing whatever they need to do, encouraging them to follow their own emotional guidance.

Wild love is about learning to love without clinging, without demands – loving with an open hand, and encouraging the other to spread their wings. This might mean bumping into our own fear and insecurity at times; but we know these feelings belong to us and are not caused by the Other. This is not love for the faint-hearted. It is love for grown-ups. It is loving while letting go. As writer Marge Piercy puts it, 'It hurts to love wide open ... but you thrive, you glow.'

Learning to love differently is hard,
love with the hands wide open, love
with the doors banging on their hinges,
the cupboard unlocked, the wind
roaring and whimpering in the rooms ...

Marge Piercy[11]

Wild love means accepting that any relationship is forever evolving, and its form might change. Love is simply love. It does not have to take any particular shape. Its form depends upon the circumstances, upon the needs and desires that that relationship can meet right now. Wild love means that we never see love as limited or exclusive. We never pin it down. We allow love to flow where it will. We welcome love with open arms, in as many places and for as many people as possible. We might hold a clear intention and desire for a relationship to be loving and lasting – and if we both love wildly, so it will be. But if a marriage turns into a co-parenting relationship, or a more flexible two-home arrangement, this does not mean the relationship has 'failed'; it has simply flowed into a different form.

My soon-to-be ex-husband and I are slowly blossoming since our separation, and our friendship has moved on. We still share spiritual ideas, and are currently co-writing a musical for our son's school. I have recovered my sense of embodiment, and my thirst for travel and adventure. I'm learning to roller-blade with my son, and to play the flute. My creativity has been unleashed. I feel spiritually awake again. I can breathe fully. On a recent solo trip to India, as I strolled along the white sands of Goa in my bikini, dipping into the warm Arabian sea for an occasional swim – feeling utterly blissed-out – I realised how much I have changed. I am more whole, more womanly, more wild. I am more gentle, open-hearted and loving. I have come home to myself. Was my marriage a failure? Not in my eyes. I learned and gained so much from it (including our wonderful child). The idea of failure comes from judgment and fixed expectations. Beyond duality, there is no right or wrong, no compulsory form, no commandments written in stone. Everything flows freely – and is guided by love, joy and freedom, rather than by the needs for approval, control or security.

Unconditional love means loving someone whatever they feel, whatever they think, whatever they desire, whatever they choose – since we love them *as they are*, not as we might want them to be. Once Matthew finally wrote to say we could no longer be close friends or even acquaintances – and confirmed this by pretending not to know me when we met – I accepted his choice, and loved him anyway. I wanted him to do what *he* wanted, not what I wanted. I could still love *him* wildly, even though he chose tame love – with fierce boundaries and rules and restrictions – which left no tiny corner for our loving friendship. Wild love is not for everyone. It is a choice that we make. Not a 'better' choice. Just a different choice, with different consequences.

A relationship of any kind will last for as long as it is meant to, for as long as it is serving us – either in helping us learn to love, or by propelling us into growth through the contrast of 'what love is not', or by reminding us of lost parts of ourselves which we need to reclaim: our hopes and dreams, our yearning, our passion, our sensuality, our emotions, our authenticity, our creativity, our dark or light Shadow.

> '*Who am I to you?*' *a lover once asked me.*
> '*You are my animus, my presence, my beauty, my free spirit.*
> *You are my everyman,*' *I replied;*
> *and he nodded, content to be all that –*
> *my tabula rasa, imprinted with my sadness, my rage and longing.*
> *He was wild and free, an artist,*

painting his life afresh each day.
Then he left, silent as a breeze, leaving me forever richer,
like a forest scattered with freshly fallen leaves.[12]

6. Be grateful and appreciative

Gratitude is a powerful magnet. Whenever we feel grateful, we attract more gifts into our lives. When I wake each morning, I make a habit of feeling grateful for all the precious gifts in my life: my beautiful home and garden, my gorgeous son, my loving friends and family, the stunning landscape around me, my fit and healthy body, doing work that I adore. Grateful for the privilege and joy of writing this book. Grateful for life itself. And grateful for all the good things that happened yesterday, and for all the good things I intend for today. Gratitude releases resistance – it opens us to receiving, to allowing miracles to happen – and is a wonderful way to start the day.

Within every relationship, appreciating all that is wonderful in the Other, being eternally grateful for their loving presence in your life, acknowledging what they do for you, or simply expressing your love and appreciation for who they are in a hundred different ways, all helps to build a deeper bond between you, and to evoke what is best and highest in each of you.

The Japanese scientist Masuro Emoto has developed a way of photographing water as it crystallises into ice. Much of the tap water from cities is so polluted that it will barely form into crystals – yet if water is exposed to words such as 'I love you' or 'Thank you' or 'You're beautiful', by wrapping written words on paper around the bottles, the water can then produce beautiful crystals. Hateful, angry or negative words – whether written, spoken or merely thought – produce dark, ugly, broken formations when the water tries to crystallise. The most stunning crystals of all are formed by sending love and gratitude.[13]

Words and thoughts are patterned energy, with higher or

lower vibrations depending upon how aligned they are with Source. Since we are 70 per cent water, Emoto's work supports the idea that every thought – positive or negative – either makes our energy more beautiful and harmonious, or more muddy and discordant. Appreciation and gratitude take us to the dizzying heights of the Emotional Scale; they align us with Source energy.

Interestingly, Emoto has found that cooked rice that is *ignored* rots even more rapidly than rice which is verbally abused. Withholding our attention – neglecting, ignoring or invalidating anyone – seems to be the most damaging action we can take, which is why both children and adults often 'behave badly', or even seem to invite punishment and abuse, when they are not given enough attention. Even negative attention is preferable to being ignored. Focusing your attention on anyone or anything is an act of love. And if that attention takes the positive form of heartfelt adoration – if you bathe them in Source energy – it can help to transform them. And it's great for you too!

7. Focus upon the positive

Why do we truly love someone? Because they connect us with Source. Because their presence makes us feel wonderful. Because they help us connect with who we really are, and bring out the best in us. The deep Self constantly affirms the other – not by putting them on a pedestal, but by seeing who they really are. Wild love means that we focus on what is best in a relationship, and in other people. Blame or criticism keeps our vibrations low, and means that we attract more of the same. Wild love means loving the other even when they are lost in shame or blame or fear or despair or distancing. It means loving them even when they are trying to tame us – without giving in, without being over-compassionate, without becoming defensive, without attacking back. It means staying Self-centred, so that we do not get hooked into our old ego defences, so we do not get entangled with their energy. It means seeing the beauty in *everything* that they are. Loving without condition.

A year or so ago, while grieving badly over my separation from Matthew, I noticed my son saying 'No' to every suggestion I made, expecting the worst at school, refusing to answer when called and generally being 'difficult' and awkward. I caught myself criticising him for being negative, especially since he is aware that our thoughts create our reality! Then I became aware of what *I* was doing. I was coming to my son with *my* pain, resistance and self-judgment, which evoked negativity from him, which I then blamed on *him*. It was, of course, me who needed to change. I spent two weeks deliberately focusing on what was wonderful about my son, reviving happy memories we had shared, feeling grateful for his presence in my life, and minimising any challenging behaviour – not in an attempt to change him, but in an effort to reconnect *myself*. Once I felt positive towards him again, my son became his usual warm, loving and cuddly self – and if he was occasionally demanding, I now saw it in a different light and loved him anyway.

Whenever we criticise or judge anyone, or tell them what *not* to do, we disconnect ourselves from Source – and in our disconnection, we attract more of the same. We get what we focus upon. Whenever we focus on problems, or what is going wrong, or what is lacking, or unhappy memories, we attract more of the same. By the Law of Attraction, critical thoughts evoke negative behaviour from the other person, which mirrors those thoughts; then their behaviour triggers more critical thoughts, and so the vicious downward spiral continues.

Instead we need to focus on what is right, what we love and what we desire. It always feels better when we focus on what is good and beautiful in the Other – and in the relationship – and *feeling* good tells us that we are heading in the right direction. As we emit more positive vibes, the Other will resonate with our energy, and respond more positively. Every relationship is a self-fulfilling prophecy.

How we *feel* is crucial here. If we say positive words that we are not resonating with, the Other will 'hear' it as flattery or manipulation – and so it is. We are far more transparent to others than we might imagine, and we have to be authentic. We cannot say positive words while secretly feeling resentful or condescending. The Law of Attraction works at an energy level, so 'empty words' make no difference to our reality. We have to shift our vibrations – to *feel* it. Life is all about energetic resonance.

8. Choose thoughts, stories and 'lessons' that feel good

Let's suppose you receive news that your mother has been rushed into hospital. You might immediately spiral into negative emotion by catastrophising, setting up worst-case scenarios of what might follow, and mentally rearranging your diary to fit in her funeral; or you might see those emotions as guidance that you are swinging out of alignment with Source. Then you might choose gentle, soothing, reassuring thoughts – such as that you don't yet know what is happening, there is no point in worrying since that emits negative energy, or perhaps that death is an inevitable part of life, and even if she does die, all is well. Whatever the situation, your task is to choose thoughts and stories that feel good – or to tap your meridians, or use flower essences, or meditate, or do anything that takes the painful resistance caused by fear or judgment out of your energy system.

However, there is no point in telling yourself stories you cannot believe. Anything you think or say but cannot *feel* is just denial. It is not changing your vibrations – which are indicated by how you feel; and it is your *vibrations* which will affect the outcome of any situation. It is your vibrations which create your reality. So if you find yourself plummeting to the very bottom of the Emotional Scale, perhaps into fear or despair or powerlessness, you might need to deliberately choose anger in order to move back towards alignment. ('I kept telling Mum to relax and take better care of herself. Why doesn't she ever listen to me?') You don't have to *express* such thoughts; you can just enjoy the private relief that comes from feeling angry rather than frightened or despairing! Once you have found relief from anger, you can probably find some thoughts based on irritation; then you are probably within reach of hopeful thoughts, and moving up towards calm acceptance or even optimism. You are moving away from fear towards love. You are getting back in the flow. As you reach for higher vibrations, new thoughts and insights become available to you, and those associated with lower vibrations simply don't occur to you any more, or feel ridiculous. Try it – it works!

> … when my heart listens
> through the cold stethoscope of fear,
> your voice in my head reminds me
> what the light teaches.
> Slowly you translate fear into love,
> the way the moon's blood is the sea.
>
> *Anne Michaels*[14]

Sometimes it helps to re-frame your family history, and choose a different story. Graham's father had spent little time with his family, visiting only occasionally in between adventures elsewhere – and always leaving them with debts to pay. Graham had always seen his mother as the dutiful, responsible, 'good' parent whom he tried to emulate; yet he had imprisoned himself by trying to avoid becoming like his 'bad' father. He strived to be conformist and dutiful, and to avoid any risks. I suggested that though his father was not perfect, he could be seen as visionary and free-spirited, and reluctantly tied to a marriage that did not work for him; whereas his mother might be seen as a martyr who was fearful and stuck. Turning our images upside down like this often frees us up (and excluding a parent from our hearts is a common cause of depression). For Graham, this gave him permission to honour his father, and value those positive 'father' qualities within himself, to free himself up. You are never trapped by your past, since it is your *current* thoughts and vibrations which create your reality. You might have well-practised 'stories' which date back to old family riverbeds, but your power is always in the present. You can choose whatever lessons you like from your personal history; but it is wise to choose lessons which feel expansive and empowering.

So what lessons emerged from my own journey with Matthew – a relationship which woke me up, propelled me out of my marriage, reawakened my lost dreams and potential, and also dragged me down through the pits of hell? There were many unhealthy elements to that relationship: trying to 'rescue', getting caught up in a drama triangle, allowing myself to be controlled and disempowered and guilt-tripped, putting my loyalty to him above my own emotional guidance. Yet I learned so much from all of that. And beyond all that messiness, shining like a beacon, was a pure unconditional love that never wavered. A love that saw all that he was, and saw that it was good. A love that knew that love is *always* good and innocent and holy. A wild and eternal love that was, and is, unaffected by the whole drama.

Can such unconditional love and trust be found in *any* relationship? In theory, yes – if we are aligned with Source. We can certainly *choose* to love self and others more wildly. In practice, unconditional love seems to occur naturally from the start in some relationships, due no doubt to a long karmic history and deep soul connection. These are blessed relationships that do not push us down our old riverbeds, but point a finger towards new vision, hope and possibility. Such love arrives like a gift of grace – if only fleetingly – and lights up our lives. Certainly, I will never be the same again.

This sweet and ancient love has left me more whole –
for all it has forced me to release.
It has stripped me of the false, and pared me to the
soul.
I will never again settle for less than is possible.
I now root to the earth and shoot for the stars.
I glimpse the heavens shimmering through at last –
And all that remains is Love.[15]

I suspect that such unconditional love – between friends or partners – will become more and more common in the years to come, as our awareness expands. Yet despite the deep love I felt for Matthew, a huge lesson I learned is never to give anyone else the power to connect us with Source. If you believe you *need* anyone (or anything) outside the self in order to feel that incredible flow of wild love, of bliss, of passion, of pure Source energy, you are in danger of becoming addicted or co-dependent. While others can certainly act as *catalysts* for the flow of Source – and it is undeniably wonderful to be in the presence of anyone you truly love – you need to know that your connection does not *depend* upon them. You cannot be separated from Love. Happiness is always an inside job.

I could have chosen many negative stories from my painful experience with Matthew – stories of abandonment, guilt, betrayal of friendship and trust. Dark lessons of fear, judgment and disconnection. But although I toyed with such ego-based stories, I chose none of them. I could tell from how they made me *feel* that they were not aligned with higher truth.

Instead I chose positive stories from my journey, lessons which feel light and loving and expansive. I now know what it means to love unconditionally. I know that love does not need to take any particular form, but that it does seek flow and expression. I have seen how fear and judgment stop this natural flow of love, and block open and honest communication – disconnecting us from who we are. I have learned from experience how being guilt-tripped controls and diminishes us. I have discovered what makes relationships dysfunctional, and how to turn this around. I have learned to listen to my emotional guidance, how to align with Source from within. I have given up being good and perfect. I now understand why love and freedom are inseparable – and how, together, they help us create heaven on earth. My experience of 'contrast' has launched huge dreams and desires in me, which are giving birth to new futures, which I joyfully anticipate. Perhaps above all, I have come to embrace the dark and the light, to live beyond duality. I have learned to love more deeply, more wildly, more boldly. I have set myself free. So much learning and growth. So many precious gifts. So much gratitude.

In *Pure Bliss*, I wrote that I suspected that my wild woman had 'yet to sing her sweetest, or roar her loudest'.[15] At the time, I wondered what I meant. Now I am beginning to understand. It might take the rest of my life – or even longer – to fully integrate my expanded awareness, but there is no shortage of time. There is no shortage of anything. Even through times of deep contrast, life is such an incredible and beautiful journey; and though we create it all, we never know what fresh surprises lie just around the corner, and where they might lead us. Life is good.

9. Everyone's needs and desires can be met

Any healthy relationship includes contrast – times of disagreement and conflict, times when you dip down the Emotional Scale, times when you seem to pull in different directions. And this contrast can be seen as a necessary spur to growth, rather than a threat. How dull it would be if we always thought alike, or wanted the same experiences! Resolving conflict by transcending the apparent duality is a major way in which relationships grow and blossom. Instead of going for the 'easy option' of control and sacrifice, this means finding authentic win-win solutions which take us to a higher level of awareness, which expand us, which increase intimacy and trust and freedom and empowerment.

Higher resolution comes from connecting with Source, by using our emotions for guidance, rather than trying to please or trying to control. When we know that guilt, anger, frustration, feeling disempowered or any negative emotion means we are stuck in ego – and find ways of re-aligning ourselves with Source – the Universe can always find a way of harmonising everyone's needs and desires. Even if it would seem to take a miracle. Beyond the ego – beyond duality – miracles happen all the time. A Source of unconditional love never calls for self-sacrifice, duty or martyrdom. It never calls on us to pay a price for happiness. Source always calls us towards joy and freedom and love. And – contrary to what society and religion have taught us – it is only when we *stop* being swayed by others' needs and demands that we can listen to our own emotional–intuitive guidance, and move towards love.

A few months ago, my parents were discussing their holiday plans. My father is somewhat disabled, and was in a negative frame of mind. He did not want to risk another fall; he did not want to go anywhere. Unusually they seemed unable to resolve the issue by discussing it. My mother began to feel frustrated, since she wanted a holiday. But instead of blaming or criticising, or giving up and sacrificing herself – instead of resonating with his disturbed energy field – she withdrew from the conversation to centre herself. She meditated, calling upon Source for a higher resolution to this impasse. When she returned to the lounge, just a few minutes later, my father was feeling much more confident and positive. They were both back in alignment with Source – and they booked their holiday. (More recently, the same dilemma was resolved by my mother deciding to travel alone to Egypt to see my brother – with my father's heartfelt support. The Universe can always find a win-win solution.)

What if – as happened with Matthew – two people want a relationship with the same person? Ideally you find a way of maintaining *both* relationships, in whatever forms are appropriate. Only tame love is exclusive. The relationships will meet different needs, and evoke different potential – and everyone involved will benefit and grow.

However, if an 'either-or' solution emerges – as it did with Matthew – the Universe is infinitely resourceful. It can deliver the *essence* of anything and everything that we desire. Only the ego thinks in terms of lack and scarcity, of competition for limited resources. So we can clarify the qualities about that person, friendship or relationship that we loved, then send our request to Source: 'Clone that one! Next time, without the complications. I desire someone who loves me as whole-heartedly as I love him/her.' Or 'I desire a friendship like that, with someone who wishes to be my soul friend.' Then we align our energy, trust in Source to deliver – and wait in joyful expectancy. This is a friendly and loving universe in which anything is possible. There are no limits other than those we choose to believe in. And when the new person turns up, we love them *exactly as they are* – without conditions, without expectations that they fit into the pre-cast mould we had in mind. Just loving and cherishing them as they are – as we love ourselves, as we wish to be loved.

> If this earth were a heaven,
> might all relationships be of loving friendship?
> No roles, no labels,
> no demands made of each other –
> just the promise, freely made,
> 'We shall love one another with an open heart –
> and cherish what togetherness we choose.'
> Then we travel our own paths,
> joining and separating as we will,
> only loving and being amazed

> *as we unwrap each other afresh each day, or each*
> *week,*
> *delighting in the beauty and mystery of our lives,*
> *honouring each other's freedom,*
> *trusting each other's kindness,*
> *and loving not one but many;*
> *loving not the false skin of the Other,*
> *but the beating heart within –*
> *the Self that is constantly emerging and being born.*[17]

10. Fall passionately in love with life

Wild love ultimately means a loving relationship with Self – and that means following our bliss, honouring our emotions, accepting every part of self without question, and reaching for our wildest dreams and desires, instead of settling for what seems reasonable or what others might expect of us. And this is what a truly loving relationship with another helps us to do.

My friendship with Matthew made me move *towards* life, towards expansion, which was partly why I found it so compelling. My marriage had pushed me into retreat, while Matthew brought out aspects of me which I had kept under wraps for years. With him, I wanted to embrace life fully – to leap into mountain streams, to scale the heights, to dance all night long, to be wild and free. I saw that he symbolised my longing to be immersed in the world, to plant both feet firmly on the earth, to love without reservation. He was my *anam cara*, my soul friend, who nourished my embodied spirit.

When he disappeared, I gradually had to learn to say an unconditional Yes to life – a wholehearted and reverberating Yes – in his absence. I had to reach out and connect instead of holding back. I had to nurture myself. I had to ground my soul. I had to stride deeper and deeper *into* the world. I had to fall passionately in love with life all over again. What a glorious task! I am revelling in it.

My 'sweet warm ghost' is still with me. We talk and laugh, walk hand in hand across the mountains and valleys, or drink wine together beside the log fire. But these days, I see him as the *essence* of my Beloved, my soul companion, my unknown future lover from whom I can never be separated – for Love knows no separation. For now, I am enjoying this honeyed time to myself, and my life is rich and warm with love in many different forms. But when I am ready, I will fully align my energy with the loving and intimate relationship of my dreams, and my Beloved will appear in the flesh. He must do so, for that is how reality works. And since my energy will be harmonised with Source, the result will be a wild and sacred love.

The greatest recipe for creating a truly loving relationship is to be in love with life – to be Self-centred, to feel complete in ourselves – so that we do not fall into needy or possessive love, so that a loving relationship is merely the icing on the cake. When we are in love with life, heaven is here and now – even in the midst of contrast, even when what we desire has not yet arrived, even when life seems messy or confusing. We trust that everything is unfolding perfectly, and that where we are right now is exactly where we need to be.

Self-love means focusing with joyful anticipation on what we desire, on daydreaming, on happy memories, on enjoyable activities, on anything that will raise our vibrations towards unconditional love and passion. We choose positive thoughts, follow our bliss, and keep our energy flowing. There is no angst about unfulfilled desires, since we know that we are loved, and can create anything that we want, if only we align our energy. And what fun we can have in the process! If we slip into negative emotion, we do whatever it takes to get a sense of relief, of increased freedom and empowerment – that breath of fresh air, that feeling of relaxation, that rush of pleasure that tells us we are aligning with Source energy. Then we take any action we feel guided towards from that higher space, doing whatever makes us feel light and expansive, and paying attention to any tension or dip in the solar plexus, which tells us that we are veering off our path.

When we are connected with Source, we are naturally 'good', warm and loving – but it comes from the heart, not from a sense of duty or loyalty or approval-seeking. It is authentic. It is real. It is who we really are, and not what others think we should be. We look at everyone and everything with the eyes of wild love – without fear, without judgment. We radiate unconditional love and joy and passion. Then we are gods in the making.

PUSHING AGAINST VS REACHING TOWARDS

Does this mean we all have to follow the same philosophy, that everyone on the planet should adopt this model – that we should go around evangelising, attempting to convince others that they too need to be deliberate and conscious co-creators, that they must love more wildly? Of course not! That is trying to change others – that is, trying to tame and control them! In any case, what works for you might not work for someone else; or not right now.

For many people (especially those born before the 1960s, or into highly conservative families), tame love is just fine. They are happy to settle for stability and conformity, or to potter along in a good-enough relationship; or they value social approval above the risks of freedom and self-expression; or they have little interest in personal and spiritual growth. And there is no right or wrong choice. Everyone is doing exactly what they need to do – even if they are limiting their potential, even if they are in the midst of huge contrast, even if they seem to be creating pain and discomfort for themselves or others. Whatever is happening, all is well.

Although I am advocating wild love, I am not pushing against tame love. If we push against tame love, it pushes right back at us. (Believe me, I know!) We get what we focus upon. Whenever we judge or disapprove of anyone or anything, they show us more of their worst aspects. We can raise awareness of issues, but there is a delicate line between raising awareness and resisting 'what is' – and resistance means that our focus and energy is split. Then we create muddy realities. Whatever we resist persists. Instead we need to reach towards what we *do* want – and set others free to make their own choices.

For more than 20 years, I was an outspoken critic of allopathic medicine, and vigorously promoted 'alternative' approaches to health. These days – thanks partly to close friends who happen to be doctors – I favour integrative medicine, since I recognise that different approaches serve different needs and circumstances, and suit different levels of awareness. Although allopathic medicine has many risks, dangers and limitations, it also has many strengths. Nothing is inherently bad or wrong. Modern medicine perfectly mirrors our current state of awareness – and if we see anything as bad or wrong, we merely hold it in place, and prevent its natural growth and transformation. We need lots of options in healthcare, and they can all work together in harmony. Likewise, I used to criticise the education system – despite knowing some fabulous teachers – and had planned on homeschooling my child. As I softened my own approach, I found a wonderful village school which supports my son's individuality and emotional well-being; and I appreciate its strengths and positive qualities, rather than focusing on what is wrong with education.

We can still envision 'what might be' for health, education and other social systems, including personal relationships, without *pushing against* 'what is' – without pointing fingers of blame, without seeing ourselves as right and others as wrong, without criticising and complaining, without trying to convince others that their approach is faulty or inadequate. Change becomes possible when we let go of our resistance, when we let go of our judgment. There is no need to go into battle, for we are all on the same side. We are all part of the same undivided whole. Radical acceptance lies at the heart of wild love.

But surely we can inspire others by our example? Yes. Yes. Yes. Our journey as individuals always serves the greater whole. It is precisely by being role models for new ways of being that we *can* change the world – since this raises the vibrations of the planet, and helps to make the energy of humanity more coherent. Our passion and hope and joy and optimism can inspire and awaken others. Instead of trying to 'sort out problems', we can reach for *solutions*. We can be the conscious creators that we were born to be. Everything that exists began as an idea, as consciousness, as a vision of future possibility. Whenever we *reach towards* what we do want, aligning ourselves with that desire – rather than *pushing against* what we see as bad or wrong – we are visionaries who are creating a new future for humanity.

Personally, I think life is much more fun if we love more wildly, and consciously make our dreams come true, with an awareness of the laws of reality creation. It is a liberating and empowering approach to life, which can help us create heaven on earth. And I have shown what a huge price we pay for living in surface reality, and limiting ourselves to tame love. But everyone is on their own unique path. Ultimately, we are all heading in the same direction – towards expanded awareness and joy – but the world needs a *variety* of models, beliefs and spiritual paths, so that we have plenty of choice. We do not have to convert anyone else to our way of thinking. In fact, we do not need 'spiritual' beliefs at all to shift into the new paradigm. All that is necessary is to move towards real love, joy and freedom – beyond fear, beyond approval-seeking, beyond duality. And that is where we are going.

RELATIONSHIPS WITHIN THE NEW PARADIGM

It is easier to remain a prisoner of the past than to become a pioneer of the future; it takes less energy, less conscious-ness. However, it blocks the flow of love and cripples our human potential. As I see it, our riverbeds of co-dependency are now standing in the way of our conscious evolution; and for many of us, the time has come to forge new riverbeds, to birth new models of relationships – relationships between people who are committed to their dreams, and to their own alignment with Source, who realise that the key to joy and freedom is unconditional love.

So what does a wild and sacred relationship look like? Any truly loving relationship gives us both roots and wings. It grounds us in the roots of unconditional love, so that we feel free to spread our wings and discover our potential. A wild, co-creative relationship helps us resonate with what is highest within us. No energy is wasted through entanglement, blaming, shaming, taming or people-pleasing. Wild love liberates us from fear and judg-ment. It makes our energy coherent. It turns us into brilliant laser beams. It allows us to sparkle and dance – to become wild and free.

These wild, co-creative relationships arise when we combine the mature ego and the deep Self. These are the healthy, supportive and truly loving relationships of the future. The mature ego gives us the ability to be authentic, and to stay in touch with our emotional guidance, our unique desires and future potential. The deep Self gives us the 'intuitive knowing' that we *are* safe and loved and good – and do not need anyone to reassure us of that. It also reminds us that any relationship mirrors our own vibrations, that the Other is never the problem. Together the mature ego and the deep Self give us the ability to love and trust this Other unconditionally: to see the light *and* the dark within them, to know that all of it is good, and to allow them to unfold in the arms of love. Together we create a synergy that makes us more than we might have been alone. In the presence of wild love, we dare to be passionate dreamers and visionaries. Our consciousness expands. Our heart opens. Our creativity flows. We become more and more aware of being multi-dimensional beings of light, dwelling in a universe of energy, consciousness and love.

In a romantic partnership based upon wild love, there is open and honest communication, emotional intimacy, fun and laughter, mutual respect, physical affection, an enjoyable (even ecstatic) sex life, frequent expressions of love – and unlimited support for each other's freedom, growth and individuality. You greet each other with love and warmth. You delight in each other's company, even while shopping or washing the dishes. Every challenge is seen as an opportunity to grow. Conflicts are resolved within the greater context of unconditional love for each other, in ways that feel mutually satisfying and rewarding, in ways that bring you closer. You feel utterly safe with each other. You can relax and breathe freely. You can share anything and everything, knowing it will be heard with love and acceptance. You 'hold' each other's wounds and melt any defences. Your deepest desires and creativity are released. You awaken and inspire each other. You connect with each other intuitively. You dive into each other's unfathomable depths. You grow and blossom like spring flowers. Your love expands into the world. You reach out to others with open arms, knowing the Other will always honour love in all its many forms. (The possibility of having an affair would never even arise.) There is a deep knowing that your soul can spread its wings, that all is well.

True love is limitless. It is only false love, conditional love, which fades and constricts and splits our energy. Wild love is eternal and ever-expanding. And it can be found not only in romantic partnerships, but with soul friends, in family relationships, between business partners, or even with our beloved pets. And the more we truly love, the more it spreads out into all of our relationships – until we blast *everyone* and *everything* with unconditional love, whether it is a stranger selling us a train ticket, or a friend inviting us for a cup of coffee, or just seeing raindrops splashing in a puddle. Love allows our energy to flow. Love heals and transforms us. Love scatters its seeds across the universe.

This really is a magical reality in which anything that we desire can happen. We have only scratched the surface of our potential as human beings – as lovers, as co-creators. Until now, we have been held down by tame love; but it is time for us to build our wings. Our culture is currently in transition between tame love and wild love – and, as always, we must learn to live comfortably in the gap between 'what is' and what we desire. It might take years, decades or even generations to learn to love wildly, but we need to be visionaries. We are dreaming this world into being, so let us have wonderful dreams. If we want a more loving and joyful and harmonious world, let us create that golden future together. One by one, we need to clarify what we want, then focus our positive thoughts and beliefs on those desires – not allowing ourselves to get entangled in discordant energy – and in the meantime, choose to be happy in any which way we can, to release our resistance.

We can create heaven or hell, or anything in between, depending upon our connectedness with Source. *Everything we experience depends upon whether our love – for self, others and the world – is tame or wild.*

♥

Wild love does not separate the world into good and bad, right and wrong, safe and dangerous. It says a profound 'Yes' to life. It affirms that 'everything within you and me is good'. It is fearless relating. It dwells in a blameless universe. It is love which gives without needing to receive. It is love without needs and demands and expectations. It is love that inspires and expands us – which sets us free.

Wild love is unconditional love. Radical acceptance. Opening our hearts. Following our bliss. Adoring the world just as it is. Loving ourselves just as we are. Loving others just as they are. No taming. No conditions. Just desires and visions that we are deliciously on the way to fulfilling – knowing that nothing 'out there' can block the fulfilment of our dreams. Knowing that we create it all. Trusting that everything is unfolding perfectly. Loving our emotions, and the guidance from Source that they offer. Enjoying the contrast that spurs fresh desires and growth. Taking ourselves lightly. Loving each step of our journey as we go. Remembering that life is about joy and freedom and growth.

Welcome to the dance! We are apprentice gods with limitless potential, who are melting the boundaries between heaven and earth. We are safe. We are loved. We are good and worthy. All is well. There is no destination – just an ever-evolving and miraculous journey. Life is this moment, and this moment, and this moment … And love is what we are.

AFTERWORD

As for me and Matthew … We did not speak again for two more years – despite living close by in a small rural community, and having many mutual friends. He did not reply to my occasional letters, and avoided anywhere we might meet. I learnt to live with the painful situation, but he was forever on my mind – sometimes with hurt and confusion, often with sadness and grief, always with love. Eventually I had some big news which led to him suddenly agreeing to meet me again. It was the first time we had spoken in two and a half years. We sat in my summer garden, and talked for hours. His marriage was still 'not going well'. He was treading on eggshells around his wife, and desperately trying to keep things stable for the children. He had found it too painful even to open my letters, but thought of me every day. My love for him remained as deep as ever. Before we parted, he said he could not meet me again to avoid upsetting his wife. Yet it had now become impossible for us to carry on pretending and avoiding each other – and in any case, the prolonged silence had not resolved our relationship. We had to find another way through. And so our journey of wild love continued ...

This story spills over into a new book. If you would like to know what happened next, see my book *Conscious Medicine* (Piatkus, 2010).

APPENDIX

EMOTIONAL FREEDOM TECHNIQUE (EFT)

Begin by accepting that you have the problem, symptom or painful memory. (This is The Set-Up phase – see below.) Then tap specific points on the body – sharply, but not hard enough to cause any discomfort – about 5–10 times each, while focusing on the problem/memory/symptom, or saying 'This anxiety' or 'This back pain' or whatever. (The exact number of taps is not important.) Every point can be tapped on either (or both) sides of the body. The order in which you tap is not important. You might get even better results if you tap each point rapidly, pause briefly, then tap again more slowly. The more *specific* you are about the symptom or problem, or particular aspect of the memory, the better the results tend to be.

I. THE SET-UP

Tap the side of one hand (the karate chop point) with the fingers of your other hand, while saying: 'Even though I have .... [this problem], I completely love and accept myself' – or words to that effect. Say this three times while tapping the point – and *mean* it!

2. THE SEQUENCE

With two or three fingers together: tap seven points sharply: inner eyebrow, side of eye, under eye, under nose, indent of chin, just below inner end of collar-bone, under arm (level with nipples) – while saying, 'this problem' (such as 'this sadness' or 'this pain in my right knee'), to keep your mind focused on it. Then tap five points on hand: top of thumb (side away from fingers, level with nail-base), index finger (the side of finger nearest thumb, level with nail-base), middle finger (ditto), little finger (ditto), then karate chop point – while saying 'this problem'.

Then tap 1) the gamut point – which is 2cm behind the knuckles, in between the ring and little fingers 2) the inside of your wrist (where a watch–strap goes) 3) the very top of your head, at the point where it begins to slope down towards the back – all while saying 'this problem'.

3. THE REPEAT SEQUENCE

Tap down body, from eyebrow to karate chop point, while saying 'this problem'.

If there is *some* improvement, but part of the problem remains, then repeat as follows:

1) Tap karate chop point: 'Even though I still have some of [this problem] left, I fully and completely accept myself.'

2) Tap as in Step 2 above, while saying/thinking about 'Remaining [problem].'

3) Or try just tapping from eyebrow to under-arm; this is often enough. Repeat as necessary.

If there is *no* improvement, repeat the Set-Up with more emphasis and conviction; or you might need to re-phrase the Set-Up. It might help to say, 'Even though I don't want to get better, I completely love and accept myself.' Or 'Even though I'm afraid of getting better, I completely love ... ' Or 'Even though I feel I don't deserve to get better, I completely love ... ' Then do the tapping. Take a deep breath.

4. CHOOSING A NEW FUTURE

Finally, **tap in what you now choose to feel instead**, or what you would like your body to do, using the same tapping points: eg. 'I now choose to feel at peace about [this event].' You can choose different affirmations for each point, just saying whatever feels right.

(Adapted and improved version of the original method – with thanks to Patricia Carrington for the Choice Method. See www.emofree.com for further details.)

GLOSSARY

Call A problem, mystery or opportunity, or a feeling such as anxiety or 'divine discontent', which calls you to wake up from your mundane life and connect with a more expansive reality. The first stage in the **hero's journey**.

Co-creator A co-creator is one who consciously aligns with Source energy in order to shape and create their reality. One who takes full responsibility for everything they experience and feel. An apprentice god. A co-creative relationship is one that helps you expand beyond the ego and release your potential – through wild love.

Co-dependency Relationships based upon mutual dependency, and the pseudo-love (approval and security-seeking) of the ego. Relationships characterised by cycles of Control-and-Sacrifice. This keeps both people trapped in lower vibrations – blocking true love and intimacy, as well as freedom and growth.

Coherence Energy which is highly integrated and harmonious, and so has immense creative power. Energy which is not split by the contradictions caused by fear, doubt, approval-seeking or judgment. See **split energy**.

Deep reality The interconnected web of energy-consciousness-love which is the 'invisible reality' which underlies the visible world, and from which everything emerges.

Deep Self The higher self or soul. The God within. Our essence. Our inner connection to deep reality and unconditional love.

Dreams The desires of your **deep Self** that give birth to new realities, and allow you to become an 'apprentice god'. See **co-creator**.

Duality Splitting self, others or the world into good/bad, right/wrong or safe/dangerous. The world of the immature ego, based upon fear and judgment.

Ego The personality that sees **Self** as separate from others, from the world and from God/Source. The immature ego is motivated by fear, guilt, anger or insecurity. The mature ego holds awareness of our uniqueness, authenticity and healthy boundaries – while also being aware of deep reality.

Emotional Freedom Technique The most popular form of energy psychology, which clears **resistance** from our energy field and so allows **Source** energy to flow. It involves tapping points on the body while focusing on specific thoughts, emotions or images.

Emotions Indicators of your alignment with (or connection to) Source energy. The primary form of inner guidance. Negative emotions such as guilt, resentment or anxiety are a sign of resistance, or disconnecting from Source; feeling joyful, loving, passionate and empowered indicates that Source energy is flowing freely through you.

Energy habits A repeated pattern of energy flow that feels familiar and comfortable, even if it is self-limiting or self-destructive – such as a familiar emotion, way of thinking or behaviour. These habits are often family-ar; that is, they were set up in childhood, and form deep **riverbeds** that become 'easy' to flow down.

Hero's journey The inner-outer journey towards reconnection with your true Self, in response to a **Call** to adventure. The transformational journey from surface reality to **deep reality**, or from the immature ego to the **deep Self**.

Intuition Messages, information and impulses to act from deep reality, received when you are in a state of low resistance – that is, when your ego is out of the way.

Judgment See **duality/Tree of Good and Evil**.

Law of Attraction The universal law that 'like attracts like', that we create our own reality on the basis on the vibrational patterns of energy that we emit – like radio signals – via our thoughts, emotions and desires.

Love See **wild love**.

Other Another significant person with whom you play out your emotional patterns or energy habits, whether healthy or unhealthy. A mirror of aspects of oneself.

Psychological reversal (PR) Contradictions in the energy system which mean that you subconsciously avoid goals which you consciously desire. See **split energy**.

Resistance Conflict between your deep Self (which is aligned with Source) and your ego (motivated by fear, guilt, blame or insecurity), as signalled by negative emotions or physical symptoms. See **emotions.**

Riverbeds of relating Repeated patterns in our relation-ships that mirror earlier relationships, often based upon **tame love**. (See **energy habits**.) New riverbeds can be formed, but this requires energy, consciousness and/or unconditional love.

Self See **deep Self.**

Shadow Denied or split-off aspects of your wholeness that are projected on to others – either as 'badness' that you despise, judge or fear, or as 'goodness' that you idealise.

Source Another word for God, All That Is, the Tao, the Beloved, the Great Mystery. The web of energy-consciousness that is 'deep reality'.

Split energy The inner conflict or neurosis which arises from being torn between following your own emotional guidance (which helps you align with **Source**) and listening to the needs or dictates of other people, society or religion. Split energy disempowers you, and locks you in ego – and is indicated by negative emotion such as guilt or anxiety, or attracting negative experiences.

Splitting see **duality**

Surface reality The superficial world of the ego. Ordinary, mundane reality in which 'luck, chance or coincidence' play a role in what happens. The reality in which mind and matter – or inner and outer reality – seem to be separate.

TAT (Tapas Acupressure Technique) A popular form of energy psychology created by acupuncturist Tapas Fleming, which involves holding points on the head while focusing on a problem, issue, allergy or trauma.

Tame love The conditional pseudo-love of the ego, which leads to 'blaming, shaming and taming'. It splits the **Other's** energy, and keeps both people trapped in ego.

Taming Making your love or approval conditional upon the **Other** thinking, feeling or behaving as you want them to. Controlling the Other through fear, guilt or insecurity.

Tree of Good and Evil The ego's tendency to separate the world into good or bad, right or wrong, and safe or dangerous. The patterns of judgment which split our energy, and disconnect us from our deep Self. See **duality**.

Vibrations The patterns and frequency of energy held in consciousness – as thoughts, emotions and desires – which create our reality through the **Law of Attraction**.

Wild love The unconditional love of the deep **Self** which loves self, others and the world as they are, while also envisioning them as they might be. The love that evokes what is best and highest in the **Other**. The love that knows we are safe, we are good, we are worthy. Radical acceptance and affirmation of 'what is'. The love that lies beyond **duality**. The expansive love that launches thrilling desires for the future, and joyfully anticipates making those dreams come true.

ENDNOTES

CHAPTER ONE: Invitation To The Dance

1 From 'Unfold Your Own Myth' in Coleman Barks (transl.), *The Essential Rumi* (Penguin, 1995), p. 41.

CHAPTER TWO: Our Looking-Glass World

1 *The Little Book of Bleeps* (Revolver Books, 2005).

2 Jane Roberts, *Seth Speaks* (Bantam, 1974).

3 See my earlier book, *Living Magically* (Piatkus, 1991).

4 eg. See Rupert Sheldrake, *A New Science of Life* (Blond and Briggs, 1981).

5 See my earlier book, *Pure Bliss* (Piatkus, 1999).

6 See Lynne McTaggart, *The Field* (Element, 2003).

7 Rupert Sheldrake, *The Presence of the Past* (HarperCollins, 1994) p. 315.

8 Amit Goswami, *The Self-Aware Universe: How consciousness creates the material world* (Tarcher/Putnam, 1995) p. 140.

9 William A Tiller, *Science and Human Transformation* (Pavior, 1997).

10 Ibid, p. 199.

11 Ibid, p. 2.

12 eg. See Esther and Jerry Hicks, *Ask And It Is Given* (Hay House, 2004); Neale Donald Walsch, *Conversations With God* series (Hodder and Stoughton, 1995 onwards); Sanaya Roman, *Living With Joy* (H J Kramer, 1986); and the many Seth books by Jane Roberts.

13 Quoted in B Toben and Fred Alan Wolf, *Space-Time and Beyond* (Bantam, 1983) p. 126.

14 Jane Roberts, *Seth Speaks* (Bantam, 1974) p. 13.

15 Larry Dossey, *Reinventing Medicine* (Element, 1999) p. 63.

16 'Abiding Chemistry' by Susan Castillo – lecturer, author and poet. Personal communication.

17 Barbara Marx Hubbard, *Conscious Evolution* (New World Library, 1998) p. 10.

18 Dean Radin, *The Conscious Universe: The Scientific Truth of Psychic Phenomena* (HarperCollins, 1997).

19 See Paul H Ray and Sherry Ruth Anderson, *The Cultural Creatives* (Three Rivers Press, 2000) - for a large-scale study of the emergence of new consciousness among millions of Americans.

20 Thomas S Kuhn, *The Structure of Scientific Revolutions* (University of Chicago, 1962).

21 Teilhard de Chardin, *The Phenomenon of Man* (HarperCollins, 1975). Also Barbara Marx Hubbard, *Conscious Evolution* (New World Library, 1998) p. 10.

22 André Gide – French critic, essayist and novelist (1869–1951).

CHAPTER THREE: The Call To Adventure

1 Robert Bly (transl), *The Kabir Book* (Beacon Press, 1977) p. 24.

2 John O'Donohue, *Divine Beauty* (Doubleday, 2003) p. 135.

3 From 'A Great Wagon' by Rumi; translated by Coleman Barks with John Moyne, *The Essential Rumi* (Penguin, 1995) p. 36.

4 Ego-based thoughts in the mid-range of vibrations can sometimes be useful as a gentle springboard to 'higher' thoughts – see chapter 6.

5 Jack Kornfield, *A Path With Heart* (Bantam, 1993) p. 229.

6 From 'The Holy Longing', in Robert Bly, *News of The Universe* (Sierra Club Books, 1980) p. 70.

7 James Redfield, Michael Murphy and Sylvia Timbers, *God and the Evolving Universe* (Bantam, 2002) p. 20.

CHAPTER FOUR: A Bridge Across Eternity

1 Barbara Ann Brennan, *Light Emerging* (Bantam, 1993) p. 41.

2 Roger Callahan, *Tapping The Healer Within* (Piatkus, 2001).

3 See David Feinstein, Donna Eden and Gary Craig, *The Healing Power of EFT and Energy Psychology* (Piatkus, 2006).

4 See www.emofree.com for full details about EFT. The website includes countless case reports and research evidence.

5 Robert O Becker, *The Body Electric* (Morrow, 1985), pp. 233-6.

6 See Richard Gerber, *Vibrational Medicine* (Bear and Co, 2001) p. 126.

7 See www.unstressforsuccess.com for further details about TAT.

8 Christiane Northrup lecture given at 'I Can Do It' Conference, Orlando, Florida in October 2005. See Christiane Northrup, *Mother-Daughter Wisdom* (Piatkus, 2005).

9 Adapted from David Feinstein's 'Energy Psychology Interactive' CD-Rom. See www.innersource.net.

10 See www.emofree.com/Research/minerals-amino-vitamins.htm.

11 Donna Eden, *Energy Medicine* (Tarcher/Putnam, 1998) p. 20.

12 Fred P Gallo and Harry Vincenzi, *Energy Tapping* (New Harbinger, 2000) p. 11.

13 Donna Eden, *Energy Medicine* (Tarcher/Putnam, 1998).

14 From 'The Journey' David Whyte, *The House of Belonging* (Many Rivers Press, 1997, 2004) p. 37. Used by permission of the author and Many Rivers Press. www.davidwhyte.com.

15 Confusingly, the triple warmer also operates as a strange flow, according to Donna Eden – but it functions very differently from the rest of the strange flows.

16 Norman Cousins, *Anatomy of an Illness* (Bantam, 1981).

17 Candace Pert, *Molecules of Emotion* (Simon & Schuster, 1998) p. 265.

18 Donna Eden, *Energy Medicine* (Tarcher/Putnam, 1998) pp. 21–2. For further ways of stimulating the strange flows or radiant circuits, see David Feinstein, Donna Eden and Gary Craig, *The Healing Power of EFT and Energy Psychology* (Piatkus, 2006), chapter 7.

CHAPTER FIVE: Does God Need Therapy?

1 From 'Wild Geese' Mary Oliver, *New and Selected Poems* (Beacon Press, 1992) p. 110.

2 Quoted in Matthew Fox, *Original Blessing* (Bear & Co, 1983) p. 88.

3 See Ibid.

4 eg. See Mircea Eliade, *The Chalice and the Blade* (Unwin, 1990).

5 From The Gospel of Thomas, in Marvin W Meyer (transl.) *The Secret Teachings of Jesus* (Vintage, 1986) p. 35.

6 See Rupert Sheldrake, *A New Science of Life* (Blond and Briggs, 1981).

7 Pat Rodegast and Judith Stanton, *Emmanuel's Book* (Bantam, 1987) p. 40.

8 Quoted in Matthew Fox, *Original Blessing* (Bear & Co, 1983) p. 89.

9 Quoted in Matthew Fox *Original Blessing,* (Bear & Co, 1983) p. 161.

10 From 'A Great Wagon' by Rumi transl. by Coleman Barks with John Moyne, *The Essential Rumi* (Penguin, 1995) p. 36.

11 Sarah Ban Breathnach, *Something More* (Warner Books, 2000) p. 146.

12 Northern Cheyenne proverb. Guy A Zona (ed) *The Soul Would Have No Rainbow If The Eyes Had No Tears* (Touchstone, 1994) p. 32.

13 From 'Sunset' Robert Bly (transl.), *Selected Poems of Rainer Maria Rilke* (HarperCollins, 1981) p. 85.

14 Monica Sjöö and Barbara Mor, *The Great Cosmic Mother* (HarperCollins, 1991) p. 52.

15 Quoted in Matthew Fox, *Original Blessing* (Bear & Co, 1983) p. 98.

16 See Neil Douglas-Klotz, *Prayers For The Cosmos* (HarperCollins, 1994) – though the quoted version was taken from the website www.sacredconnection.ndo.co.uk.

CHAPTER SIX: Choosing To Be Happy

1 From 'Moving Water' Coleman Barks (transl), *The Soul of Rumi* (HarperCollins, 2002) p. 79.

2 From 'The Winter of Listening' David Whyte, *The House of Belonging* (Many Rivers Press, 1999, 2004) p. 29. Used by permission of the author and Many Rivers Press. www.davidwhyte.com.

3 Esther and Jerry Hicks, *Ask And It Is Given* (Hay House, 2004) p. 44.

4 Quoted in Matthew Fox, *Original Blessing* (Bear & Co, 1983) p. 43.

5 From 'Have You Ever Tried To Enter The Long Branches' by Mary Oliver. Quoted in Roger Housden, *110 Poems of Love and Revelation*, (Harmony Books, 2003) p. ix.

6 Abraham is a group of spiritual teachers channelled by Esther Hicks. See Esther and Jerry Hicks, *Ask And It Is Given* (Hay House, 2004) p. 114.

7 Quoted in Matthew Fox, *Original Blessing* (Bear & Co, 1983) p. 161.

8 Candace Pert, *Molecules of Emotion* (Simon & Schuster, 1998) p. 265.

9 From my poem 'Love Does Not Thrive In A Thimble'.

CHAPTER SEVEN: Reclaiming Your Authentic Self

1 Joseph Campbell, *Pathways to Bliss* (New World Library, 2004) p. xxvi.

2 Ibid p. xxiii.

3 Nora Weeks, *The Medical Discoveries of Edward Bach* (C W Daniel, 1973) p. 23.

4 For details about Lakeland Essences, see the resource list at the end of this book.

5 From 'A Great Wagon' by Rumi – translated by Coleman Barks with John Moyne, *The Essential Rumi* (Penguin, 1995) p. 36.

6 Joseph Campbell, author on mythology (1904–1987).

7 Christina Baldwin, *One To One* (M Evans & Co, 1977) Quoted in Susan Seddon Boulet's 'A Woman's Diary' (Pomegranate, 2005).

8 Karen Kingston, *Creating Sacred Space With Feng Shui* (Piatkus, 1996) p. 50.

9 Quoted in the CD set by David Whyte, *Midlife and The Great Unknown* (Sounds True, 2003).

10 Elizabeth Lesser, *Broken Open* (Rider, 2004).

11 From my poem 'Wild Love'.

12 Ibid.

13 Ibid.

14 W N Herbert and Matthew Hollis (eds) *Strong Words*

(Bloodaxe, 2000) pp. 148–9.

15 Mary Oliver, *Winter Hours* (Houghton Mifflin, 1999) p. 98.

16 John O'Donohue, *Divine Beauty* (Bantam, 2003) p. 80.

17 From 'Sweet Darkness' David Whyte, *The House of Belonging* (Many Rivers Press, 1997, 2004) p. 23. Used by permission of the author and Many Rivers Press. www.davidwhyte.com

18 From 'The Journey' Mary Oliver, *New and Selected Poems* (Beacon Press, 1992) pp. 114–5.

19 Sarah Ban Breathnach, *Something More* (Time Warner, 1998) p. 117.

20 Ibid, p. 57.

21 From my poem 'Wild Love'.

CHAPTER EIGHT: A Foot In Both Worlds

1 From 'The Summer Day', Mary Oliver, *New and Selected Poems* (Beacon Press, 1992) p. 94.

2 Abraham is channelled by Esther Hicks. Jerry and Esther Hicks, *A New Beginning II* (Abraham-Hicks, 2001).

3 From 'And The Days Are Not Full Enough', Neil Astley (ed), *Staying Alive* (Bloodaxe, 2002) p. 130.

4 From 'The Summer Day' – in Mary Oliver, *New and Selected Poems* (Beacon Press, 1992) p. 94.

5 The cancer personality was first described by Galen in 2nd century CE. It is still controversial in medical circles but commonly observed by practitioners, and there is increasing research back-up over the past 50 years – eg. see Bernie Siegel, *Love, Medicine and Miracles* (Arrow, 1988) pp. 78–83.

6 From my poem, 'Before I Scurry'.

7 Annie Dillard, *The Writing Life* (Perennial, 1999).

8 From 'Someone Digging In The Ground' by Rumi, translated by Coleman Barks with John Moyne, *The Essential Rumi* (Penguin, 1995) p. 107.

9 William Tiller, *Science and Human Transformation* (Pavior, 1997).

10 From 'What To Remember When Waking' David Whyte, *The House of Belonging* (Many Rivers Press, 1997, 2004) p. 26. Used by permission of the author and Many Rivers Press. www.davidwhyte.com.

CHAPTER NINE: Turning Lead Into Gold

1 Richard Gerber, *Vibrational Medicine* (Bear and Co, 2001) p. 467.

2 From my poem 'Miracle'.

3 See my earlier books, *Living Magically*, *Stepping Into The Magic* and *Pure Bliss* (all published by Piatkus).

4 Thomas Moore, *Dark Nights of the Soul* (Piatkus, 2004).

5 Deepak Chopra, *The Deeper Wound* (Harmony, 2001).

6 From my poem 'Separation'.

7 From my poem 'Under The Same Sun'.

8 Jay Ramsay, *Alchemy: The Art Of Transformation* (Thorsons, 1997) p. 143.

9 See Robert A Johnson, *The Fisher King and the Handless Maiden* (HarperCollins, 1995) for an excellent analysis of how scapegoating is an inevitable result of our 'wounded feeling function' in patriarchal society.

10 John O'Donohue, *Divine Beauty* (Bantam, 2003) p. 173.

11 Thomas Moore, *Dark Nights of the Soul* (Piatkus, 2004).

12 From 'A Great Wagon' by Rumi; Coleman Barks with John Moyne (transl.) *The Essential Rumi* (Penguin, 1995) p. 36.

13 John O'Donohue, *Anam Cara* (Bantam, 1997).

14 Jay Ramsay, *Crucible of Love* (O Books, 2004) chapter 4.

15 Contrast is a key concept from the channelled teachings of Abraham.

16 See Ilya Prigogine, *From Being To Becoming* (Freeman, 1980).

17 Brendan Doyle, *Meditations with Julian of Norwich* (Bear & Co, 1983) p. 48.

18 Marianne Williamson, *The Gift of Change* (HarperSanFrancisco, 2004) p. 188.

19 Immaculee Ilibagiza, *Left To Tell* (Hay House, 2006).

CHAPTER TEN: Tame Love

1 From my poem 'Icarus'.

2 From 'He Wishes For The Cloths of Heaven' W B Yeats, *Selected Poetry* (Pan, 1974) p. 35.

3 John O'Donohue, *Divine Beauty* (Bantam, 2003) p. 150.

4 Thomas Moore, *Dark Nights of the Soul* (Piatkus, 2004) p. 135.

5 Mary Oliver, *West Wind* (Houghton Mifflin, 1997) p. 46.

6 Ibid.

7 Coleman Barks (transl) *The Soul of Rumi* (HarperCollins, 2002) p. 27.

8 Chuck Spezzano, *If It Hurts, It Isn't Love* (Hodder & Stoughton, 2001) p. 109.

9 Gaslighting means invalidating someone's feelings or needs by implying they are crazy, or attributing it to 'mental illness' (eg 'That's just your depression talking').

10 From my poem 'Love Does Not Thrive In A Thimble.'

11 Marshall B Rosenberg, *Being Me, Loving You* (PuddleDancer Press, 2005) p. 10.

12 Many abusive relationships involve 'borderline personalities' who are clingy, possessive, controlling and terrified of abandonment, yet struggle with emotional intimacy. They split the world into black and white, and often flip between idealising and devaluing their partner. They can be emotionally numb, moody or fly into unpredictable rages, and you might find yourself 'treading on eggshells' around them – and giving to the point of exhaustion. For further details, see Jerold J Krreisman, *I Hate You – Don't Leave Me* (Avon, 1989) or Paul T Mason and Randi Kreger, *Stop Walking On Eggshells* (New Harbinger, 1998).

13 Marianne Williamson, *Enchanted Love* (Touchstone, 2001) p. 222.

14 From my poem 'Love Does Not Thrive In A Thimble'.

15 *A Course In Miracles* (Arkana, 1985) p. 136.

16 Marianne Williamson, *Enchanted Love* (Touchstone, 2001).

17 Thomas Moore, *Dark Nights of the Soul* (Piatkus, 2004).

18 Denise Linn, *How My Death Saved ★y Life* (Hay House, 2005).

CHAPTER ELEVEN: Riverbeds of Relating

1 Thomas Moore, *Care of the Soul* (HarperCollins, 1992) p. 28.

2 Bert Hellinger, *Love's Hidden Symmetry* (Zeig, Tucker & Co, 1998) p. 94.

3 Bert Hellinger, *Acknowledging What Is* (Zeig, Tucker & Co, 1999) pp. 4-5.

4 Bert Hellinger, *On Life and Other Paradoxes* (Zeig, Tucker & Theisen, 2002) p. 34.

5 Foundation for Inner Peace, *A Course in Miracles* (Arkana, 1985) p. 77.

6 Abraham, channelled by Esther Hicks. Workshop recorded on 5 January, 1991.

7 Barbara Ann Brennan, *Light Emerging* (Bantam, 1993) p. 186.

8 Danah Zohar, *The Quantum Self* (Flamingo, 1991) pp. 168–9.

9 From my poem 'Love Does Not Thrive In A Thimble'.

10 See references to Bert Hellinger's work in the Further Reading and Other Resources section.

CHAPTER TWELVE: Wild Love

1 From 'Doubt Shall Not Make An End Of You' Brian Patten, *Love Poems* (Unwin, 1984) p. 16. Now published by Flamingo/HarperCollins.

2 From my poem 'Love Does Not Thrive In A Thimble'.

3 Robert A Johnson, *We: Understanding The Psychology of Romantic Love* (HarperCollins, 1983) p. 191.

4 William Tiller, *Science and Human Transformation* (Pavior, 1997).

5 Maria Housden, *Hannah's Gift* (HarperCollins, 2003). Highly recommended to anyone who has suffered the death of a child – or anyone who wants to be reminded of the gift and wonder of life.

6 Oriah Mountain Dreamer, *The Dance* (Element, 2003) pp. 157–8.

7 Hale Dwoskin, *The Sedona Method* (Element, 2005).

8 Hal Stone and Sidra Winkelman, *Embracing Each Other* (New Word Library, 1989) p. 184.

9 Eg. See Lee Carroll and Jan Tober, *The Indigo Children* (Hay House, 1999); Doreen Virtue, *Indigo, Crystal and Rainbow Children* – CD (Hay House, 2003).

10 eg. Byron Katie, *I Need Your Love: Is That True?* (Harmony, 2005).

11 From 'To Have Without Holding' Marge Piercy, *The Moon Is Always Female* (Knopf, 2004) p. 40.

12 From my poem 'Wild Love'.

13 Eg. Masuro Emoto, *The Hidden Messages In Water* (Beyond Words, 2004).

14 From 'What The Light Teaches' Anne Michaels, *Poems* (Bloomsbury, 1999) p. 136.

15 From my poem 'Wild Love'.

16 Gill Edwards, *Pure Bliss* (Piatkus, 1999) p. 31.

17 From my poem 'Love Does Not Thrive In A Thimble'.

FURTHER READING

Rudolph Ballentine, *Radical Healing* (Harmony, 1999).

Melody Beattie, *Codependent No More* (Hazelden, 1987).

Melody Beattie, *The Language Of Letting Go* (Hazelden, 1990).

Sarah Ban Breathnach, *Something More* (Warner Books, 2000).

Barbara Ann Brennan, *Light Emerging* (Bantam, 1993).

Joseph Campbell, *The Hero With A Thousand Faces* (Fontana, 1993).

Joseph Campbell, *Pathways To Bliss* (New World Library, 2004).

Deepak Chopra, *The Path To Love* (Rider, 1997).

Larry Dossey, *Healing Beyond the Body* (Time Warner, 2002).

Neil Douglas-Klotz, *Prayers For The Cosmos* (HarperCollins, 1994).

Oriah Mountain Dreamer, *The Dance* (Element, 2003).

Hale Dwoskin, *The Sedona Method* (Element, 2005).

Donna Eden, *Energy Medicine* (Tarcher/Putnam, 1998).

Gill Edwards, *Living Magically* (Piatkus, 1991).

Gill Edwards, *Stepping Into The Magic* (Piatkus, 1993).

Gill Edwards, *Pure Bliss* (Piatkus, 1999).

Masuro Emoto, *The Hidden Messages In Water* (Beyond Words, 2004).

Beverley Engel, *The Emotionally Abusive Relationship* (John Wiley, 2002).

David Feinstein, Donna Eden and Gary Craig, *The Healing Power of EFT and Energy Psychology* (Piatkus, 2006).

Matthew Fox, *Original Blessing* (Bear & Co, 1983).

Matthew Fox, *One River, Many Wells* (Gateway, 2001).

Richard Gerber, *Vibrational Medicine For The 21st Century* (Piatkus, 2001).

Amit Goswami, *The Self-Aware Universe* (Tarcher/Putnam, 1995).

Henry Grayson, *Mindful Loving* (Gotham Books, 2004).

Bert Hellinger, *Acknowledging What Is* (Zeig, Tucker & Co, 1999).

Bert Hellinger, *Love's Hidden Symmetry* (Zeig, Tucker & Co, 1998).

Esther and Jerry Hicks, *Ask And It Is Given* (Hay House, 2004).

Marie-France Hirigoyen, *Stalking The Soul: Emotional Abuse and the Erosion of Identity* (Helen Marx Books, 2004).

Maria Housden, *Unravelled* (Element, 2004).

Barbara Marx Hubbard, *Conscious Evolution* (New World Library, 1998).

Byron Katie, *I Need Your Love: Is That True?* (Harmony, 2005).

Elizabeth Lesser, *Broken Open* (Rider, 2004).

Lynne McTaggart, *The Field* (Element, 2003).

J Keith Miller, *Compelled To Control* (Health Communications, 1992/1997).

Thomas Moore, *Dark Nights of the Soul* (Piatkus, 2004).

John O'Donohue, *Anam Cara* (Bantam, 1997).

John O'Donohue, *Divine Beauty* (Bantam, 2003).

Candace Pert, *Molecules of Emotion* (Simon & Schuster, 1998).

Dean Radin, *The Conscious Universe* (HarperCollins, 1997).

Jay Ramsay, *Crucible Of Love* (O Books, 2004).

Paul H Ray and Sherry Ruth Anderson, *The Cultural Creatives* (Three Rivers Press, 2000).

Jane Roberts, *Seth Speaks* (Bantam, 1974).

Sanaya Roman, *Living With Joy* (H J Kramer, 1986).

Marshall B Rosenberg, *Nonviolent Communication* (PuddleDancer, 2003).

Rupert Sheldrake, *A New Science of Life* (Blond and Briggs, 1981).

Rupert Sheldrake, *The Presence of the Past* (HarperCollins, 1994).

Jacquelyn Small, *Awakening in Time* (Bantam, 1991).

Chuck Spezzano, *If It Hurts, It Isn't Love* (Hodder & Stoughton, 2001).

Hal Stone and Sidra Winkelman, *Embracing Each Other* (New World Library, 1989).

William A Tiller, *Science and Human Transformation* (Pavior, 1997).

Neale Donald Walsch, *Conversations With God* series (Hodder & Stoughton, 1995 onwards).

Marianne Williamson, *Enchanted Love* (Touchstone, 2001).

SELECTED POETRY

Neil Astley (ed), *Staying Alive* (Bloodaxe, 2002).

Coleman Barks (transl), *The Soul of Rumi* (HarperCollins, 2002).

Robert Bly, James Hillman and Michael Meade (eds), *The Rag And Bone Shop Of The Heart* (HarperCollins, 1992).

Jane Hirshfield, *The Lives Of The Heart* (HarperCollins, 1997).

Roger Housden (ed), *Risking Everything: 110 Poems of Love and Revelation* (Harmony Books, 2003).

Roger Housden (ed), *Ten Poems To Change Your Life* (Hodder & Stoughton, 2003).

Roger Housden (ed), *Ten Poems To Open Your Heart* (Hodder & Stoughton, 2003).

Roger Housden (ed), *Ten Poems To Set You Free* (Hodder & Stoughton, 2003).

Alan Jacobs, *Poetry For the Spirit* (Watkins, 2003).

Anne Michaels, *Poems* (Bloomsbury, 1999)

Mary Oliver, *New and Selected Poems* (Beacon Press, 1992).

Brian Patten, *Love Poems* (Unwin, 1984).

Marge Piercy, *The Moon Is Always Female* (Knopf, 2004).

David Whyte, *Everything Is Waiting For You* (Many Rivers Press, 2003).

David Whyte, *The House of Belonging* (Many Rivers Press, 1997, 2004).

OTHER RESOURCES

Abraham – Channelled by Esther and Jerry Hicks. Books, tapes, CDs, videos, workshops in the USA etc. See website: www.abraham-hicks.com

EFT (Emotional Freedom Technique) Training CD-Roms, workshops, practitioners and a wealth of free articles and information. See website: www.emofree.com

Energy medicine Books, videos, talks, workshops, courses, etc. with Donna Eden, David Feinstein and others. See website: www.innersource.net

Energy psychology There are many different approaches, but I particularly recommend EFT, TAT and Emo-Trance. For list of trained UK practitioners, see website: www.theAMT.com

Flower essences Australian Bush Flower Essences www.ausflowers.com.au; Alaskan Essences www.alaskanessences.com; Californian Flower Essences www.flowersociety.org; Bailey Essences www.baileyessences.com; Indigo Essences www.indigoessences.com; Bach Flower Remedies www.healingherbs.co.uk; Lakeland Essences www.livingmagically.co.uk; essence suppliers: www.healthlines.co.uk

Hellinger For healing the family soul. Books, videos, workshops, private practitioners. See website: www.hellinger.com or www.hellinger.co.uk

Non-violent communication Books, tapes, videos, workshops etc. on healthy communication skills – beyond duality. See website: www.nvc.org or www.liferesources.org.uk

Sedona Method Books, tapes, videos, workshops, etc. See website: www.sedona.com

TAT (Tapas Acupressure Technique) Workshops, videos, etc. with Tapas Fleming. See www.tatlife.com

Living Magically For details about workshops with Gill Edwards, self-help CDs, Lakeland Essences, etc., see website: www.livingmagically.co.uk

Or contact: Living Magically, Fisherbeck Mill, Old Lake Road, Ambleside, Cumbria LA22 0DH, United Kingdom. Tel: (015394) 31943. Email: LivMagic@aol.com

INDEX